THE BELLY
OF THE
BEAST

Life Inside a
Gated Community

TIMOTHY DAVIDSON

Timber Hollow

The Belly of the Beast
Life Inside a Gated Community
All Rights Reserved.
Copyright © 2021 Timothy Davidson
v9.0 r1.2

The opinions expressed in this manuscript are solely the opinions of the author and do not represent the opinions or thoughts of the publisher. The author has represented and warranted full ownership and/or legal right to publish all the materials in this book.

This book may not be reproduced, transmitted, or stored in whole or in part by any means, including graphic, electronic, or mechanical without the express written consent of the publisher except in the case of brief quotations embodied in critical articles and reviews.

Timber Hollow

ISBN: 978-0-578-24322-1

Cover Photo © 2021 Karen Phillips. All rights reserved - used with permission.

PRINTED IN THE UNITED STATES OF AMERICA

Table of Contents

Introduction i
In the Beginning 1
Richard A. Mcgee Academy 24
Reporting for Duty at Mule Creek State Prison 33
The Hole 56
Visiting 66
Ethnicity and Gangs 74
First Watch 84
Third Watch 90
Second Watch 104
Thunderdome, the Infirmary, and the Psych Ward. 126
Discipline 141
Prison Rape 148
Escapes 153
Famous Characters 174
And Just Some Interesting Ones 188
Department Waste 195
Capital Punishment 202

Inmate Hijinks	207
Weapon Stock	229
Interesting and Dirty Staff	234
Sports	245
The Day We're All Waiting For	249
Epilogue	255
Acknowledgements	259

Introduction

PRISON IS THE Beast. It will ingest convicted felons as well as some staff members, digest them and extract the part that needs to remain within its' caustic, tumultuous, fetid tract. The Beast will excrete things at times but what's left is always bubbling, gurgling and steeping within its chaotic confines.

This memoir is an accurate account of my 25 years inside the walls of a California state prison. I'll tackle the riots, stabbings, gang fights, smuggling and various tactics utilized by inmates to avoid detection of illegal acts. I've also witnessed staff manipulation, extortion and shootings; the sexual behavior of convicts and staff; the hundreds of ways prisoners try to beat the system; and hundreds of fascinating characters and incidents. Daily life is reduced to its' most basic components of wants and needs.

Some names have been changed or omitted, and some of the subjects' physical characteristics, ethnicities or gender may have been altered to further obscure their identities, but all of the events actually occurred. The prison system is but a cross section of society with both good and bad capacities. I have my share of both, but am somewhat atypical of my former brethren. Hell, I don't even particularly like doughnuts.

I do not intend this to be a hit piece on the California Department of Corrections (CDC). Overall, I think they do a pretty good job of achieving their major objectives: protecting the public by preventing escapes and keeping the inmates from harming themselves or each other, as well as giving them every opportunity to flourish both inside the Beast and outside if the make it outside of it's belly. Many of the events chronicled here are beyond the capabilities and responsibilities of the state. The CDC more reactive than proactive. When an incident arises, they make adjustments to deal with it as the circumstance occurs, and that's understandable. Given convicts' resourcefulness, adaptability and creativity, it would have been impossible for the CDC to anticipate all the guidelines necessary to prevent prisoners from behaving in ways that are disruptive or dangerous to themselves and others. The convicts will also adapt to those guidelines and modify their ways to live within them or...circumvent them. It isn't always the biggest and strongest who survive, it's the most adaptable.

This is but a snapshot of the CDC that I experienced during the time-span of my career and might bear little resemblance to the CDC from decades ago or in the future.

The CCPOA—our union—likes to claim that we "walk the toughest beat in the state." I guess it's true in the sense that 100 percent of the folks we are surrounded by and dealing with every day are convicted felons, many of whom have committed the most heinous and callous of crimes. Many of my fellow peace officers working as street cops or with the California Highway Patrol (CHP) tell me they wouldn't want my job. I wouldn't want their jobs, because at least I knew the people I was dealing with were convicted felons and I treated them accordingly as far as any security concerns. On the street, you don't know which ones fall into that category. Street cops could interact with the most innocent-appearing folks who'd pull a gun and end their life at any moment.

Corrections is one of the very few occupations where you can be involved in a lighthearted conversation with your partner: eating lunch, spreading a little manure around, talking about family, sports or any benign subject one minute, and then be confronted with a life-or-death situation the next moment. It may be witnessing an inmate or staff member being disemboweled, or having to make an instantaneous decision to end a man's life. You could be seconds away from being relieved and heading home to your wife—or maybe to your child's birthday party—and suddenly be assaulted, end up in an ambulance, or respond to a serious incident. Then you're stuck for the next eight...to who knows how many more hours dealing with the situation and its' aftermath.

Those who have worked inside for a while feel there is a distinction between correctional officers and prison guards, and between convicts and inmates. Convicts know how to do time and don't bother staff with petty crap. Inmates have a sense of entitlement, whine and snivel about everything and are constantly pestering officers to give them some special treatment because they are experiencing something that is causing them an inconvenience or interfering with their comfort level. Most prisoners consider being called a convict a compliment.

Guards don't sweat convicts over petty issues and instead focus on behavior that is going to endanger other inmates or staff and put us on "Front Street," which can cause our supervisors to bring heat down on us. Correctional officers can be "badge heavy," getting off on bossing inmates around and being unrealistic about expectations of inmate behavior. I think there were a few officers who had been burglarized , assaulted or robbed at some point in their lives and took the opportunity to transfer the rage they had for the actual perpetrator onto the inmates they dealt with every day. They treated every convict as if they were the guy that ripped the tape deck out of their Ford Pinto twenty years ago. Fortunately, most of those would be weeded out prior to graduating from the academy if they displayed any attitudes or behavior that would deprive prisoners, or staff of their right to fair and equal treatment. You can't make Chicken salad out of Chicken shit. I always told the residents that how I treated them was entirely up to them. If they knew how to act, we'd get along; if they didn't, we would clash, and they would lose.

I met some really great convicts and some pretty sleazy staff members. A study conducted by Stanford University in 1971 divided students into guards and prisoners. The study concluded that those who were acting in the role of the guards became abusive and authoritarian towards those in the prisoner role. I tried to be introspective periodically and ask myself if I'd fallen prey to that phenomenon.

I don't intend to have this memoir make me sound like some sort of bad-ass. I was just lucky at times when things started to go sideways. It's also a lot easier to be brave when you've got a baton and pepper spray on your belt, as well as another officer above with a rifle aiming at anyone's chest who threatens your well-being.

I also don't want to give anyone the impression that I was the perfect officer. There were numerous officers far better at the job than I was. I was lazy at times, falsified cell search logs, slept on the job (as long as there were no inmates out.) and other shortcomings. I certainly tried to be vigilant as far as security factors were concerned but the fact that I didn't always do the two required cell searches every day defies that proclamation.

I've committed many crimes. I was a skilled shoplifter, used illegal (at the time) drugs, had a vandalistic phase and offer no excuses for it. I don't see any of it as being hypocritical. I didn't put any of these people in prison. I was homeless and lived on the streets for about six months back in 1970. There was a time during my unrestrained youth when it looked like the only thing that was going to beat me to prison was the headlights on the bus.

I want to issue a disclaimer here and apologize in advance to my friends or anybody who prefers the company of their own gender for cuddling purposes. Homosexuality is a prominant facet of incarceration and I use some terms and descriptions that some might find offensive. I hope not and I've asked several of my friends in that category to read related excerpts from this memoir and so far...they've all given it their stamp of approval.

There are a lot of infamous people spending quality time at Mule Creek State Prison, with whom I interacted with along the way. Some of the legendary convicts I had daily interaction with during my career were; Tex Watson (the main killer for the Manson gang and was my clerk), Lyle Menendez, Rick Stevenson (Tower of Power lead singer), Suge Knight, Andrew Luster (Max Factor heir) and a host of others, whom I will expand on later. I had to go before the shooting review board three times after discharging my weapon to quell disturbances on the yard. The last time was for the morning when the prick who stalked and murdered TV actress Rebecca Shaeffer was being stabbed by Janeane Garafolo's cousin and I was compelled to negatively reinforce his behavior. I will relate that entire incident along with the other two shootings I needed to do in later chapters. I tracked down and received written permission from both parties to describe that morning, including my conversation with the assailant in the hole afterwards and will relate his account of that morning. I got Tex Watson's signature to describe the interactions I had with him over the years. Tex disclosed things to me about the Tate/LaBianca murders that I didn't know and very few other people do either, which I will describe in detail in another chapter. It was a much more complicated and convoluted story than the simplistic one the DA used to in order to get the conviction. It really had very little to do with the whole race war/Helter Skelter version most people have come to accept.

Prison is a complete subculture and ecosystem with its' own set of rules, laws and behavior expectations, and not just from the State. The prison population also has its' own set of behavior parameters and will enforce them in a much more timely and harsh manner then CDC can. There are no secrets in prison. Somebody always knows and will always tell. Within the Beast, frank words and direct dialogue are the preferred language. Nobody is concerned about anybody getting their feelings hurt over race, sexual preference, gang affiliation, socio economic standing, education or appearance. They are only concerned about the intended message being effectively conveyed and received.

On that note, there a certainly a few punctuation boo boos in here. Hey, sue me...it was edited by a prison guard. All that matters is the reader grasping what I intended to convey.

People who have never entered the Beast have the faulty belief that it's just a bunch of crooks lying and stealing from anybody they can inside. That notion is partially accurate. However, the phenomenon of honor among thieves applies, too. If a prisoner makes a deal or tells somebody they're going to do something, they better do it, or the consequences will be swift and impactful. As Charles Manson once said, "Crooks will catch crooks before cops will."

Most people think that cigarettes are the prison currency from all the old movies they've seen, but since tobacco was outlawed years ago, the current currency is ramen soup, jars of coffee crystals and postage stamps. Respect, however, is the ultimate currency.

I want to state here that there are some very decent human beings incarcerated in prison. Everybody has greatness within them, we just have to nourish in order to flourish, many variables will enable or hinder that process. Some convicts just made a mistake when they were young or in a moment of passion, but in my opinion, the vast majority of them need to be in there because they have a high "me" priority. Meaning if they want your car, money, dope or ass, they're going to take it. The ones in that category don't have a true north on their moral compass. Many of them behave the way they do because of horrific experiences from their upbringing. Damaged people damage people. We can debate whether it's nature or nurture that gives them that perspective, maybe their mother stood in front of the microwave while pregnant, but they seem to have a higher incidence of it than most of us. It's not rocket surgery.

No matter how much I liked or had a high opinion of an inmate as a human being, I still had to observe barriers of propriety. The convicts realized this and rarely crossed the invisible line we both knew was there. Sometimes, like around Christmas, Thanksgiving or the Super Bowl, that gulf between us would narrow, but it was always there, except for some dirty staff who chose to cross the line.

Most of us were taught how to do our jobs by the inmates when we were new at the institution. They would tell me that I was supposed to do this or that, and, factoring in my wariness that it could be an attempt to get something over on me, the majority of their advice was intended to keep the "normality" of their regimented day intact.

"Normal," however, is just a setting on a washing machine.

Many people are like the moon. They have a dark side you don't see. It's interesting to hear a mother, brother or friend of somebody on trial for an ugly crime and hear them state, "My son/brother/friend could never do that! He is incapable of anything so horrible." It's an example of Centristics; they contaminate our conclusions and it takes many forms. It can be egocentric, geocentric, theocentric, ethnocentric, or any other form of the phenomenon that causes us to believe that ourselves, our religion, city or ethnicity is the best one. Geocentric can be spread over a large area such as a nation, a city, a neighborhood, even a street.

As for me, I've always loved prison movies and books. *Papillon* is my favorite book and I read it every five years or so. Such a fantastic adventure. *Escape from Alcatraz, Blood In, Blood Out,* and *American Me* are a few films I love. I was talking to a shot caller (or gang leader) for a Mexican gang (the Sureños) about *American Me,* and he told me that the star, Edward James Olmos, was "green lighted," meaning he was going to be hit. One of the female stars had already been murdered as well as some who worked as "Technical advisers". I asked him why Olmos, and he said it was because he'd told their secrets. I asked, "What secrets? Everybody knows you guys sell dope, extort and kill people that piss you off, just like all gangs!" I believe that even though Olmos had a green-light hit out on him, he's certainly not in hiding, which tells me he may have made a cash settlement with the Sureños. He has had a couple lawsuits filed against him from some of the Mexican Mafia members depicted in the flick, most notably Joe "Pegleg" Morgan, who was portrayed convincingly by William Forsythe. Just my opinion, though.

When people find out what I did for a living, they constantly ask me questions about what it's like inside those walls. It seems to fascinate them, there's been a lot of TV shows on the subject lately. So pour yourself an adult beverage, nibble on whatever you deem fun, take a puff of your meds, get into your flannel snuggies, get your dog(s) on the blanket and let me take you inside the security perimeter, the razor wire, within the gun coverage, into the dingy, musty dayrooms and cells, kitchens, chow halls, the gun towers, and onto the yard. You'll hear the raw dialect, hear stories that will greatly disturb you, meet characters who have committed the most sinister acts and realize what human beings are capable of doing to another life form, as well as what they are capable of enduring themselves.

Let me take you now, inside the Belly of the Beast!

In the Beginning

LET'S GO BACK to where and when this reporter was hatched. It all started on Aug. 19, 1951, which gives me the privilege of being a Leo, King of Beasts. The blessed event occurred at Patrick AFB in Cocoa Beach, Florida. As you may have surmised, my dad, Capt. Ross Davidson, was in the Air Force. Thirty-five missions as a B-17 pilot over Germany. He eventually retired as a full colonel after 28 years.

My mom, Mildred Gene Davidson (nee Davis) was called "Micky" by everyone, because she hated the name Mildred. She was cheerful, sunny, smart, lovely . She bore a resemblance to actress Gene Tierney, made even more amazing by the fact that they shared the same spelling of that name. She was an amazing woman who took on the chore of raising three hellion boys mostly by herself. Even when my daddy wasn't off playing war somewhere, he wasn't especially attentive. I don't bear any resentment toward him, though. We were never abused or neglected in anyway, they both did what they thought was right and we were provided every opportunity to flourish. That's all anyone can ask of a parent.

It has been very difficult for any woman I've met to live up to the standards of integrity and the upbeat, giving and unselfish approach to life I came to expect from women after growing up with her devotion to putting a husband and three bratty boys before herself. No Oedipus complex here, I just came to appreciate those traits in a woman. She went back to college after us three brats got into high school and used to edit the newspaper ads for Weinstocks, a local department store, so I like to think that any writing talent I may have comes from her. A true wordsmith, she could knock out the Sunday New York Times crossword in no time.

Mom and Daddy were polar opposites on the political spectrum, but that wasn't really a problem. I always held their same approach that ones' political conclusions are not a good barameter of ones' qualities as a human being, as long as either side doesn't insist that their viewpoint is the only valid one. Politics certainly lends itself to centristical influence and we all make conclusions based on the evidence we deem to be credible. Somebody who takes the approach that anybody who hasn't come to the same conclusion they have is wrong are guilty of the centristic phenomenon that leads to conflict. This is how wars happen. We badmouth others for things we do ourselves, but when we do it, we feel we had some compelling reason, and our actions are justified but that nobody else's would be.

Neither of my parents ever took a drink, a puff on a cigarette, or uttered a cuss word in my presence. I was born an 11-pounder, and perhaps that was why Mom decided not to go through that ever again. That big baby grew up to stand 6'5" and around 255 pounds but is still a big baby. I was the last of three boys; Mark was three years older and Marty was two years older.

My mother's side of the family was the Hardgraves, and one of her cousins, Ruby, married a famous fellow. There were over 20,000 people at his funeral in Oklahoma in 1934, and he was the "number one" man in his profession. His name was Charles Arthur Floyd, but was better known as "Pretty Boy," and robbing banks was his game. My friends all thought I would end up in prison. We just didn't know what color I would be wearing. One of my mom's other claims to fame was dancing with Jim Nabors in high school. Rock Hudson never forgave him...

Here is our family when I was about 5 years old. I'm on my Dad's lap and was pouting because the photographer was taking too long and I wanted to play with my cousins. Marty is on the left and Mark on the right.

Daddy bought a lot of acreage when we first arrived in California and always advised me to invest in land because "They don't make it anymore." My oldest brother, Mark, got his broker's license and I tried to as well (kind of) but it was all Greek to me. Daddy liked to come across in business as some inbred hayseed, but after a deal was completed, that same hillbilly rube would be wearing the other person's shirt. His philosophy toward the banks he secured loans with was, "If you owe them a little bit of money, they've got you, but if you owe them a lot of money, you've got them." They did everything possible to help him succeed.

We left Florida for Baltimore after a year and I have few, if any, memories of either place. Thank goodness my dad had an old 16mm wing camera from the war and we have lots of films of those days, including being there for opening day at Disneyland in 1955. I do remember that he once told me, "Treat every man like a gentleman. Not because they are, but because you are." A vague memory of Baltimore is that one night Daddy somehow arranged for Doc Blanchard to come over for dinner. Blanchard had been a huge football star at West Point in the '40s and was the first junior ever to win the Heisman Trophy. He was known as "Mr. Inside," and his running mate, Glenn Davis, was "Mr. Outside," so named for their running styles. Fortunately, Davis wasn't there, so we got to eat inside that snowy Baltimore night.

By the time I was about three, we moved to Birmingham, Alabama, which is where my dad grew up. His dad, Martin Luther Davidson was the postmaster of Birmingham. Daddy attended the University of Alabama and played trombone in the Alabama Million Dollar Band. In 1941, Alabama played Texas A&M in the Cotton Bowl and won the National Championship. Daddy loved to tell people that he played for Bama in the Cotton Bowl and leave it at that. If they asked what position he played, he would admit he played trombone. I've told the story many times myself and usually omit the trombone part, until the timing is perfect to drop the punch line. To this day I live and die with the Crimson Tide, and I'm so grateful daddy got to see them rise to prominence again before he passed in 2012. They just won championship #18 in January of 2021, and I watched it with all my inbred cousins.

After living in Birmingham for about a year, my dad and his three brothers moved their families to California. We settled in Carmichael, a suburb of Sacramento. After finishing first grade there, my dad told us we were being transferred to Japan. A family friend drove us to San Francisco and dropped us off at Fort Mason, where we boarded the Sultan, a small, converted troop transport that certainly wasn't a luxury cruise ship. We cast off for the 14-day trip across the Pacific Ocean. We lived most of that time at Yokota AFB. Maybe we were just insulated because we lived on base, but I never detected any animosity from the Japanese I encountered. I'm sure all those who were allowed on base were heavily vetted to ensure they harbored no resentment after the war.

We bought a house for $1,400 and had two maids and a houseboy. Living large. Our primary maid was Aiko and she was very cheery and capable. When I was about eight, my mom wasn't satisfied with the job I was doing getting myself clean, so she assigned Aiko to bathe me. One day when Aiko leaned over the tub, I copped my first feel. Hey, a young boy has to be resourceful when opportunity knocks! In retrospect, it was wrong of me to take advantage of this young woman who probably felt she needed to keep her mouth shut in fear of losing her job.

Every night while we lived in Japan, a tanker truck would drive through the neighborhood spraying a mist of DDT out the back because of diseases mosquitos were carrying. They put some kind of fragrance in it and it smelled really sweet, so my buddies and I would ride our bikes behind it, inhaling the tantalizing aroma. Any questions about my arrested development and why I turned out the way I did should be answered right there.

After three years in Japan, we moved to Colorado Springs and I loved it—except it was too far from an ocean. But I was lucky: I went from having Mt. Fuji outside my bedroom window to a view of Pikes Peak. I enjoyed the snow, and everyone kept their tire chains on all winter. We lived there just one year, then it was back to Carmichael. If we would have stayed there longer, I would have attended Wasson high school and been a classmate and teammate of Rich "Goose" Gossage, the great Yankee pitcher who was the same age as me. I also used to ice skate at the Broadmoor Arena, where I watched a gorgeous Peggy Fleming practice her skating.

I started sixth grade at John Barrett School about two weeks into the school year. It was a scene where all these kids had been classmates since kindergarten without anybody coming in or going out of the class. So I had to fight most of the boys to assume my place in the pecking order. There were two guys in the class who had been held back a year, so they were bigger than the rest of us. Fortunately, they were too involved in fighting each other to bother me.

It was when the Beach Boys ruled the radio waves and hot rods ruled the streets. Sam Barris, brother of legendary Hollywood car designer George Barris lived two blocks away. His kids both went to Barrett and a couple times the Batmobile and Munster Koach were in his driveway. I got to sit in both of them.

I got my first job as a paperboy for the *Sacramento Union* and had to get up at 4 a.m. to make my deliveries. I didn't have a bike, so Daddy took me to Bobs' Cycle Center in the neighboring suburb of Fair Oaks. They've moved a few blocks from there since, and I just recently bought another bike from them. But in 1963, I simply *had* to have a Schwinn Varsity 10-speed like all the other kids. Daddy, ever the Scotsman, said the store on base had one called a Huffy with all the same features for about $20 less, and he thought that was the smart move. I was devastated at the prospect of having to endure the stigma of being the only kid at school with a Huffy! Compliance was mandatory there. I pleaded with him not to do this to me and finally he relented. *Whew!* To this day, my family and I refer to any lesser-desired product as being the "Huffy" of whatever the category is.

I was a horrible student but they just pushed you through back then, especially if you were an athlete. So after somehow graduating from eight grade, I began my high school experience at Del Campo in 1966. My freshman year I got five "Fs" out of six classes, I think I passed Speed listening… One frustrated teacher asked me, "I can't figure out why you struggle so much. Is it ignorance, or is it apathy?" Unable to grasp the irony of my responce I answered, "I don't know and I don't care." During my senior year my girlfriend Lorna did all my homework (It was her idea) but she couldn't take the tests for me. I'd have done a lot better on the tests if they hadn't had so many idiots seated around me...Lorna later was Carole King's personal assistant for 40 years and married her guitar player. I read Ms. King's autobiography and she mentions her frequently. See Lorna Beth, if we hadn't broken up you never would have met your soulmate.

That year was memorable because a new student arrived named Johnny Baker. He was better known as "Dusty" Baker, and his family was the first black family in Carmichael. He was the perfect guy to integrate the area because he was total class and the best athlete in the area. It didn't matter if you were a zit-faced freshman or whomever; he would know your name and take the time to talk to you. Dusty and I used to go to Memorial Auditorium in downtown Sacramento for the boxing cards, and one time we saw a young kid who was having his first professional fight. His name was Ken Norton and it lasted one round, with both of them on the canvas several times before Norton finally had his opponent (Harold Dutra out of Half Moon Bay) hearing Brahms' "lullaby".

One day I took Dusty and a few others out to the base to meet a sergeant, Fred "Preacher" Lewis, who was working for my dad and was also a professional boxer. We're cruising down Madison Avenue towards the base, with Dusty driving the canary-yellow Oldsmobile 442 that he got as a signing bonus from the Atlanta Braves. I'm a passenger in the car next to him, a GTO. It's about 4 p.m., and the guy driving the GTO starts trying to bait Dusty into a drag race. Next thing I know we're going down Madison at about 110 mph, door to door! Madison wasn't quite as crowded back then, but it was still stupid madness. Nothing bad came of it, but we were idiots. I was in that same GTO one day with that same driver and he's flying down Mapel Lane, which is a Carmichael neighborhood street with a few bends in it, at about 115 mph. We blew right by the house where the girl I would marry 15 years later was probably playing in her yard. Thank goodness that little 9-year-old wasn't out in the street at the time! It was in that backyard that we tied the knot. I never got in a car with that fool again, and, once again, I am fortunate to be here today.

You would think that Dusty was the most famous person to come from Del Campo High School, but there was a guy in my class named Scott Patterson who was on the cover of *Time* and *Newsweek.* He was drafted, and when they put him on the plane to fly to boot camp, he hijacked the plane to Canada. Can you imagine what the other draftees were thinking? Back then they took hijacking pretty seriously. I remember him as being our "Commissioner of entertainment" at Del Campo; he was in charge of lining up the bands to play at our dances. He was pretty clever when he gave his speech at the school assembly to ask for votes along with the other candidates vying for the same position. He utilized lines or titles from various songs in the Top 40, and when he closed his comments, he said, "If any of you don't vote for me, don't think twice, it's all right." Thank you, Bob Dylan. The plane he hijacked landed in Vancouver. There was conflict between Canada and the United States over whether or not Canada would extradite him back to America for prosecution. Perhaps he should have belted out a few verses from "Gimme Shelter."

While at Del Campo, we played a basketball game against Rio Americano, which was about 15 minutes away and in a bit more affluent area of Carmichael. All those Olympic swimmers like Debbie Meyer and others from the Arden Hills Swim Club went there. One of the Rio song leaders in particular caught all of our eyes. Her name was Barbara Klein, but she became much better known in *Playboy* and on *Hee Haw* as Barbi Benton.

Once the football season ended my senior year, I was introduced to the Devil's lettuce. The majority of folks in my generation had already taken Timothy Leary's advice to "Tune in, turn on and drop out". I even dropped acid a few times. The first time was in the morning before class with several of my buddies. We all had PE together 3rd period and it was fun to share our observations up to that point. Never did any of that after 1970 and have never tried Coke, Heroin, Meth or any of the other substances.

One night when I was about 17, I was sitting in Sambo's, a pancake house that evidently disappeared due to incorrectness, when a man sitting at the table next to me asked if I knew anybody wanting to buy a car. He said it was a 1956 Chevy, wanted $50 for it and he lived a few minutes away. I went over there with him, took it for a spin around the block and made the deal. At the time I was the meat carver at a Hof Brau and had a few bucks in my pocket. My dad had always told me he'd pay half for my first car so he got off easy with that $25 commitment...so did I. The 1956 Chevy is still the most beautiful car ever built and I got a lot of use out of it until it succumbed to various afflictions. That car was a rolling bust with all sorts of illegal paraphernalia and lurid tales within its' doors. It's a miracle I wasn't busted numerous times.

Toward the end of my senior year, my middle brother, Marty, who had been attending UC Berkeley (a great place to learn how to read and riot) became quite involved in the radical anti-war movement. One weekend he brought a couple of friends up and it was my first experience with real '60s political subversion. One of the guys was Willie Brandt (no, not the German chancellor) who was the founder of a fanatical group called the Berkeley Revolutionary Army, or something like that. Marty told me that these guys had a bunch of plastic explosives, and a couple of years later, Willie was arrested for having a bomb factory. He brought along his girlfriend who was named Wendy Yoshimura, a few years later she was Patty Hearts' roommate. It was at her apartment where the cops busted in and arrested both her and Patty.

I was in Berzerkely during the People's Park demonstrations. The roof of Martys' apartment was just a good Molotov cocktail's throw from a lot of the conflicts; the Peoples' Park fiasco was just within range. He continued to socialize with extremist friends. Marty had a roommate named Willie Wolf, who eventually became infamous as "Cujo." He was Patty Hearsts' lover in the Symbionese Liberation Army. He ended up dying in the L.A. shootout and fire along with the leader, Cinque, and most of the other SLA members. I met several people who later became members of the SLA.

On the lighter side, there was a basement at Marty's house that was a music studio and housed many guitars, drums and keyboards. The gent who lived next door used to come over and jam with us. His name was Eddie Mahoney, but he later became known as Eddie Money.

In the spring of 1970, when I was 19, my father got tired of his lazy, hippie-bum son and kicked me out of the house. I lived on the streets for about six months, sometimes in my 1956 Chevy when it was running. My diet consisted of whatever I could shoplift from the local stores, mainly beef jerky, Snickers bars, and hunks of cheese. I was so hungry, I went to KFC to lick other people's fingers. The American River was my bathing facility. The old Fair Oaks Bridge was the hangout, and if you've ever seen a movie called *The Stunt Man,* that bridge is prominently featured in it. I jumped off that bridge well over a hundred times.

I did have one income source during this time. Despite my emaciated condition, I was still wide enough across my back to slide about ten records up my shirt and tuck it in. I charged $1 a disk and my friends would give me a list of desired platters and I would hit Tower records to do the job. At least the other local stores got paid for the Snickers and jerky for a couple of days...

Enjoying a nice afternoon buzz during my hippie bum days.. Now why would my 28 year Air Force Colonel, who's political leanings were just slightly to the right of Darth Vader want to kick this future law enforcement officer out on the streets?

When the winters' chill and rain came, shorter hair, being clean, having available food and going back to school didn't seem so bad. I had dropped to around 150 pounds of solid steel and sex appeal (NOT!) so I moved home, got freshly shorn and received my GED (Didn't graduate with my class due to being so rebellious...and disinterested). I then started classes at American River College in Carmichael. Some of my buddies there were very handsome dudes. So whenever we were out on the prowl (Wearing shirts without a natural fiber in them if you don't count the dog hair) and if we met some girls, I was gonna get the one with the good personality. That's okay, she was, too.

I once met a girl at ARC who was three or four years younger than me and had attended Bella Vista High School in Fair Oaks, one of my school's rivals. She took me to a Bella Vista party and I hear her saying, "Hey, Gordon, I brought somebody here that's as big as you!" Well, "Gordon" turned out to be Gordon King, who later that year would be the number one draft choice of the New York Giants as an offensive tackle. She was wrong about one thing: I wasn't nearly as big as Mr. King, and after he came over and sized me up, he fortunately decided I wasn't worth the energy to flick against the wall. Thank you, Mr. King.

Around this time, one of my buddies went up to Chico State University, which had the reputation of being the No. 1 party school in the nation. I would go up there most weekends that spring of 1972 to evaluate whether that rumor was true. His roommate was a guy that years later would be one of my sergeants at Mule Creek. When Chuck Berry performed in the campus gymnasium, the atmosphere was thick with the pungent aroma of NorCal green bud. None of us had ever heard of the opening act called the Doobie Brothers, and when Mr. Berrys' back up band didn't show up, the Doobies graciously stepped in and backed him up. Talk about bumbling into a splendid moment!

In the summer of 1974, a buddy got me a job as a lifeguard in El Dorado Hills, up in the foothills above Folsom. A lifeguard is the greatest job in the world. Doesn't matter how much of a dork you are, put that lifeguard label on you, and the girls will have their crushes. I still have Facebook contact with several of them, even though they live all over the nation now. Being a lifeguard was kind of like working inside the Beast—both required a whistle and being able to administer discipline. Not too many inmates obeyed me though, when I ordered them to sit on the bench for 30 minutes.

That fall, after the pool closed for the year, I got a job with the biggest construction company on the West Coast: Teichert Construction. Did a lot of different jobs there including their gold reclaiming project. I became a foreman of a small group that basically took care of the land they owned, which was extensive. We'd put up fences, take down fences, paint houses, plow firebreaks, things like that. Teichert owned a lot of houses, too; they needed land so they could eventually consume the layer of old riverbed gravel about 20 feet under the dirt covering. Two buddies and I moved into one of those houses and paid $75 a- month rent. That's $25 a piece.

The Farm. My bedroom was front right. Upstairs was the lounge. Crop was out back, behind the barn. We installed that A/C unit upstairs, which made about 50 square feet tolerable in the summer.

I had a company pickup, a flatbed truck, a van and a few tractors at the house, plus a key to the gas pump, so it was *on*. We made it into the ultimate bachelor pad. A crop we were growing of about 200 plants out behind the barn added to the ambience. We never sold it, but just used it ourselves and gave it away to all our friends. This was back in the day where we just kept blazing one joint after another trying to get higher. Eventually we learned when you do that, you don't get more high, you just get less weed.

The first year of our crop, we planted a row of corn around the outer perimeter of the pot to conceal it from the ropers who sometimes walked around the cow pasture that surrounded the place, changing the irrigation flows. When harvest time neared, the cattle broke down the fence to get to the corn and ended up eating most of the product. That gave them the munchies, and they wolfed down all the corn then covered the rest with poop. I can just imagine when those cattle burped up a few of those cannabis cud balls to chew on and then laid waste to tons of hay they never before realized was so delicious. Maybe they even experienced paranoia about their tenderloins ending up on someone's plate. Too bad they didn't have alfalfa-flavored Doritos.

Gold mining is really hard work—you're lugging around the heaviest elements on earth. Between humping containers of water, black sand, gold and mercury, it's a chore. We would have to carry buckets of all these things up and down five flights of stairs at the gravel plant, usually in bad weather, making the steps quite slippery. A 100-pound container of mercury is about the size of a quart of milk. This was the thing that finally caused the hernia I'd had for eight years to become painful enough for me to realize surgery couldn't be any worse. We also weren't smart enough to be aware of how unhealthy being exposed to mercury was, so between the DDT in Japan and the mercury here, how could I not be a little unhinged?

One day it was raining. Whenever that happened, we would have to apply some belt dressing to the inside of the conveyor belts to prevent them from slipping at the ends near the pulley. One worker was applying the dressing, slipped and lost his balance. When he put his hand down to keep from falling, it went inside the belt and was pulled around the turning pulley. It snatched his entire arm right out of the sleeve. Most of us were down in the break room eating lunch when the man came in, staggering. We threw him on the floor and tried to apply pressure to what was left of his arm until an ambulance could arrive. Nice man and a good worker, but his career was over, and I began to realize maybe I should find another vocation.

Teichert was a great company to work for, they were a very conscientious and took good care of their employees. Every Friday I would pick up my check from the very pretty and bright black woman who handed them out. It definitely raised a few eyebrows when she was my date at the Christmas party. Fridays always were exciting in the construction industry, it was payday, so it was all about getting paid and getting laid.

There was a girl named Sherry who used to come over and hang at our place—"The Farm" as we called it. She was very pretty and fun, and later became successful under the name Sherilyn Fenn and was a big star in the *Twin Peaks* nighttime soap opera. She also starred in several movies, including *Boxing Helena,* and played the lead in *The Elizabeth Taylor Story*. She dated Prince and was engaged at one time to Johnny Depp. We were very proud that she realized her dream. We talked frequently about it with her, and it was something she really strove for, and I'm glad she made it. Hope she still remembers warmly those carefree days with "The Farm Boys."

Every summer, Teichert would give me a crew of teens from Oak Park, one of the lower-income areas in Sacramento and have me try to keep them out of trouble and put a few bucks in their pockets. One year, they also gave me two guys from Del Paso Heights. The Oak Park and Del Paso factions didn't especially have warm and fuzzy feelings towards each other. One day, we were painting some houses near the gravel plant and the older women who lived there called Teichert and complained that they'd been robbed. Turned out, the two dudes from the Heights had broken into the house and stolen the women's social-security checks. One of the fellas from the Park told me which two did it, and I fired them on the spot, leading to one of the Heights' chaps alerting me that I'd better start bringing a gun to work. The dude that ratted them out to me had a brother who became well known throughout CDC for being involved in the last murder of a CDC staff member, a sergeant at San Quentin. I became acquainted with him on *Alpha* yard at Mule Creek years later.

One of those dudes from the Heights is on death row for doing the same thing, except this time he decided to kill the two elderly women. That guy drove an old, raggedy-ass Cadillac Tuna boat back then, and one day I noticed one of the gas drums we had in the storage barn was losing gas at a higher rate than it should have. Obviously, this fool had gotten ahold of one of the keys and was coming out there at night to top off the tank of his lead sled, so I switched the labels on the two drums in there: one for gasoline and the other for diesel. We never saw that old tuna boat again. It was a valuable experience that would benefit me greatly in my prison career. Most of the guys were good kids and I learned some cool dialect I didn't hear in Carmichael.

I began seeing the girl I would eventually marry seven years later. I had dated her older sister a year or so earlier and invited them both to the inaugural "Farm Party." We had spent about 10 months turning the place into party central and when they showed up, I did my best to cut Pam out of the herd and we danced the Bump all night long to Barry White, Ohio players and the Commodores, with a few quiet moments of the front porch swing in between. I had two tickets to Earth, Wind & Fire the next weekend, but she said she had to study for finals. I didn't know people like that existed, but the following Friday night we had our first date. We saw the original *Rocky* and were together for the next 30 thirty years or so. She bore me the two sweetest kids in the world. Pam was seven years younger than me and was Del Campo's homecoming and senior ball queen, as well as student body president.

I was quite taken with her appearance, as well as her intellect, character, sunny disposition and ambition. I tried to be helpful on her quest to attain her doctorate degree, but she really didn't need anybody's assistance. It's like that slogan. Behind every successful woman, there's a man . . . checking out her butt.

No, that is not a perm...Richard Simmons eat your heart out!
Back in early dating with Pam & picking the 'Fro.

Even though we're no longer married, she lives five minutes away and we are great friends. She's still a classy human being and is mostly responsible for me finally realizing that it was time to grow up (One of these days I'm actually going to). She did a great job raising our two kids while she got her Masters and Doctorate degrees.

I spent a couple years waiting tables in historic Old Sacramento at a place named Fat City. Almost all the waiters were gay and it was commonly referred to as "Fag City". It was here that I met Kevin Henderson, who would later be a softball teammate, roommate, golf buddy and a guard at Folsom who primarily helped me get through the selection process for CDC. One of those waiters was especially flamboyant, swishy and years later I was working in R&R and guess who came sashaying off the bus, It's hard to sashay in leg irons and waist chains but he pulled it off. He recognized me and I reassured him that he'd have a full dance card there at the Creek. Seems like you don't see too many homosexuals who embrace the Country Western, Cowboy persona but this guy was a real Brokeback Buckaroo. I guess there's nothing wrong with a little ridin', ropin' and redecorating...

After that I returned to college, this time at California State University at Sacramento and two years later I received my BA in Journalism and Communication studies. Finally, I had become a good student! It was easy because I was taking classes I liked, and since I was now with Pam, other things like chasing *girls* weren't part of my distraction. Most of my classes were in the speech and drama building where another gent by the name of Tom Hanks was also getting his diploma. Still waiting on that role as the bad guy in your next flick Tommy.

One of my professors got me a summer job at KROY, a local rock radio station doing news and traffic. While working there, I also got to go to the 49er and Raiders' training camps. This was 1981, and I went to the 49er camp in Rocklin, CA and interviewed head coach Bill Walsh, who was very nice. I asked Coach Walsh if he had a minute for an interview, and he graciously agreed to my inquiry. That year, the 49ers ended up winning their first Super Bowl. Still waiting on my Super Bowl ring Mr. Walsh for my contribution towards the winning Super Bowl Mojo.

Even though I wasn't working there anymore, KROY hired me the next year to go to Raiders' training camp in Santa Rosa. There I interviewed Marcus Allen, Jim Plunkett, Lyle Alzado, the late John Matuszak and Matt Millen. Lyle Alzado was extremely polite to this cub reporter, as were most of them. Plunkett was the only one who was a jerk to me, but maybe he was having a bad day or just didn't like the way I looked and acted.

Most pro athletes pad their personal statistics: I was taller than most of them except Matuszak. Alzado and Millen came up to about my chin but they were thick, wide and solid and could have easily thrown me over the goal posts. Matuszak had a head the size of a grizzly bear! He walked by me going toward the locker room and I asked if he would mind doing an interview. Matuszak brushed by me, saying, "Give me a few minutes," and continued into the locker room. I figured he had blown me off and I started looking for someone else to interview but, then after about five minutes, he came walking back out and said, "Okay, let's do it." I was shocked, and he was very cooperative.

Al Davis walked by and I asked if he had a few minutes to talk and he brushed me off by stating I should talk to "The Man," which apparently meant the coach, Tom Flores, who was walking beside him. Mr. Flores was very kind and gave me a nice interview. Both Flores and Bill Walsh were very skilled at giving answers that were in that 20- to 30-second range that they knew could be used in a radio spot.

Marcus Allen had been the Raider's first round draft pick that year. He had been holding out for a few months, but had signed his contract that morning and ran straight out onto the practice field after doing so. I was standing there as he came off the field following the morning session and asked him if he would allow an interview. He accepted, despite complaining about having blisters on his feet. So… allowing for a little creative license, I did Marcus Allen's *first* interview as a professional!

The next summer I got a job as the announcer for the Lodi Dodgers, the L.A. Dodgers' Class A affiliate. Yep, stuck in Lodi again. I had lots of fun doing that and met many players who later made it to the big league. Before one game, I had to go down to the dugout and tell Kent Hrbek, who was playing for the Visalia Oaks, to pack up because he was going to "the show" with their parent team, the Minnesota Twins. His euphoric hug almost broke my ribs.

Being a minor-league announcer meant I operated the scoreboard and was also the bouncer. I had to come out of the booth on many occasions to give numerous fools the bum's rush out of the ballpark. Every Thursday night was "beer night," and you could get a 12-ounce Budweiser draft beer for 25 cents. By the third inning, most of the crowd was pickled and disorderly, which meant I didn't get to spend a lot of time in the broadcast booth. We also had many giveaways from local merchants, and, being a poor college student, I would make up names for the winners like: Ben Dover, Rusty Trombone, Buster Hymen (Pastor Hymen on Sundays) Harry Cox, Lance Boyle, or Hugh Jorgan. I then kept the free pizza or Whoppers for myself. As long as the merchant got his company's name blared over the airways, I don't think they cared. I did that job the following summer, too.

Sometimes, after the games, I'd take a few tokes with the umpires. I won't use their names, but two of them have been working in the major leagues for several decades now, and I've seen them umping World Series games. Sometimes they make calls that have me wondering if they blazed up before the game.

I soured on the idea of a career in broadcasting. Remember that feeling you got whenever you had to get up in front of class and give a speech? I had that feeling every day I was scheduled to work and decided I wasn't going to live that way. So I got a job with the Oakland A's Baseball Club. I worked with one other guy and a supervisor, covering the Sacramento area, trying to get companies to buy season tickets. Companies could use them as incentives for their top employees and as gifts for their loyal customers, then write them off as a business expense. We would work the area all week, then go to Oakland for the weekly marketing meeting on Friday at the Oakland Coliseum. Our bosses told us that the top agent would be given a high-level marketing spot. I was the top sales guy, but the job went to a lady who'd caught the roving eye of someone who mattered. Allegedly...

A few months later we were having an Easter Seal benefit meal at a local hotel in Sacramento, and the A's sent three or four players to appear and speak a little. One of them was their second baseman at the time. I learned later he had purchased a bit of the Devil's dandruff from my partner's father. I feel comfortable talking about this because he was later traded to another team and had many well-publicized issues with the booger sugar.

After that, I starting working for IBM, mostly in the electronic typewriter division like the Wheelwriter. I jumped around from company to company, utilizing their three-month "training" salary, leaving just as it was about to expire, and then going to their competitor for the next three months. Eventually, a good friend felt sorry for me, bouncing here and there, and gave me a job selling computers inside a small store. One of their products was Wang computers, and they had us wearing buttons with sayings like, "Ask me about my Wang," or "My Wang works wonders." I knew nothing about computers and my friend realized that, but it just shows you what a great friend he was and still is.

I walked into that store on the first day and realized I was completely out of my element regarding anything about computers. I was terrified each time someone walked in and would start asking questions. I did somehow manage to sell a system to actor Timothy Busfield, who lives in Sacramento. He, along with his brother, run a local theatrical venue. Within the first hour of work, I went into a back room and called my old roommate, who I met while waiting tables. He was now a guard at Folsom, and I said I was ready to start the process of becoming an officer. I'll be forever grateful to Kevin Henderson for all the help he gave me getting into the CDC.

I had on about a dozen occasions gone into Folsom Prison and played softball against the convicts. The prison was always looking for teams willing to come in and play the fellas, but my wife, Pam, was not so cool on the idea of me going in there. The guards had a team in the Folsom recreation league called "The Bulls" and I knew a lot of them, having competed against them for years in that league. It was a great league, and Louis Tiant from the Boston Red Sox, along with Dave Revering, the former New York Yankee first baseman, played in it. It was always exciting to go inside the prison, and we always whipped their asses.

I didn't think Pam would be too happy about the thought of me working as a corrections officer, but when I got home after that day at the computer store and told her what I was thinking, she said, "Go for it!"

The trips into Folsom to play softball were quite interesting. First, we had to pass a warrant check, and then agree that we understood that if any of us were taken hostage, the department would not negotiate for our release. It was fascinating to think about all the killings that had taken place on the yard where the games were played. Unlike more modern facilities, there is only one yard there, and if you've ever seen the TV movie *The Jericho Mile,* that track is part of the field where we played. As we warmed up, a lot of inmates kept asking us if we were any good, because they had to get their bets in. I needed to give the inmate team our lineup so I went into their enclosed dugout. They all looked at me like I was crazy to come into such a confined spot surrounded by killers. I guess I'm just not smart enough to be scared. The guy who ran their team was a big black man, and I was told he had a fairly large role in that *Jericho Mile* movie, but I've never watched the flick.

The players were very polite to us because they loved having outside teams come in and they understood that if there were any problems, that would be the end of that. Anything to break up the daily routine was welcome. There was a basketball team that would come into Mule Creek State Prison every year and play the cons, but it was some type of religious organization and after the game they would preach about seeing the light. Everybody knew they were coming a week or two in advance, and I'm sure that was also the case whenever we went into Folsom. I never knew of any softball teams coming to the Creek. Man...would I have loved to sock a few taters against the Mule Creek felons, but it wasn't allowed.

The last time I went in there to play, we went to the new part, called New Folsom back then. It is now known as California State Prison Sacramento. It had a much different vibe. These inmates were Level 4s, the worst level, and they weren't very polite to us. We played one game each in two different yards, and the convicts booed and jeered as we entered their space. They yelled out a lot of disparaging remarks intended to frighten us, and it probably worked on a few. The inmate umpires told us that because there was no outfield fence, any ball hit onto the track was a home run. I hit one well out there, and their left fielder ran onto the track and caught it about 25 feet beyond the grass...the umpire called me out! On the next yard, I hit a ball that cleared the table area beyond the track. Their left fielder went all the way up onto the basketball court and caught it around mid-court. I was called out again. I found out later that the umpire was Angelo Buono, better known as the Hillside Strangler. It then made sense why he took such delight in facilitating my failure, he just liked watching people choke...

Before the game, there were three big, completely inked-up White guys standing behind our bench—there really wasn't a bench, just the area where we kept our bags—and I asked them who the money was on and one of them snorted, "Who do you think?" I later learned those three were Blue Norris, Cornfed Schneider, and Art Ruffo, three of the heavy shot callers from the Aryan Brotherhood (allegedly). Norris and Ruffo were later killed by their own people (allegedly). It was Cornfed, the man who had been deemed "The most dangerous man in California" who asked me the rhetorical question. More on him later in the chapter on gangs, quite a story.

We beat them handily.

I ran into numerous prisoners over the years who remembered me from those games. Of course, most of the inmates remember me from my time *as Big D at the Creek*.

Richard A. Mcgee Academy

AFTER SOMEHOW HOODWINKING the selection department into clearing me, I entered the correctional academy in Galt, which is about a 45 minute drive from my home. I had been assigned to San Quentin. I wanted to go work at Folsom because I knew so many from softball in the Folsom league. But there were no openings there, and the seven spots available at Mule Creek had already been taken. Most of the cadets knew somebody at the selection office who processed them during the evaluation phase and had been alerted earlier in the day of which institutions had positions available and they had already called the institution to claim a position. My mail didn't arrive until the afternoon, so I got shut out of my first preferences and the "Q" seemed like it would be interesting to walk those historic tiers and death row.

The academy is a few miles north of Lodi, so I was used to the trek. It was a Saturday and some of the cadets reported on Sunday too, but most of the weekend was spent getting your uniform, your hair cut to an acceptable length, linens for your bunks as well as lounging by the pool. Lots of checking out prospects of the opposite gender going on there and then. Our bunks and lockers were the same ones used by the inmates.

That Monday morning there was a meeting in the gym for all the cadets. The academy was an old Catholic school, there was much screaming from the sergeants and it became clear this was real and serious. Several people walked out and quit right then once they realized how intense this paramilitary endeavor was going to be. Some were probably not prepared for the prevalence of profanity, which would make a longshoreman blush, but if you couldn't handle hearing a lot of very crude cussing, you probably weren't going to excel in this profession. There were about 30 cadets in each company and about seven or eight hundred total. All in all, training was a six-week program back then. That is, until later some cadet sued the state for not paying overtime after 40 hours a week. So the state decided to make it last 16 weeks after that. Glad I didn't have to stay there that long.

The academy day typically started at 0400 hours, and first thing would be physical training (PT). It would consist of a rotation of several options including running in formation, aerobics, self-defense, weights and calisthenics. That would go until around 0530 or 0600, and then you had until 0800 to shower and shave, do your assigned side duties and eat chow in whatever order you preferred. Your shoes had to be perfectly shined and uniform perfectly pressed. Back then we wore a tan shirt with brown slacks that made us look like UPS employees, but now the cadets wear olive green CDC jumpsuits right from the first day. A great deal of our off-time was spent shining shoes, ironing clothes and studying for academics. Several cadets would make various trades in exchange for doing chores for others. I had snuck a Sony Walkman in and would lend it to another cadet who would iron my clothes with military precision and put a great shine on my shoes. The different genders were all together for everything except for sleeping, but that was just in another row of dorms.

Cutting up at the Academy. These are the UPS like uniforms we wore until graduation. Both of these two cadets were headed for Pelican Bay.

I lived in a bay with 22 other fools and there was no air-conditioning, just a large fan at the opposite end from my bunk. I was there from July through August, so it was quite hot in the dorms, classrooms, shooting range, chow hall and everywhere else. There was no TV and we never knew what the temperature was, so the weather just broke down into three categories: not too hot, hot, and real fucking hot. Seemed to me that the latter was the usual condition. I never once used any of the top sheets or blankets provided because it was sweltering at night. The Walkman tape player I had smuggled in would have gotten me in trouble if it had been discovered by any sergeant, and they did on occasion do locker searches. It was worth it to listen to music and the Giants games while lying in the bunk.

At 0800, classes would start and they continued throughout the day and frequently until as late as 2100. We learned early on in classes about hostage situations. The inmates, as well as staff, know they could take over at any time, but the inmates also knew that no matter what they did, they wouldn't be leaving the grounds. The CDC has a non-negotiation policy, and the inmates know of the department's commitment not to stray from that procedure. First off, if you are taken hostage, your chances of being sexually assaulted regardless of your gender are very likely. The inmates will make you take off most, if not all, of your clothes. This will leave you feeling particularly vulnerable and humiliated. They will then put your clothes on to create confusion in the event of intervention by SERT (Special Emergency Response Team). Sometimes the inmates may force you to wear their clothes. If SERT threw flashbang grenades, and if there was any gunfire, we were to remain proned out, because the SERT guys may not know whom is whom. Near the end of my career, there was a female cop who was taken hostage at a different prison and was fortunately released but did endure the typical assault. She resigned shortly afterward.

There really have only been a few righteous prison takeovers. Everybody knows Attica. Alcatraz had a good one, too, but there's haven't been very many compared to some of those South American joints. Typically, if the inmates can take over, they break into the pharmacy right away for some joy pills. I heard about one where after the inmates got their issues from the drug store, they sought out a few Chesters (child molesters) and rats on whom to instill some prison justice. They apparently rounded up a few and took blow torches to their skulls. Who says those vocation programs aren't working?

Each week at the academy, we would be awarded liberty for a few hours on Wednesday evening and on weekends if we passed various inspections. Because I lived 45 minutes away, it was great to go home and see my wife and one-year-old son, Sam. Those from the faraway ends of the state never left for the entire six weeks. Several of those, including staff, took advantage of the opportunity to become better acquainted with the opposite gender regardless of their marital status. I must admit, I was somewhat surprised at that behavior.

Most cadets who bombed out of the academy flunked due to academics or not passing the shooting range. The .38 pistol gave many of them problems. Some of the sergeants and cadets took advantage of certain females who were struggling on the range by offering to take them to a private range during liberty for personal instruction. There was little doubt about what their aim was. After we graduated, one of the sergeants that I had really thought was a good guy was doing late-night duty with one of the female cadets. We were required to do at least one shift of security duty during our six-week stint. They were in the office in the middle of the night, nobody else was around, and at one point, the female cadet turned around towards the sergeant, and there he was, with his pants unzipped and brandishing Ole Blue. He was fired.

The shooting range was given a full week of training time and was an interesting experience. Some had never fired a weapon and it showed. We had to qualify with four different weapons: The Mini 14 rifle for the yard gunners and towers, the H&K carbine for inside the housing units, the .38 revolver, and the 12-gauge shotgun that was used mostly for transports. The H&K used a unique 9mm projectile called a "Glazer" round. It was a bullet made of Teflon that was filled with small BBs, and when it hit a living tissue, it would burst and the BBs would spread out and do some serious damage, remaining within the victim. The H&K was very good for inside the housing units because the Mini 14's .223 round would pass right through the body, ricochet around, and probably hit a few other people. The H&K was a great weapon—it was accurate and relatively quiet and didn't have much of a kick. For some reason I was never clear about, CDC stopped using it and started using the Mini 14 everywhere, including the housing units. I never knew of one being discharged inside, but I wouldn't want to be in there when it was. Not only was the prospect of being hit by the bullet bouncing around those walls and floor upsetting, but it would be really loud! Most officers had only used the Mini at the range with ear protection on, but having discharged it on several occasions during incidents, I can vouch for the sound it makes when fired.

The .223 round is the same one used in the M-16 that was common in Vietnam and has been getting a lot of mention due to so many of the recent school shootings because it's what an AR-15 spits out. It's a relatively small projectile in diameter, but rather long. It has a whole lot of gunpowder behind it and tends to deflect around once entering the body, causing a lot of organs to be damaged. If you were in a unit when one was fired, your ears would be ringing for weeks, if you didn't get hit by a ricochet. The Mini 14 used a "Peep" sight, which is a circular disc at the rear sight with a hole in the middle of it. I never liked it. You have to align the front sight in the middle of the hole but you can't see very well what's off to either side of the sight. When I fired shots later in my career, I had to keep peeking over the rear sight before squeezing the trigger in order to make sure staff wasn't running into the melee from the side.

Before I joined the department, CDC used the 30-06 rifle, and it packed quite a punch. They also used birdshot in the shotguns, which was not very effective in knocking down anyone. Birdshot has a whole bunch of small BBs and simply doesn't have much stopping power. The inmates told me stories about planning to hit someone; they would just put two coats on and get busy. I also met a few OG sergeants (original gangster, as any staff or inmates with a lot of time in were called) that showed me scars on their legs from trying to break up fights and getting hit with birdshot. They would tell the gunner not to worry about hitting them, to just to go ahead and shoot. By the time I got in, we were using 00 buckshot, which has much fewer, but much larger pellets, and if you got shot with one of them, you were not likely to get up or even survive. They would really tear up some flesh.

When I first rolled up at the Creek, we had the Special Emergency Response Team and they were there to intervene in hostage situations. SERT used slugs in the 12-gauge, just one big hunk of lead, which had a much bigger kick than the pellets. The larger the projectile(s), the bigger the kick. I had a lot of respect for some of the smaller women that fired the shotgun. One woman in particular, who was destined for Pelican Bay was so petite she could have used my socks for a sleeping bag, really got rocked by the recoil but regained her stance and kept firing.

Once we arrived at our institutions, we would be required to qualify on the range every 90 days. Early on, we would go before or after work and get paid overtime for the approximately two hours it involved. But later on, in a cost-conscious move, we would be relieved from our post, drive out to the range, which took about two minutes and was behind the Level 1 dorms, and qualify. There was a time when the department decided it would be a good idea to have a group of officers on each watch who could be called upon to do emergency medical transports, and that those officers should be more capable with the weapons, especially the .38 revolver. Prior to that, the watch sergeant would call his favorite cops whenever an emergency transport was needed and it was always the same two guys. Resentment grew that the same two guys were getting all the overtime. I was one of those chosen to become part of the medical transport group and it was a pretty tough course of fire. We only had about half as much time as regular qualifying to complete each aspect of transport range, which involved shooting six rounds, emptying the spent casings, reloading utilizing a speed loader, and firing the next six rounds within a certain time frame and hitting the target silhouette enough times to pass. This scenario was repeated from 10 yards farther back for each aspect from four distances. Regular range only had three distances. Finally, one course of fire would have to be completed using our weak hand just in case we had gotten wounded or our strong hand had become useless for whatever reason. It was tough, but I always passed. It's amazing what just 10 yards farther away from the target can do to your accuracy when the barrel is only four inches long. We were also taught to use the speed loaders without looking down at them and keep our eyes focused on the target or adversary while reloading. I always worked on my quick draw and fire technique because I subscribe to the philosophy that if you shoot first... you shoot last.

There were several times at the academy when I kinda did one of those movie zoom-outs and would reflect on the amazing series of events that had led me to this time and place. It might be standing in formation for inspection, at the shooting range, marching, PT, studying or lying in my bunk, but I would have one of those moments when it felt like I was looking down on myself and was hit with the astonishing fact that I was really there, working my way to become a correctional officer. So many variables had led me to the moment, so much good fortune.

Towards the end of my stay, we went to Sierra Conservation Center, a prison in Jamestown, for on-the-job training. We did searches and tried to learn from staff in real-life situations. Whenever the cadets came to MCSP in my years there, the water pressure dropped to a trickle from all the toilets flushing down dope in the cells. Those cadets were thorough.

In the last day or two, we did physical testing. Not too tough—we had to do 30 push-ups and sit-ups, as well as run two and a half miles in under 30 minutes. Gravy.

Before I graduated, I heard some scuttlebutt that a female scheduled to go to Mule Creek had failed range. My heart fluttered. I ran to the phone, called downtown to the central office, and asked to be put into that position. Because I was the first to request it, I got it! What a relief. Although it would have been fascinating to walk those historic tiers and yards of San Quentin, California's first prison, I was going to have to commute to the Bay Area for at least a year and put in a hardship transfer request and hope for the best, but not now. I couldn't wait to tell Pam that night in our evening phone call, and it was a big load off of both our shoulders that I would get to spend a lot more time with Sam during those critical first years..

Finally, after six weeks of obeying orders, passing tests, 12-hour days, and marching around, I was ready to graduate. Back then, they had a big party the night before the ceremony and it got pretty wild. It was at some hall near Elk Grove (where I had seen the great high-school basketball player Bill Cartwright play my alma mater) about 15 minutes or so from the academy. We had been warned about numerous cadets getting busted for DUI on the way back and never getting their badge, so I was wary. But not too wary to stash a bottle of bourbon near the academy grounds in a cornfield, and a few of my buddies and I had some nightcaps before we had to sign in at 0100. They no longer have a graduation party, I guess due to the likelihood of losing too many new guards.

The next day was intense. We were graduating at the Spanos Center in Stockton, and we were all pretty hung over. Marching into the auditorium wasn't so easy. This was the first time we had been able to dump our UPS uniforms and wear our CDC ones. The ceremony was long and boring, but eventually I got to walk across the stage and was handed my badge: #44087. My wife, mom and dad were there, and we were all so proud as Pam pinned the badge on my uniform shirt. The ne'er-do-well, hippie-slacker youngest son had finally accomplished something!

Reporting for Duty at Mule Creek State Prison

THE TUESDAY AFTER academy graduation, it was time to venture out to Ione, to Mule Creek and begin my 25-year endeavor of correctional duty. Ione is a small, sleepy little motherlode town in the Central California foothills and was the former home of jazz great Dave Brubeck. The area was the kind of place Wrangler jeans with a big belt buckle, cowboy boots and hat were the standard wardrobe. Half the residents either worked at the Preston Castle (The Youth Authority institution right beside Mule Creek) or Mule Creek. Most residents believed there were only two types of music, Country and Western. That was fine with me—I liked both—and because of my family's Dixie roots, I was comfortable with the lifestyle. Ain't nothing wrong with a little drinkin', cheatin' and losin'. It was the kind of country living where if you heard somebody say they had lost their home to a fire, that meant it had burned all the way down to the axles.

The Preston School of Industry is an interesting place. It's over 140 years old and has had numerous well know inhabitants. Merle Haggard, Actor Rory Calhoun, tennis star Pancho Gonzales, Eddie "Rochester" Anderson from the old Jack Benny show, Former heavyweight champion Eddie Machen, Black Panther leader Eldridge Cleaver and serial murderer from the Sacramento area Gerald Gallegos all shared an address there. Gallegos was convicted of kidnapping young couples, raping the female repeatedly before murdering both of them, all with the assistance of his wife Charlene. He died in prison many years ago, she did a couple years after claiming he forced her to do it. I just recently found out she's living about five houses down the street from me. It closed down a couple years before I retired and we had to absorb a bunch of their staff, pushing many of us down the seniority list. It is rumored to be haunted and every Halloween they conduct haunted tours inside.

I met with the other six fish cops, some of whom I had seen at the academy but didn't know they'd been assigned here until now. We gathered in the administration building outside the secure perimeter, and after an hour or two of orientation, we had our pictures taken and were issued our CDC identification cards.

Naive, raw but eager fish cop with only 25 years left to do. Grew the soup strainer the first few years of my career, trying to look like a seasoned guard.

Then we walked through the sally ports and checkpoints into the watch office. The watch sergeant was Sergeant Stark and he was right out of central casting with his bushy mustache and country drawl. We were issued chits: small, coin-like objects with our names stamped on them, which were used to check out cuffs, keys and weapons. Years later, Lieutenant Stark lived on the 18th fairway of a golf course close by, and I played with him several times there. He always gave me carte blanche to go into his garage and grab a few barley pops from the fridge anytime I played the course. Sometimes, I would leave a few in there as an appreciative gesture. Of course, this Scotsman would take Stark's premium beers and leave some generic swill.

Mule Creek was only three years old at that time and staffed mostly by relative newbies. There were a few OGs there, because even if they only had five years or so under their belts, they would have seniority, which meant they would have better choices for shifts, days off, vacation preference and overtime. At the academy, they really don't teach a lot of things that you use in everyday situations at the prison. Most of that just comes with experience and watching the OGs go about their business. I always picked their brains during slow times, and most all of them were more than willing to give their opinions. Hell, it could save both of our lives. I was always impressed and grateful whenever some green-around-the-gills fish cop would hit me up for advice on specific situations. I would create scenarios for them like, "What would you do if a cell fight broke out during count?"

The Belly of the Beast

The Entrance building. One of the 2 places to enter the security perimeter and the one we used daily unless driving a State vehicle inside. We entered right where the roof shade is, had our IDs scanned and passed through the sally port, which was operated by Tower 1. The left part of the building is Visitor processing. You can see part of one of the visiting patios to the right of Tower 1.

When you're new, the inmates will ask you for permission to do something rather than go to your more experienced partner. It was difficult to know at that stage of your career if it was allowed or a good idea. Over time, I developed a set of questions I would ask myself whenever confronted with such a circumstance. First, could it affect security? Second, if I let one guy do it, I have to let everybody do it too, will that create a problem? Last, could it get me in a wreck with supervisors, staff or even residents? The answers would provide my response to his question.

One thing we learned is that if you see your partner involved in a conversation with a felon, regardless of the nature of the encounter, you immediately went to their side to provide support. It didn't have to be hostile or threatening in any way, you just needed to be in close proximity to him/her. The convicts would keep an eye on which officers adhered to this policy and it could determine when and where they might execute an assault on a cop.

There are three main facilities at the Creek for about 3,600 inmates: Alpha, Bravo, and Charley yards along with the minimum dorms outside the secure perimeter. Each is basically the same. They all have five housing units, a chapel, education area, vocational area, kitchen and chow hall, medical office, laundry, gym, canteen, and program office, which is where the supervisors and counselors are. All the yards have a softball/soccer/football field, a basketball court, horseshoe pit, volleyball court and some workout stations, which are basically bar dips, pull-up bars and things like that. An asphalt track surrounded the yard and was just under a quarter-mile around. There were always two housing unit walls for handball games at each end of the yard. One belonged to the Norteños (Northern California Mexican gang members) and the other to the Sureños (Southern California Mexican gang members) because few of the other ethnicities tended to play handball. We used to have the "weight pile," which was a large collection of barbells and dumbbells, where the weights were welded on to prevent them from being taken apart and becoming weapon stock. Different ethnicities had gained ownership of certain benches through intimidation, areas of the weight pile by strong-arm tactics, as well as different parts of the yard via bullying in order to establish their turf.

There is virtually no shade on the yards other than near the buildings in the later afternoon, but it was out of bounds to be near the walls. Ione is very hot in the summer and it was always funny to see a long line of blackbirds standing in the long shadow of the yard light poles on those sweltering days. Even yard birds have common sense.

View of Charley yard looking towards the program area. Laundry, Canteen, the clinic are visible towards the left. The tall building is Charley gym with OBC, the yard gunner booth above it. To the right of that is Main Kitchen and vocational education. This photographer was standing about 10 yards from where the .223 round discharged by me from OBC tore up the sod during my first shooting. Full story to follow.

There was a heavy punching bag on each yard as well, and you'd see guys beating the hell out of it; most of the time it was intended as more of a warning to other inmates than a workout. Whether you could really bang or punched like a wimp, the inmates on the yard would certainly take notice and treat you accordingly. The inmates weren't allowed to do any martial arts on it or kick it, so whenever I was in the yard gunner spot, I would frequently have to admonish them over the PA system.

Another view of Charley yard. Murals were all done by inmates and were prevalent around the entire institution. Some very talented residents. Inmates utilizing the workout stations which replaced the weight pile after a few fellas used the dumbbells on the dumbbells. Wind sock was for judging the wind direction if chemical weapons needed to be discharged.

Upon my arrival at MCSP, the Hispanics were on lockdown and had been for a couple of months from a major donnybrook on *C* yard between the Northern and Southern Mexicans. It was one of only two times when an inmate was actually shot at MCSP. He was sniped in the ass with an H&K 9mm from the back window of housing unit 15, but he survived. Poor guy, he got socked up and clubbed with softball bats from the Southerners, then pegged in the ass from the H&K, and finally hit with batons before staff realized he'd been shot. The other shooting victim was a few years later from the yard gunner on *A* yard with the Mini 14 and it was a scrap between Bloods and Crips. He also survived.

Warning shots were practically a daily event when I first arrived. Any one-on-one fistfight would frequently result in a warning shot being fired, but later on, they changed the criteria for utilizing them. It became necessary for the same elements to be present for deadly force to be used, but a warning shot could be deployed if, as a last resort, it might possibly stop the threat without taking a life and could be done safely. In my early career, the policy was "shoot to disable," which basically meant aim for his extremities, but later on it was changed to "stop the threat." The best way to do that was aim for center mass. During the "Shoot to disable" period, all of us knew that if we shot a inmate between the eyes or in his heart and consistently had perfect scores at the range during quarterly qualifying, we could be subject to lawsuits or disciplinary action. The victim's family or even CDC could claim we intended to kill the felon instead of disabling him so we all knew it was a good idea to intentionally throw one round off the target at the range.

The Creek has for the last several years been a "Sensitive Needs" institution. It used to be called a PC—"Protective Custody" joint—which meant that if an inmate needed extra protection, he would be sent to us. So the majority of its clientele were child molesters (Chesters), gang dropouts (retirees), rapists (tree frogs), snitches (double agents), or some notorious person who needed to be hidden away to keep someone from taking them out for the prestige. If O.J. Simpson (who knew O.J. stood for orange jumpsuit?), Michael Jackson and Robert Blake had been convicted, assuming they weren't condemned, they almost surely would have ended up at the Creek. Too bad...I could have gotten some great stories about them.

When inmates arrived at Mule Creek, they would go on orientation status for about 10 days. Upon arriving at their housing units, one of the officers would give a little speech outlining the program and expectations. Here is the one used by C/O J. Baker, one of the Creek's true OGs.

"Welcome to Mule Creek State Prison.
You are on the softest yard in the state of California.
You were snitchin' to get here and we expect you to continue your efforts.
We're looking for drugs, weapons and money.
You kick (down) We kick (down).
We got TVs, Radios, Fans and packages.

If that doesn't entice you we will throw in a case of soups, a punk and a bed move.
Everyone on the yard is tellin' so your job is to get off first!
We're lookin' for Black (Tar), (China) White, not green bud or tobacco.
REMEMBER, DROP A DIME, STOP A CRIME!"

J-Bake had a real knack for keeping it real. The only speech I gave to inmates arriving into the mental health housing unit I worked in was to advise them not to eat the Milk Duds on the shower floor...

When I first "drove up" to MCSP, *A* yard and *C* yard were main line yards, meaning they accommodated general population inmates who did not need to be protected from inmates that might object to them being snitches, rapists, gang drop outs, or Chesters. *B* yard offered such protection. *B* yard was probably the softest yard in the state and was full of inmates not welcome among the state's finest offenders. Some called it Camp Snoopy. No other yard in the state provided any inmate the opportunity to do time without getting caught up in gang activity or being terrified about being held accountable for his behavior by true convicts. Most joints you will be either predator or prey, but now with these protective yards it's possible to do your time fairly safely. When Scott Peterson had his death sentence for murdering his wife and unborn child in the Bay area overturned, I heard a lot of people saying to let him go to main line and he would be taken care of by the population. That was the old days fokes, now they can live out their days in safety.

Many of those on *B* yard had "green light" hits out on them, and if a righteous gang member had the opportunity to hit one and didn't handle it, they could be subject to having a contract issued on themselves. This became a problem because sometimes inmates from different yards would be in proximity to each other in R&R or the infirmary. R&R stands for receiving and release, and is where inmates are processed in when they come off the bus or return from a medical or legal transport. It also processes inmates out for parole, transfer, or transport. We had different holding tanks for each yard in both places, but the inmates still could pass each other in the hallway as they were being moved from the tank to see the doctor, and they would definitely take advantage of the opportunity. So MCSP converted all the yards to PC then later changed the term to "Sensitive Needs." Sounds much nicer.

I remember one time when a cop from a northern county was in R&R to pick up several felons for a trial. The proper protocol in such a situation would be for him to apply his cuffs on the prisoner first, THEN remove ours so he is never unrestrained. This guy didn't follow that protocol and as soon as he removed our cuffs from one convict, BOOM...he bombed on an enemy convict who still had cuffs on. Live and learn buddy.

I suppose it's a good idea to have places where inmates can be relatively safe but I must admit, it's tough to watch some of these guys who have done horrible, disgusting things to children or women strut around the yard without any concerns of being assaulted. I'll relate a story here about one Chester that is especially disturbing, so *WARNING!* Skip down to the next paragraph if you don't want to be absolutely enraged and sickened. Seems this, um, "individual" decided he wanted to have intercourse with his newborn daughter and after not being able to gain entry, used a razor blade to perform his version of an episiotomy to allow him access. A puke like this would have gotten stuck within hours of arrival in prison before the introduction of "Sensitive Needs" yards.

Snitches are also viewed low on the totem pole. However, in order to be allowed to come to MCSP, in theory anyway, the inmate couldn't be gang affiliated, show any predatory behavior, and had to "debrief," which doesn't mean removing your underwear, but is code for ratting out your former gang members. As a result of this, any inmate who had done time at the Creek and got transferred to a main line joint had some "splaining" to do to the other inmates. In the old days, being a rat was pretty much a death sentence, but they all now know they can go to one of these "Sensitive Needs" joints and be surrounded by other rats and Chesters. Tellin', or rattin', is pretty common. They're all tellin' now, and we frequently knew when something was about to jump off well before it did.

There was a fellow on Alpha yard who was always ratting out convicts on the yard who were dealing dope. He did it because he was a "Distributer" himself and wanted to eliminate the competition. He wasn't even slick about it. I frequently overheard him on the dayroom phone calling the squad and when I was the Plaza cop he would be hanging around the yard gate wanting to be escorted to the squad office. All the convicts knew it but nobody moved on him.

If it hadn't have been for Susan Atkins spilling the frijoles to her cellies in County jail, the entire Manson gang probably would have never been caught. How many of you knew the cellmate she ratted herself and the gang out to was Virginia Graham, who later parlayed that opportunity into a daytime TV talk show called "The Virginia Graham Show"? Another quick fun fact...the bailiff at the Manson trial was Rusty Burrell, who later became well known as Judge Wapner's bailiff on "The Peoples Court". He was also the bailiff at Patty Heart's trial.

I had an Aryan Brotherhood member tell me how they found out who the rat within their midst was. If they suspected that someone close to them was tellin', they would inform three or four of the ones whom they suspected of a different area where they had buried a weapon on the yard. Then they'd watch to see where the goon squad came with their metal detectors and did some digging. That location would tell them whom the rat was and he would usually have a little daylight shone upon his inner organs.

The "gooners" are the security and investigation squad that scrutinizes the behavior of inmates and also staff. The dots have to be collected before they can be connected. There are about eight of them and they are selected from officers that apply for the position. Frequently they are observed with suspicion from other custody staff who may feel that they are out to get staff when they should be more focused on inmate transgressions.

If an inmate got busted for an offense and wanted to lessen the discipline he was going to face, he might give up a few others to get a more favorable outcome from the charges he was facing. There is a saying inside the Beast: "Those who squeal get the best deal." I had an old convict tell me that in the earlier times, inmates wouldn't really talk to us at all for fear of being thought of as a snitch. He said that if they were talking to a cop on the tier or at their cell they would speak in a very loud voice to make sure everybody could hear what they were saying . . . and not saying.

There is something called a "squeal mark" or sometimes a "snitch stripe," which is caused by slicing a snitch from the side of his mouth along his cheek to his ear with a razor blade to leave a scar and forever brand him as a rat. It's not unlike the branding used throughout history to identify someone guilty of adultery or an escaped slave. It's the scarlet letter of prison.

Sometimes the inmates would rat themselves out to avoid having to carry out an order or act that was likely to get them in a wreck. I had a convict working as a clerk in the main kitchen who was supposedly an Aryan Brotherhood member. He had been instructed to hit a particular fellow white boy who had fallen out of favor with "the Brand," which is another name for the Aryan Brotherhood. He told all the big mouths on the yard about the hit he was to execute, knowing it would get to the right staff members. Those of us in main kitchen knew about it, along with the yard supervisors and the squad. As soon as the inmate hit the yard after work, he was immediately "arrested" and taken to "the hole." He had accomplished exactly what he'd planned. It appeared to the Brand leaders that he was being a good soldier and was en route to complete the hit, but was unable to through no fault of his own. He saved face.

Rats are equally disdained within the custody staff, too. Even we looked down at the inmates tellin' on their own boys unless it was something serious. I always told the inmates, unless it involves someone getting hit who doesn't have it coming, I didn't want to hear it. Tellin' is not appreciated among our brethren either; getting the "snitch jacket" is not something you want to have. Protecting fellow staff and not making any incriminating statements towards them is referred to as the "Green Wall," and it's still true, up to a point. We would try to cover for our partners if they did something against policy. But nowadays, I think most staff is concerned about covering their own bottoms without putting their career in jeopardy in order to protect a coworker who has done something stupid. I've had partners do ridiculous things that put me in a tough position between having to bend a little truth to save their asses and risk getting myself in a wreck by getting caught up in their lies. CDC was very clear about making false statements and it would usually result in dismissal. If a cop was terminated, it frequently wasn't because of the act itself, it was for lying about it. When I would get caught up in such a cross, I might do what I had to do to protect my partner (providing it wasn't too outrageous), but I would also let him/her know afterward that they better not ever put me in that situation again. I can remember times when an officer felt that another had not observed the Green Wall and told the truth, which got them in a wreck, and the offended officer would put a hunk of cheese in the other's mailbox or leave some cheese on their car windshield as an indicator to all that this person was considered a rat. I used to tease the B yard inmates when I worked as the food truck driver that when distributing that days meals from main kitchen to the yards that we had to send a double order of cheese to B yard.

There was also something called "Parking Lot Therapy," which meant trading blows outside the walls for some disagreement or plain dislike for a fellow staff member. It was understood that whenever a conflict got to this point, regardless of what had transpired, that this scrap was the end of it; the administration was never supposed to find out about it. Although I've heard it was not uncommon at other joints, the only time I ever witnessed any parking lot bouts at the Creek was when two females officers were slugging it out.

Almost all of the inmates at MCSP were hiding from something, so as a rule there weren't many large riots. Most of the fights after the SNY (Sensitive Needs Yard) transition were one on-on-one and usually due to drug or gambling debts or someone feeling like another was trying to swoop on his punk. But in my first 10 years or so there, we had our share of wars between rival gangs.

Regardless of whether they're in a "safe space", Chesters occupy a special place of disdain. And they're frequently people that you know like a family member or neighbor. In a main line joint, if an inmate was suspected of being a Chester, he would be told by convicts he needed to "produce paperwork," which meant show his court records to the others about his crime. Usually, if he was indeed a Chester, he would immediately tell an officer he needed to get off the yard, and he would then be sent to administrative segregation—possibly another yard or institution. Sometimes the inmates would let him stay on the yard but he would have to pay "rent." Rent was giving the other inmates all or most of his canteen or having relatives on the outside send money orders into the other inmates' accounts. Sometimes they would let him remain on the yard, too, if he could get a job in the watch or program office, keeping his ears open for valuable information from staff that weren't being vigilant about who might be within earshot. If a Chester can get a job as a clerk in the program office on their yard, he would be typing all the write-ups from staff and reports that might contain sensitive information about rivals. There was a clerk on B yard who was educated and personable. I found out later he had been a Captain in the CHP but had a weakness for underage children. I remember another inmate on *B* yard who was about to be transferred to Folsom talking all kinds of stuff about how he couldn't wait to get there because he was sick of being around "all these Chesters!" Well, turns out he was one himself and three days after arrival at Folsom he was found with his throat slit and a rolled-up *TV Guide* shoved up his ass. Someone was "channeling" his anger.

On my first day I was assigned as a floor cop in housing unit 14 on C yard. There were two floor officers, one control booth officer, and two hundred convicts. Nobody on the ground anywhere in the joint had any guns. The only guns were above the floor or above ground level, so no inmate, in theory anyway, had the opportunity to get their hands on one. I had to have total confidence in that control officer paying attention and knowing where I was at all times. It's not really a given that every one of them actually *would* shoot if the situation required them to do so. The climate in the prison world now is such that some would be hesitant to shoot anyone for fear of losing their job, their freedom, or getting sued by the inmate's family.

Most of us, including free staff, like teachers and cooks carried alarms. They looked like a garage door opener, and could be activated in an emergency. They were programed to set off the alarm in the area they were in and wouldn't work if you took it away from that area. When activated, it would make a loud buzzing sound and a spinning blue light would come on outside the building so that it was easier for staff on that yard to identify where the problem was. It would also make a high-pitched noise inside Main Control, and a little red light would show on the institutional diagram telling staff where it was. Then they would announce it over the radio. A routine alarm would be a "Code 1, Alpha yard!" or "Code 1, Building 9!"

When I first got there I would sprint towards the alarm because I wanted to show the inmates I was prepared to handle some business, and I knew they paid close attention to who was in shape and ready to get busy. In later years, I realized it was more important to be under control as you responded in order to have something left in the gas tank once you arrived in case you had to fight one or more convicts. The vast majority of alarms were false after someone accidently bumped into something that pushed the button but we had to respond to all of them as if it were truly an emergency. A few C/Os did have their careers end after getting injured from slipping or tripping during responding to an alarm. It was especially tough during the rainy season to run across the yard that was all muddy and torn up by sporting events. There were a few cops that had gotten injured on their day off but didn't go to the doctor right away so they could come into work, fall out, and then claim they were injured on the job, making them eligible for workman's compensation. This was risky, not only because of the chance of being busted for fraud but also there was always the possibility that the state doctor might decide you would be unable to continue your career. If you did suffer a career-ending injury, you would usually get 50 percent of your salary, tax free, for the rest of your life. Not too bad, but I never met anybody that did it intentionally.

In those early years at the Creek, when responding to a fight, I'd tackle one or both of the boxers to break it up. But really, CDC doesn't want you doing that. It's best if you see a fight to hit your alarm or call a "Code" on the radio, note the time, pull up a chair and take notes (or bets). Then once we have a large enough numerical advantage, go ahead and dog pile them. Usually after a minute or so, the inmates would be tired and looking over at us like, "Aren't you going to stop this?" If we were in a scrap with one of them and they were on the losing end, they might be trying to reach for our alarm and push the button themselves.

I was having a chat with a convict one time about whether or not it is a good idea to let the inmates fight it out in order to alleviate tension or beefs that some of them may have with each other. If it is allowed to fester, it could build up and result in a more serious assault. I told him, "Look, you see us (I was a yard cop at the time) hanging around in front of the program office. If you have a problem with a guy, you can go to the other end of the yard and put 'em up. It gonna take us a minute or so to become aware of it, and another thirty seconds or so to run to that end of the yard, so you have maybe two minutes to slug it out. But when we get there and order you both to get on the ground, you better kiss dirt!"

In the real early days, whistles were used and we were all required to have one on our person at all times. I had the same one for my entire career and never blew it once and only recall hearing a whistle maybe once or twice in my twenty-five years. I think they should be used more because it can't be set off accidentally like an alarm, which I rarely carried. When there were sporting events on the yard, the inmate referees used those New Years Eve type of party horns instead of whistles. It prevented any panic or confusion that a disturbance might be taking place. By the time I got there, whistles had been mostly replaced by electronic alarm, which produced a very loud buzzer sound when activated. Shortly after beginning my career, I was attending a local high school basketball game and when the buzzer sounded to end the first quarter, I nearly jumped out of my skin.

I recall playing in a softball tournament in Richmond near Oakland back in the mid-Seventies and we played a local team called Swahili Incorporated. They all had their names on the back of their jerseys like: Stabber, Pimp, Pusher, and one named Chinchilla Chuck. Someone with our team had a whistle and would blow it intending to fire us up, but when he did, most of the Swahili team dove on the ground and as did a few in their crowd. We know where *they* had spent some time. It was kind of intense for us lily-white boys but we bought some boo (weed) from their first baseman, "Big Red," and everything was cool after that. It's always good to contribute to the local economy to endear yourself to the indigenous inhabitants.

For the last seven or eight years of my career, CDC decided we were all required to wear protective vests. These were not bulletproof vests but were called "stab resistant" vests. Not stab *proof,* stab resistant. They were very hot and bulky, uncomfortable, and pretty worthless. If a convict wanted to stick you, they'd go for your neck, your femoral artery, or your side where there were not plates in the vest. Plus, being so tall, the thing only came down to above my belly button, meaning a convict could easily still give me a C-section. Once the administration started really sweating it, I did wear one for the last two years of my career but I took the front plate out so it was more comfortable. If a sergeant came up to me and would pat my back to see if I had mine on, it felt as though I did.

Every day, yard would be recalled at 1600 hours in order to conduct count. One of the yard S&Es (search and escort officers) would have brought the mailbags in from the mailroom by this time, and each floor officer would take the mail for the tier they were working and sort them in the order of cells. It was not unusual for there to be around fifty to seventy-five letters on each tier that we had to deliver. After conducting count, we would walk our tier, approach the cells, and call the name of the inmate. He would recite the last two numbers of his CDC number and if it was correct, we'd drop the letter(s) on the floor and kick them under the door, which had about an inch of clearance on the bottom.

You had to be vigilant to prevent mail from falling into the wrong hands, and it had to be a little tough on the ones that never or rarely received any correspondence from the outside world. I didn't feel too much compassion, though, because I felt they must have done things to alienate the people who loved them. I was also wary of any "podium pals" hanging around the officer station while we were sorting the mail, because they might be looking to see if they could read the return address or name on a letter in order to hit, pressure or extort an inmate's family. This was especially important at an SNY joint where dropouts and snitches are hiding out, and a "sleeper" could be trying to find out where another inmate's family is living. A sleeper is an inmate who has convinced a counselor or administrator that he needs to be protected from another inmate's ire in order to gain access to a specific felon that is already on a sensitive needs yard in order to do harm to him. Even if the podium pal wasn't a sleeper, he could sell or trade that information to someone on the outside via a phone call or letter.

Back to my first day in building 14, after count cleared, I was sent over to the chow hall for my first evening mealtime. Not to eat, of course, but to cover the inmates. There is no lunch hour provided in a CDC shift for the officers, so we just had to eat when the opportunity presented itself.

The inmates would enter the chow hall in a line and approach the slot where an inmate worker would shove a tray out through the slot. The inmate would then go sit at a four-seat table. The tray slot was blind, meaning that the inmates working on the steam line inside couldn't tell who was next in line. Therefore, the servers were unable to give their homies any extras or mess with the food if they could tell the recipient was an enemy. The inmates in line would try to use various tapping codes on the painted-over windows to alert their buddies behind the glass to give them a bonus, the hungry man tray or even an extra spoon. Conversely, if the inmate worker knew the next tray was going to an enemy, they could either mess with their food or give them the "Childs plate". There was however, an officer standing by the tray slot checking them as they came out.

Charley dining hall, the place I covered on my first shift. The inmates would enter and walk along the rail on the right, proceed to the end wall and receive their tray through a blind slot to the left of the letter "B". They would then fill their cup with either coffee or juice from the containers in front of the "B" then take the next available seat. The gunner up in the booth would walk back and forth between this side and the identical one on the other side. On Alpha yard dining (Level 4) there was a gunner on each side.

That cop would be looking not only for extra food on a tray but also for not enough food. He would also double check for a spoon and fork. The inmates would sometimes leave the area, get to their table, and either pocket some food or utensil—perhaps give it to a friend/

homie—and then go back to the tray window and claim he had been shorted some food or wasn't given both his utensils. This is one of the ways an inmate would get metal stock to make a shank. At the end of the meal, the kitchen cop would have to count all the silverware to minimize the chances of weapon stock falling into a convict's hands. With about 1,200 guests on each yard, it was pretty much impossible to make a completely accurate count after every meal. Usually, the kitchen workers would form groups of 25 utensils and the kitchen cop would count the groups. Then he would randomly count a pile now and then to try to deliver the workers from temptation. If a pile was found to be short, the inmate has plausible deniability so why wouldn't they pilfer one now and then? Good, hard steel that's already in a shape easily formed into a sticking device will fetch a tidy sum on the yard or curry favor with the shot caller of your subset. Later on, the inmates were issued a fairly heavy-duty plastic spoon and fork, and it was their responsibility to keep them clean and bring them to the chow hall. This was a smart move.

When the inmates approached the table to sit, they were required to take the next available seat and not mill around and get a seat with their buddies. They would always try to take their sweet time, loitering around the coffee or juice containers, and stalling if they didn't care for the supping candidates in order to try to get to a different table. While they were filing in along the narrow walkway leading to the tray window, they frequently would try to move past other inmates to join up with their homies, but this was against the rules. Most cops didn't sweat it, but I always did. Anytime I saw one doing that, I would go over and escort them to the back of the line. I didn't like it whenever I saw someone moving towards another one with his back turned. If you got distracted by something and eventually noticed there was an empty seat that had been skipped moments earlier, you and everybody else in there knew you just got beat.

Once seated, inmates were also not allowed to stand up until everyone had finished their meal, and the officer who was not watching the tray window would tell each row when they could leave. That officer would try to time each row's release effectively because the inmates drop their trays off at the dishwasher area on the way out, and we didn't like it any time too many felons got bunched up in a pack; it would be easier to stick someone in a group and get away undetected. After dropping off their tray, they walked out the door, and a cop would be standing next to a tub filled with water. The inmates would have to show both of the utensils to the officer before dropping them into the water tub, that was before they were issued the plastic ones.

There would be about five or six officers standing outside the chow hall, and inmates would be randomly be selected to be put "on the wall" and patted down. Usually, all we found was fruit or sugar packets they were trying to collect for fermenting Pruno (prison wine) but occasionally we would catch them trying to get out a metal spoon.

As that meal progressed, I noticed the volume level in the chow hall really started to escalate. The concrete walls of the room intensified this, and I found it very alarming. There was a gunner in a booth above the floor and I kept looking up at him to see if he was concerned but he didn't seem to be. I asked the other officer in there with me about it and he told me that it was actually a good sign, and when things got real quiet, then it was time to be nervous.

After the meal was complete—usually it took around two hours to feed the gym and five housing units—we would have about 30 minutes before evening yard and dayroom opened up, which would be at 1900. This break between chow and evening program was usually when the officers would break into their lunchboxes.

Yard and dayroom would usually open around 1900 and we would run an unlock at 2000 so inmates could come inside, go outside, or pick up/drop off something in their cell and perhaps return to the yard. Once yard and dayroom were recalled at 2100, my partner and I each would count one of the two tiers in the building. Each had fifty cells with two bunks apiece so it was easier to do a negative count, which meant noting the empty bunks and subtracting them from one hundred instead of counting actual persons. This count is conducted at 2130 hours and rarely had outcounts, unlike the 1630 count, as nobody would be at work, at school, or in visiting. I would rarely allow inmates to engage me in conversation while conducting count, as they would try to distract me from focusing on counting if there was an escape or something going on farther down the tier, and they wanted to give their buddies time to cease their activities.

Sometimes there wasn't anyone assigned to a certain bunk, but also, he could be working in the chow hall or somewhere else. If you called in a bad count, the Main Control sergeant would ask which bunks were empty and they could track down if there was a valid reason for it. Years later, I worked in Main Control and the sergeant in there had me set up and take the counts on many occasions. It's fascinating and complicated. I'll expand on that later.

After getting relieved from my post that first shift, I drove home feeling exhilarated and proud. This new job didn't feel like work to me. I was just hanging with the fellas, talking bunk with them. It came easy and was something for which I had the physical, intellectual and emotional aptitude to handle. It also helped me appreciate that I was able to lie next to and cuddle with my wife. I held her extra close that night...and that was just one of the reasons why she was delighted about my new career...

I had to wait until my second day on the job to have the most embarrassing moment of my career. I was sitting in the dayroom with my partner and was fiddling around with the set of handcuffs I'd been issued for that shift. For some bonehead reason, I started to wonder if I could put it on my hand, click it to the first notch and still get my hand out of it. I got my answer when I clicked it on the first tooth and...you know it...I couldn't get my hand out. In those days, we didn't have a cuff key on our key ring in most positions, so I had to ask the control-booth cop to pass one down so I could unhook myself. Of course there was a key up there, but this veteran cop saw the opportunity to milk some entertainment out of this rookie's stupid behavior. They could see I wasn't even smart enough to be an idiot. He said he didn't have one but if I went next door to Ad Seg, they would help me out. I hid my hand in my pocket and headed over to Seg while the control booth cop called over there to alert staff in there about the dimwitted fish cop and their opportunity to have some fun at my expense. I sheepishly walked up to the first C/O I saw, explained my predicament to him and asked him to remedy my crisis. Even though every cop in Seg has a cuff key, he claimed he didn't have one but sent me over to another floor cop to take care of it. There are five floor officers in Seg plus the sergeant. Each and every one of them claimed to not possess a key and passed me off to the next one for their merriment. Finally the sergeant felt sorry for me and unhooked me. I'll be forever grateful to Sgt. Cliff Brown for ending the fiasco and taking pity on me. I think he became a Captain later and has been over to my man cave for football since he's also a Cowboys fan. He was also our running back when Mule Creek played the Youth Authority team from Preston next door in the Bull Bowl. It was a charity game and was televised locally. I played defensive end after not have pads on for about 30 years. Good thing I was on vacation for a week after the game which we lost.

Throughout my career I would work with staff that heard of that incident and remarked "Was that YOU? I heard about that but didn't know who the lame was." I deserved the ridicule and knew that the embarrassment was well earned. I laughed right along with them but never heard of anybody ever being curious enough about cuffs that way to do such a dimwitted move.

The Hole

THE NEXT DAY I worked third watch, which was from 1400 to 2200, and was assigned to Administrative Segregation (Ad Seg) which is also called "the hole." These guys were there because they got in a fight, got busted with dope, a weapon or pushed somebody down on the playground. Sometimes, though, as I said earlier, they might be there for protection. They were in the cell pretty much all the time except for a shower three times a week or to go to the small Ad Seg yard about three times a week for about two hours. They got their meals through a tray slot in their cell door and any time they came out of their cell, they had to back up to the tray slot, stick their hands out, and have cuffs put on before the door opened. Sounds like it would be easy for the cops in there, but it was a lot of work. You were pretty much cuffing guys up, taking them to one of the six showers in the building, closing the grill door to the shower after they went in, uncuffing them, and giving them the razor that was assigned to them. Then you took a different inmate back to his cell and got another to put in a different shower. Ad Seg was the only housing unit that had locking grill gates to the showers. There was a box on each tier with the razor assigned to that bunk in it, and all the disposable razors had the handles cut way down so there was just a little stump; this was a precaution against providing the inmates anything they could make into a weapon. The razors were replaced whenever the inmate in that bunk left and a new one took over that bunk in order to discourage the spread of HIV or Hep C.

Some inmates were either very skilled or double jointed. There were times I'd escort an inmate back to his house (cell) from the shower, close the door, and before I could get my cuff key ready, the convict would hand me the cuffs through the tray slot. Nice of them to wait until they were back in the cell.

Years later, I was doing an overtime shift in there and there was this one absolute POS that had raped, stabbed and set a nurse on fire in Carmichael. Somehow, she survived and he acted as his own attorney during the trial, so when he cross-examined her, he really hammered her. You know the saying, a man who acts as his own lawyer has an idiot for a client, so he got a life sentence, which is way too lenient. One day, this loser had a few letters for mail pick up, but I walked on by his cell. He yelled, "Hey, get my letters!" I politely declined and he started in with a barrage of obscenities towards me. He was a classic "Cell door warrior" as inmates were called for the bravado they exhibit as long as there's a door between us, not unlike todays' "keyboard warriors" on social media. They liked to talk and act tough, but as soon as the door was opened or you encountered them on the dayroom or yard, they'd pee (figuratively) all over themselves. This phenomena applied to some staff as well. There were a few cops that talked and acted tough up in the control booth but if they ever did a swap or changed positions and were then on the dayroom floor or yard…they were meek and accommodating to inmates. I leaned in close to this jerk's window, towering over him, and said, "I know a lot of nurses in Carmichael." He immediately shut up and kept his mouth shut from then on.

On the day shift, which is second watch, 0600 to 1400, after doing morning chow, the main duty the officers have is to run out the yard. Ad Seg has a small yard adjacent to the building, which is separated into several different areas. Two main sections that are approximately 20 yards long by 12 yards wide and have a basketball hoop, a shower nozzle (the tower officer could turn off the shower because the inmates would run to it if any tear gas or pepper spray was being used for an incident), and a back wall can be used for handball. There are also several small, fenced areas within the yard not much bigger than a cell, which are used for "walk alone" status convicts. These are ones that have been deemed too dangerous or vulnerable to be exposed to any other inmates.

There was once was a felon in one of the small, walk-alone enclosures and he decided he'd had enough of Ad Seg and prison in general. So he climbed up the chain link fence and over the razor wire. He got sliced up pretty good but managed to get over the fence and began running toward the vehicle sally port by Tower 7, which was about 200 yards away. He got there and tried to squeeze through the narrow gap between the inner sally port gate and the perimeter fence, which was not very large but he did get an arm and part of one leg through the gap before Ad Seg staff tackled and cuffed him. He visited the infirmary and was returned to the hole. The officer who worked in Tower 7 that day was number one on the seniority list and was known affectionately by inmates and staff as "Beer Can Bob." He told me he had the Mini 14 leveled on the intruder and if he would have gotten through the gap and gained admittance into the sally port, that inmate was going to be the recipient of at least one .223 round. The administration was really caught off guard. I don't think it really ever occurred to them that anybody could make it over that fence without being so torn up by the razor wire that he would be unable to continue any escape attempt. They figured it was an isolated incident and I don't recall them changing anything regarding the fence or policy. To my knowledge, it has never happened again.

When I first got to Seg, officers would bring a few inmates inside from the Level 1 dorms to clean. That was until they caught them passing kites (prison notes) and dope under the cell doors. After that, the officers did the cleaning. Inmates in Ad Seg can't come out of their cells without being in handcuffs, so it would be pretty hard to mop.

The inmates who were eligible for the Ad Seg yard each day would be brought outside in cuffs and wearing only boxer shorts. They would be allowed a towel and handball. They would be placed into the sally port leading to the yard and stripped out by an officer standing on the outside, and then the other gate would open and they could enter the yard for about three hours of "recess."

The two main sides of the yard were used to separate the inmates who might have been from rival gangs. If a fight broke out, the yard cop would say, "Yard down!" on the radio and staff would respond from within the building to assist in quelling the incident. Officers would never enter the Seg yard and would have to hope that the wood or rubber projectiles, gas, or fatigue would end the scrap. Staff from C yard would not respond to Ad Seg fights and they were handled strictly by the Seg staff.

The Hispanics would usually try to put on a show to their rivals by doing a big, organized callisthenic session. The activities could be observed by their adversaries through the windows of their cells in that side of the Ad Seg housing unit. The Norteños and Sureños alternated having yard, and the Northerners in particular would try to make a big show of it. All Norteños were required to participate. They would even chant various slogans espousing the superiority of their faction as cadence for their exercises.

Years later, the prison installed a gun tower on the roof overlooking that yard. I wanted that job and got it. I had several weapon options available to me up there to utilize depending on the level of appropriate response. There was the 40mm with various rubber projectiles and gasses for simple fights, the Mini 14 for incidents that involved the imminent threat of life or death scenarios, but the coolest thing was the water cannon. It was brand new in the state and had never been used in an actual incident. Not only would it shoot water at high enough pressure to knock a grown man down, you could flip a switch and pepper spray would be included in its powerful stream.

Every morning after I helped serve chow and picked up the empty trays, I would go out on the yard and search for anything that might have been stashed the previous day for a buddy to pick up. Could be dope, a weapon stock or a kite. I also had to check all the fasteners holding the chain-link fence to the poles in order to make sure they hadn't been removed either for a potential escape attempt or to make into a weapon. The areas where a fastener was were spray painted red so if any had been removed it would be easier to spot. Once I had lugged all the weapons from the building's control booth onto the roof and over to the tower, I would have to pressurize the water cannon and test fire it to get all the air bubbles out of it. Since it was in its early stages of deployment, it was pretty temperamental and sometimes wouldn't work. I would frequently spray the windows on the adjacent housing unit and wake up the inmates. One time, my sergeant told me to hose down the whole yard for the purposes of cleaning it, but I forgot to check the pepper spray switch and proceeded to spray the whole yard with it. Once I realized my error, and it was *not* intentional, I drenched it thoroughly with just the high-pressure water. When the inmates came out for yard though, they all began complaining that their feet were on fire!

While I was working that tower job, an officer had been busted for "muling" dope in for two inmates, and both prisoners had gotten sent to Seg for their role in the caper. They were both out on the yard one day and I was conversing from above with them. I said, "You guys did us a favor by getting a dirty cop out of the department." One of them replied, "Well, you'd be surprised what someone might do for five thousand dollars." As he spoke the words, he intently watched my reaction with a sideways glance to this dollar figure, hoping I might be just such a someone and pick up the slack of shipments coming in, especially because being in Seg had put a crimp in their supply. Sorry fellas, I don't need a new Evinrude.

The Ad Seg yard had a very tall net on the side that faced the regular yard on *C* facility. It was put there to discourage the *C*-yard inmates from getting tobacco, dope or kites to their homies who were vacationing in the hole. Inmates would get a handball, make a slice in it, then stretch it partially open and stuff the contraband in. The screen was installed and it was about 50 high, but handballs could still be thrown over by a strong-armed felon. It was a lot harder, though, and sometimes it might land on the wrong side of the split Seg yard. If the package ended up in the wrong hands, negotiations or threats would ensue to remedy the situation. Do NOT cross anybody who's going through heroin or nicotine withdrawal.

Building 12, Administrative segregation...The Hole! Note fence screen on left where the Ad Seg yard is located. You can just barely see the roof of the Seg yard gun booth right above the blue cart. Red curb indicated inmates were not allowed to loiter in the area.

When I was in the gun booth, I knew when I heard certain types of yells or whistles from *C* yard that there was about to be incoming contraband. Since the net was so high, the inmates really had to wind up and give "the package" a mighty heave to clear the obstacle, so it was pretty easy to see them doing it. If I noticed prisoners in Ad Seg hanging around the wall looking like a delivery was imminent, I would radio the yard cops on *C* yard and get them to come over and search the ones I'd identified for them. Later, we also had high-quality cameras focused on the area for when inmates denied throwing the goodies.

There were times during the winter when the Ad Seg residents would still come out to the Ad Seg yard in hopes of receiving a care package from C yard. They'd come out there with rain coming in sideways and thirty-degree temperatures, clad only in boxers, because they were "Jonesing" for something.

I liked the position as Ad Seg yard gunner because I was outside and could enjoy the weather, listen to the radio (which is against the rules, but someone had brought one in and we all knew to hide it in the ceiling panels before leaving). The excitement made the day go by faster. I must admit that I really wanted to be the first in the state to use the "squirt gun," but in the nine months I worked that post, there was not *one* fight on the yard. There were a few scraps when I was on my days off but not while I was up in the tower. I'm not making any inference that the fights didn't happen because the inmates were afraid of my rath. That may have just been a coincidence.

There were several cameras focused on the Ad Seg yard, and sometimes there would be fights that weren't seen by the gunner. Now, *no* one can see everything that happens out there, but if these incidents went on for a while, and I saw tapes of a few that did, that officer would have some 'splaining to do. One time, the sergeants were reviewing a tape of a fight that went unseen, but the gunner's boots could clearly be seen, propped up on the windowsill by one of the cameras while the scrap raged on. He/she was either asleep or blabbing on the phone. There were also some explicit sex acts caught on camera that I heard about but fortunately never saw.

One inmate who had been caught before on camera getting busy with his queen, was informed he was being transferred to another joint. He didn't particularly want to leave the Creek—why leave the wedding suite on the yard? The morning he was supposed to be escorted up to R&R for the bus, I was picking up his tray after breakfast when he made a big show out of taking a huge handful of pills and stuffing them into his mouth. I told the Seg Sergeant about it, and obviously, we had to take the possibility of an overdose seriously. We began to prepare to pop the cell door and go in to get him. Since all

Seg inmates are supposed to be in cuffs whenever they are in contact with staff, and he was already showing that he was too drowsy and unwilling to approach the tray slot in his door to cuff up, we had to go through protocol before entering the cell. Once all the policies had been observed, the control cop opened the door and we hastily entered, slapped some restraints on him, and placed him in a wheelchair for transportation to the infirmary. He was acting like he was passed out but we were all pretty sure this was just a ploy to avoid being transferred. I kept making little wise cracks and he was unable to keep from laughing. It turns out he had taken a handful of vitamin C tablets, so other than not having to worry about contracting scurvy during the voyage to his new address, he was fine. He was loaded onto the bus and probably found some new royalty at the new pen.

One of the tasks that occurred in the hole was a cell extraction. These can happen in any housing unit or holding cell but there's a higher incidence of them in Ad Seg. Usually the inmate will "paper up," which meant putting some papers on the inside window of the cell door so we couldn't see him. The law says we had to be able to see inmates in case they were trying to harm themselves or escape. When resolving the issue by talking to them doesn't work, an extraction team would be formed. A lieutenant or an associate warden would usually come over and try to talk him out as a last resort, but when that wouldn't work, we prepared to go in and get him.

In the old days, we would get him out however we needed to, and it wasn't always pretty. Usually it would involve about six or seven officers. The shield man would be in front, one would be behind him with a baton to hit the inmate's fingers if he tried to grab the shield, then there would be several others with leg irons, hand cuffs, etc., to secure him once they got control. Since I was one of the bigger guys there, sometimes they wanted me in front as the shield man, but in reality, you want a short, stocky guy because of leverage. I remember one relatively new guy who was the shield man on an extraction and the inmate rushed the team as they entered the cell. When the felon hit the shield, it knocked a few of the officer's front teeth out. So after completing the extraction, we had to locate his Chiclets on the floor.

Now they video the entire procedure to ensure that the inmate can't make claims of abuse. They'll use pepper spray initially through the tray slot to try to get him to come out, but usually he'll put his mattress against the door, limiting the pepper spray's effect. Almost every time, the inmate will pee (comply) just before we bust open the door and rush him. The whole scenario is usually created to get some meds, a cell move, some attention, or to try to show the other inmates he's tough.

One time, a lieutenant who has now been out of the department for years, was in charge of the extraction. We had the taser back then, and after getting the team all suited up and prepared to enter the inmate's cell, the guy decided it was time to comply. The lieutenant informed him that once his officers had suited up and the situation had gotten to that point, it was too late, and after the door was opened, he deployed the taser and let the inmate do the Funky Chicken for a minute or so. All involved staff appreciated that the lieutenant didn't let that gent manipulate the system to get what he wanted, but that's also probably one of the reasons why we don't have the taser anymore.

We had one interesting felon in Building 13, which is right next door to Ad Seg on *C* yard, who went by the name of a famous Egyptian prince. He was a pleasant enough guy and was always laughing and smiling, but later he transferred over to *B* yard and didn't smile or laugh anymore when I instructed him in the chow hall to tuck in his shirt, take off his hat, and take the next available seat at the table like all the others. I would kid around with inmates more if I only worked in that location one day a week or was there on overtime, but if it was a position I worked every day, and was responsible for any problems that might occur there, I was a bit more of a stickler for the rules. This gent had been a football star under his real name at a high school near Sacramento and was drafted by an NFL team after playing college ball in Northern California. He didn't last in the pros and ended up in the Miami area with some cult of kooks whose leader was a criminal/charlatan who went by Yahway Ben Yahway. Turned out the cult was basically trying to take over an apartment complex and some of the residents were not keen on that notion, so because this chap was in charge of security within the cult, he was involved in dispatching the naysayers. When the heat came down for the murders, he peed and copped a plea, ratting out all the others in exchange for being given leniency on his sentence. He did 10 years of a 22-year sentence and ended up being put in a witness protection program.

He was living in the foothills in an affluent community and passed a bunch of bad checks so now, he gets to do "All day" (Life) at MCSP. Obviously, if there's anybody still buying into that cult, this gent would be in danger of getting hit, so that's why he's at the Creek. I recently saw on the news that one of the cult members has been quite visible in the front of Donald Trump rallies carrying a sign stating, "Blacks for Trump." I heard him interviewed and, whoa, dude . . . what color is the sky in *your* world?

In the world of Ad Seg, at least, a glimpse of the sky was a commodity, and few inmates wanted to spend much time in "the hole."

Visiting

NEWER OFFICERS ARE often put into visiting because it's always been considered "out of bounds" for any gang activity. You'd have mortal enemies standing or sitting next to each other without incident, no matter how much tension there might be between the factions at the time. However, it's also where the vast majority of contraband enters the prison. Visiting has its' place in keeping families together, giving inmates a sense of hope and incentive to clean up their act, get out and enjoy all the outside world has to offer That's providing they grasp the concept of living within framework and rules of society.

I was working as the strip officer in Alpha visiting early in my career. Who wouldn't want to spend their day observing the nappy doughnuts of a bunch of convicts? The first time I ever met Tex Watson and Lyle Menendez was stripping them out and having them pose in a some of undignified positions.

An inmate will send a potential visitor a questionnaire to fill out, mainly involving the person's important information so they can be checked for warrants, etc. Once approved, the visitor will come to the joint, enter the visitor processing center, then will have to pass through a metal detector before walking to a separate sally port right next to the one staff uses. Next they proceed along the walkway from the sally port to that yards' visiting room where the officer will call the inmates' unit to have the cop there to inform him he has a visit. Usually, he knows he'll be getting a visit so he'll be sitting around with his hair slicked back and all spiffed up. The inmate must wear full state blues, and he will enter through the strip room, get patted down, and then be allowed to go into the visiting room where his honey or friend will be waiting.

They're allowed one kiss upon arrival and one when they leave. Of course, that privilege is heavily abused and the *one* kiss becomes a long, make-out session unless the officer has the stones to enforce the rules. There are rules about excessive contact, but most of the staff doesn't stick to the rules. I always did. Most of the visitors are family but also plenty of convicts who are romancing lonely and homely women that they usually met through some sort of pen pal thing, and they use them to get some rubbin' and cuddlin' as well as to bring in dope, send in money for their books, take in or out information. These inmates couldn't care less about what happens to these ladies if they get busted and will dump them upon parole.

There's a building near the visitors processing called "Friends Outside" and they try to provide assistance to the visitors. For instance, if a visitor shows up and is dressed inappropriately to enter the visiting room and is not going to be allowed inside, Friends Outside has clothing options that might remedy the issue. They also provide rides to and from the joint and a few other services. Sometimes, if an officer is deemed to be a little too attentive or accommodating to an inmate he/she might be referred to as "Friends Inside."

When I first started, there were too many pelvic exams and hernia checks happening under the tables. So the state sawed off the legs and made them too short to hide any lurid behavior. Inmates and visitors were assigned a table by the floor cop, and they were supposed to sit facing the officer podium with their hands on the table. Obviously, the suspected mules and the ones with priors for fondling got assigned front row tables. There were also officers (not me, of course) who assigned the relatively attractive ladies in relatively short dresses to the front row too.

The Belly of the Beast

Inmates and their visitors can go out on the patio, but they either have to sit at one of six tables out there or keep walking in a counter-clockwise direction. They weren't allowed to stand still if they weren't sitting or walk in a clockwise direction. Regardless, it was still easier to get a little tug on the ol dumbstick out there. Another perk? The visitors can bring in $20—only in a clear plastic purse, and the inmates can't handle the money. There are all sorts of vending machines in there; these guys really grub out!

And as for the hard stuff the vending machines don't stock? The way most of the dope comes in is when the inmates arrives, the visitor puts the balloon of smack (heroin)—the Mexicans pronounced it, "Hairen"—Booger sugar or devil's dandruff (cocaine), Shurm, (PCP) crank (meth), or chronic (weed) in their mouth and passes it during the arrival kiss. The inmate can either swallow it then or leave it in there for a minute until no one is looking then remove it and shove it up his ass. They are allowed to use the bathroom in the strip room and the officer stands in front of the toilet with the door open. He may have some lubricant on his neck, hair, or maybe he already greased up his "nappy doughnut" prior to arrival. Trust me, I've seen videos of these dudes transferring drugs and it's remarkable how fast they can "take it to the hoop." Some resourceful entrepreneur needs to come up with an applicator for the balloons similar to ones used to insert tampons; he could make a fortune and they could sell them in the vending machines in the visiting room.

Visitors can buy photos and one of the inmate porters working in visiting will take them with a Polaroid camera. We count the number of pictures available on each roll and after a picture is taken, it must be shown to the officer on the floor, signed and dated to be sure there aren't any gang signs being flashed or any other inappropriate behavior.

There was once a bust involving a Native American felon after his female visitor brought in some smack for him. The Indians are allowed to wear a "medicine bag" around their necks, which is a fairly small, leather pouch containing whatever they consider to be "good medicine." As a rule, these things are considered sacred, religious objects and are not searched or messed with by staff. So this guy's wife, who is also wearing her own medicine bag (containing heroin) around her neck comes into the visiting room. At some point, while walking around on the patio, they switch bags. So he now can go back to his cell with the fire powder around his neck and she can leave wearing his pouch, which contains the money payment. Clever, except the gooners (security guards) were watching some palefaces nearby, observed the switch, and had some reservations about his behavior. They popped him as he was being stripped out to leave and got her as she was going out through visitors' processing.

If an inmate swallows the drug, he can either puke it up upon returning to his cell or wait a day or so to pass it. And even though he's stripped out when he leaves visiting, he can get it up there far enough to avoid detection unless he has a tampon-like rip cord hanging out of his ass. Although the strip officer is supposed to have them squat and cough, who really wants to stare at those nasty turd cutters anyway all day? There were times visitors would even put the bindles in the diaper of a baby. Known Chesters were not supposed to be anywhere near a baby being changed or even hold them.

The security and investigation squad (goon squad) is often in a separate room called "the fishbowl," watching the visiting floor through cameras that can move around and zoom in on something. It's no secret. One time, a squad officer zoomed in on the chest of a rather busty officer in the room to admire her assets. He forgot she had a monitor right there at her desk and saw herself being leered at on the screen! She brought it to her supervisor's attention and that dude got in a wreck with them. He later got fired for other indiscretions, but that was one of the straws that broke the camel's back.

In the cases where the squad has seen something they believe was an inmate either swallowing dope or "keystered" it, the prisoner will be taken to the BCS cell. BCS stands for Body Cavity Surveillance. Very complicated process. First, he's stripped out, then he's issued two pairs of underwear (one is put on backwards) then two jumpsuits (also one backwards) making it harder to get anything out through the fly. Then the ankles of the jumpsuit are taped up and he's put in leg irons and waist restraints. All of this to prevent him from squeezing the drug out of his ass and onto the floor of the cell, where he could claim that it was before he even arrived.

From there he goes into the cell, which has been thoroughly searched prior to his entrance, and where the toilet has a plastic bag put on it. He either lays on a mattress or sits on the stainless steel throne with an officer sitting in front of him, watching. When he does take a dump, the officer has to hold the bag and squish it with his hands looking for the dope. This could go on for days! Not a great job. I had that post a few times on OT and would tell the inmate if he didn't poop during my stay with him, I'd give him an extra lunch. Never had to do the bag squish thing, thank goodness.

One guy passed out the poopy bag and when they looked through the it, they found three balloons of dope. He was ready for this ordeal to end and return to a cell in Ad Seg but then he says, "Did you get all five of them?" Back on the crapper, Homey. It's such a degrading event and so uncomfortable for them, if they have anything they'll usually cop to it and try to get it out before having to endure days of humiliation and discomfort. I've known of guys being in there for four or five days and nothing was found before they were finally allowed to go back to their cells.

I've also seen inmates walking around without their shirts on who have nice zipper scars running the length of their torsos from having balloons burst in their stomachs.

Whenever there was a good bust in visiting on a weekend, it was always interesting to watch on Monday to see who was spending all day and night hiding out in their cells because they're too dope sick to come out. The inmates jonesing for drugs would frequently have to wait and hope they could make the connection the next weekend although they could probably cop from a backup source on the yard. Supply and demand made the price fluctuate, and a recent bust would mean prices would go up as opposed to when there was a glut.

Sex acts were fairly common in visiting and anything from hand jobs to BJs to actual intercourse happened. If inmates are caught doing any of these or with contraband, they are usually put behind glass for non-contact visits for a while. There's a lot of kids and religious folks in the visiting room and they don't need to be seeing that stuff.

There were occasions when a female visitor would show up and because of snitch info, prior busts for muling stuff in, or because of a conversation overheard on the dayroom phones by staff about her bringing his meds in, she would be offered the choice of being stripped out by female staff or leaving immediately. The strip outs were thorough and involved using a mirror at times held between the legs of some of the more rotund women to observe fully all the nooks and crannies in which a bindle could be stashed. The reality of the situation was that the visitor knew that refusing to at least try to get the payload by staff was not going to go over very well with a bunch of junkies who had already paid for the smack, which they needed right now inside the Beast. They could suffer much harsher consequences from them as opposed to the ones the state could hand down if they got popped for muling in some heroin.

When I was new, I was working the visiting room and I got a call from an officer in visitor processing to keep my eye on an inmate I'll call Winters, because they suspected he had gotten a little tug job the day before. So I watched him, and Tower 1 was watching, and so was someone in processing through binoculars. There was some excessive contact but not too much. When he left and was stripped out, the officer discovered his shorts were full of baby batter. So staff eavesdropped on his phone calls that evening and him and his female visitor were talking about how staff couldn't stop them, and that they were going to escalate their mischief the next day.

The next day, he arrived at the strip room to enter the visiting room and the strip cop told him they had a new policy that included stripping out every third inmate coming in and he was the third. He shuffled around and asked if he could use the bathroom first. The officer said, "No, get nekkid!" Winters started undressing and when he got to his boxers, he hesitated, and then dropped them. As he did, a small plastic bag of "man mayo" plopped on the floor. Turns out he was bringing it in for the girl put on her sandwich! I guess he had mighty tasty Miracle Whip. Hey, I warned you there are some twisted folks involved in prison culture and there would be some gross stuff here.

When I was a fish, I got put in visiting often, and one time, a convict who had held a high cabinet position with the Black Panthers had a visit from his attorney. I won't use his name, but he was up there in their hierarchy. He told me that he and his female attorney were entitled to a private meeting room, adjacent to the visiting room. I was a raw rookie, so I allowed them to go into the room where, as I found out later, she gave him an "oral" interview. A few years after that, he was rightfully released without a new trial or anything after some evidence surfaced about the guy who testified against him being full of shit.

Weddings are fairly common in the visiting room too. Nothing like 50 or so of your closest adversaries witnessing the blissful event. And no, a hand job on the visiting patio does not constitute consummation. If they weren't lifers or sex offenders, they could get on the waiting list for some "Boneyard" time. "The Boneyard," as it's known to staff, involves conjugal visits. Only spouses or immediate family can enter the Boneyard, and it consisted of six two-room apartments where the inmates were basically unsupervised for three days. All they had to do was step out of the apartment door four times a day to be counted by the tower officer. The inmates are piss tested on the way in and the way out. Obviously, a ton of dope comes in and the inmate will just refrain from partaking for those three days.

Manson family murderer Tex Watson had four kids from conjugal visits, and eventually the public outcry about that resulted in a law being passed stating that no lifers or sex offenders would be allowed to go to the Boneyard. Tex was not convicted of any sex offenses but certainly qualified as a lifer. Every time a local TV news program ran a story on the new law, they showed Tex's picture, so he caught a lot of heat from affected inmates who looked at him as the reason why they could no longer get an issue from their wives.

The Hispanics would frequently bring in their whole *familia*, including the grandparents.

There was a VCR in each apartment and a collection of tapes they could choose to have the officer put in there. Most of those with young kids, I'm sure, were wearing out those copies of *The Lion King* and *Aladdin* while Mommy and Daddy took another "nap."

One time, a woman showed up for a family visit with her inmate "brother," but when the processing officer, Desi, who happened to be a carpool partner of mine, started searching her suitcase, there were all sorts of negligees and Victoria's Secret stuff in there, and, well, that visit was terminated before he could get his issue. Maybe they would have let her in at a joint in Dixie but California doesn't accept that arrangement.

Visiting definitely has beneficial traits as far as keeping families together and giving incarcerated folks some hope and incentive to behave inside the Beast in order to return to life outside the gated community. This also is where the vast majority of drugs, money, threats and information is exchanged. This Covid-19 pandemic has seriously limited visiting and accordingly has affected the supply line of dope coming in. The only place drugs or other contraband can come inside the walls is from dirty staff or quarterly packages, which I will explain about later.

Ethnicity and Gangs

CDC BREAKS DOWN ethnicity into four categories: white, black, Hispanic and other. It's amazing how even the numbers are between the first three. I have often wondered if judges take this into consideration when sentencing offenders to prison. Like, maybe they get an up-to-the-minute list of the breakdown and decide whether or not they need to incarcerate more whites or whatever. "Other" mainly consists of Asians, Native Americans and South Americans, etc. Many Hispanics would claim they had Indian or Guatemalan blood so whenever the Northern and Southern Mexicans went on lockdown, those guys would be out and about, and able to pass kites, food or dope under the cell doors of their homies locked down.

Each gang had someone who was considered the leader, or "shot caller." He would be known as the guy who "had the keys" to that yard. If he transferred out or fell from favor, someone else would be "passed the keys." Some of the guys selected to be the shot caller for some of the gangs were not the sharpest tools in the shed and I often wondered how these lames rose to such a position of power. In a land of the blind, the one-eyed man is king.

We always knew who currently had the keys to each flavor and I always found the majority of them to be gregarious and personable, even likable. They kept their distance from the day to day criminal activity and let the subordinates handle those tasks, but make no mistake about it, most of them would slit your throat in a second if it served to benefit them in some way.

In order to become a member of most gangs, you had to be "jumped in." That means three or four of them beat the snot out of you. You were allowed to fight back, so it was basically a four-on-one brawl that lasted for a few minutes. After it was over, everyone rejoiced in celebrating the new member. Some gangs had the "blood in, blood out" rule. Meaning you had to "put in some work." That meant assault or kill somebody the leaders ordered you to, and if you decided you wanted to discontinue pledging the faternity, you would be the target of another pledge doing his initiation. Once the state initiated so many SNY yards, it is a lot easier to get out of a gang, but they could always put a green-light hit on your family.

Sometimes, OGs are allowed to "retire" after putting in so much "work" over the years. But if something jumps off on the yard between his homies and their rival, he would still be expected to contribute, and I think the vast majority of them would do so willingly.

At this point, the Asians are lying low and not doing any flexing, but if they were ever to get enough numbers inside, I'm sure that would change. They seem to prey on only their own people on the outside—home-invasion robberies—because they know that most that come over from the old country don't trust banks and keep all their money stashed in their homes. I don't know if I should feel disgusted that they prey on their own, or relieved that they leave Americans alone for the most part. We had one Vietnamese inmate whose name was so long and confusing it looked like an eye examination chart. The inmates (and staff) just called him Charley.

Each ethnicity has several gangs within them. The blacks have Crips, Bloods, 415s (Bay area) and Black Guerilla Family. The whites have the Aryan Brotherhood, Nazi Low Riders and a local group, the Sacramaniacs. The Mexicans have Northern, Southern, 18th Street and Border Brothers. The name MS-13 has been thrown around on conservative media lately as a border security issue along with Fentanyl. No doubt the border should be secure and we should know who's coming in as well as going out but all the Border brothers I spoke with all shared their observation that the wall will stop nobody. I rarely heard any mention of MS-13 during my career. Who knew that the biggest threat to this nation would become domestic terrorists. Fentanyl is coming in mainly through the U.S. Postal service. It's so powerful and concentrated a shocking number of doses can be contained in a single letter. There is an offshoot of the Norteños from Fresno called the "Bulldogs," named for the football team at Fresno State University. They later decided to go out on their own and were known as F-14s. Dumb move, as they now had enemies at both ends of the state and it got so bad they basically have their own prison now. I think DVI is one. I'm sure there are sub-factions even there that keep things lively on the yards.

I must give the Hispanics credit for being extremely clean. When I did any cell search, and we were supposed to do two randomly every day, you could tell it was a Mexican by how neat and organized it was. When they went for visits, their clothes were always immaculately cleaned and pressed.

When I think about the Norteños and Sureños, it always amazes me that they could meet another inmate inside whom you really liked but just because of where he's from, he had to be your enemy. I guess that's true in any conflict, tribalism takes over. The cutoff point between north and south was Bakersfield. Outside the walls, they would almost break it down to streets and blocks to designate who you ran with, but inside they were either north or south. That is until the blacks or whites were having issues with them; then they were all Mexicans.

Same with Bloods and Crips. If there were problems between them and another ethnicity, then they were all just black. I think it's true in all facets of life—a common enemy will unite the worst of adversaries. If some aliens from another world were threatening Earth, we would all be Earthlings, and all our petty disputes would seem insignificant. An expansive example of Cosmocentrism.

The Norteños were the Nuestra Familia, wore red, and used the number fourteen in their identity because *N* is the fourteenth number in the alphabet. The Sureños were the Mexican Mafia, wore blue, and used 13, because that's where *M* falls in the alphabet. The Border Brothers are Mexican nationals. They would all amaze me whenever they'd play volleyball using only their heads or feet!

The Sureños were by far the biggest gang due to their numbers inside. They pretty much control what goes on inside with the whites, with whom they're affiliated. The Norteños are aligned with the blacks. I was told by a Sureño one time that in addition to the geographical reason, they also disliked Norteños because they tried to "look like niggers." I wouldn't agree with his phrasing, but there was a difference in the appearance of the two Hispanic gangs. Norteños were more likely to have longer hair, greased up, or in some flashy do. And the Southerners almost always kept their hair quite short. I had one guy who claimed he was half Russian and half Mexican. I called him Vladimir Puto.

Some of you may remember a documentary from 1922 about an Eskimo man named Nanook and was titled "Nanook of the North". We had a resident that ran with the Nortenos but claimed to actually be of Eskimo descent. He was a friendly gent and was always bragging about what a ladies man he was on the streets. I would remind him of his prospects of enjoying some female companionship inside the Beast were basically nonexistent and hung the moniker on him of "No nookie of the North".

Among the Whites, the Nazi Low Riders are fairly new and although the Aryan Brotherhood has great influence, their actual validated members are quite low. They have numerous guys who are loyal to them and will claim membership, but mostly they're just wannabes. If the AB catches anyone with one of their tattoos without being an actual member, that fool is gonna get punctured. Their identifying marks are the shamrock, lightning bolts, and 666. If you have ever wondered where the term "Peckerwood" comes from, It has to do with the back of a Woodpecker neck has a red patch on it, so if you identify as a Peckerwood... you might be a Redneck.

Although the ABs only make up about 1 percent of the prison population, they are responsible for 20 percent of all murders. The Cosa Nostra recruits ABs that get out of prison for hitmen. I had one AB tell me, "If we want to hit you we don't care if you're sitting in the Warden's office, we'll hit you there. If the Warden tries to interfere, we'll stick him too.

I mentioned Cornfed Schneider, deemed the "Most dangerous man in California" who had made gruff remarks to me during a softball game in New Folsom earlier so I'll expand on his story now.

He was transferred to Pelican Bay. Some of you may remember two attorneys in SF who had two enormous dogs who attacked and killed a lesbian in their apartment building in 2001. I only mention her preference because it may register to some since it was portrayed that way in the news. Cornfed had purchased those dogs while incarcerated but gave them to the attorneys after they slaughtered all the sheep and pets of a Mormon woman he had befriended and who had agreed to keep them. When she informed him they had to go, he advised her, "Things can happen to you out there". She's now in protection.

Cornfed had fashioned a shank out a ladle handle and while in court, he produced it and stabbed an attorney several times with it. They weren't sure how he got the weapon into the courtroom, until they found out the lawyers wounds had fecal matter in them...

After that, he sued the state for "excessive Xrays of his bowels" and won.

When he was being transported to a trial in SF, CHP closed the Bay Bridge down in order for him to be transported across it.

The attorneys who had the dogs were convicted and sentenced to a few years in the joint. Prior to being incarcerated, the lawyers legally adopted Mr. Snieder. Searches of his cell allegedly revealed some photos of the woman engaged in some sex acts with the male dog who was named Bane. Why would they adopt a grown man in prison? The laws back then would allow them to have conjugal visits with their "Son". We all know how important maternal love is for getting a boy on the right path.

The DA who prosecuted them in SF was Kimberly G...who is the ex wife of California Gov. Newsome and lately has become the companion of Lil' Don Trump. I guess they have forgiven her for prosecuting some White supremacists.

The ABs didn't especially care for Charles Manson but allowed him to live because several of the "Manson women" got approved to visit numerous members of "The Brand". They were "Muling" in both drugs and information, and taking information out of the joint...allegedly.

I had a Mexican Mafia soldier let me in on a tactic they'd use to hit somebody that was in protective custody and they couldn't get near enough to take him out. If a member was going on trial for something that happened during their prison stint, they would subpoena the intended target to testify. They would also subpoena one of their soldiers as a witness to the charge. When that happens, the trial can go on for weeks and the inmates usually stay in the County jail for the duration. Sometimes the jails either aren't as equipped or maybe weren't made aware of the danger if these two felons came in contact with each other. They might encounter each other in the jail's dayroom, yard or a courthouse holding tank. Many hits have taken place in these circumstances.

I had one guy in Building 1 who was as white as the driven snow but identified as a Crip. He would only live with blacks and spoke in their dialect and phrasing. I was kinda surprised that the shot callers allowed this guy to be a Crip, and there was a lot of suspicion about him possibly being a double agent, what his motivation was, and had some hesitation before they allowed him in. There were certainly no blacks in the Aryan Brotherhood. I had a run-in with that gentleman when I was the control booth cop in Building 1. I did or said something that pissed him off and he shouted, "FUCK YOU!" to me during dayroom. This was not an uncommon utterance to hear from an inmate and was not considered write-up worthy. It was rather inflammatory however and I wanted to deescalate the situation without calling him out in front of his homies. I opened the sally port door and allowed him to step outside where I could talk to him from my back window without any of his peers witnessing the dialogue. Once outside, his demeanor changed dramatically. He was very contrite and apologized for the verbal outburst. I told him that I would appreciate it if he would refrain from making such shouts that could incite hostile behavior from other inmates caught up in the emotion. If I had tried to have this conversation with him inside the building he would have continued to flex up and not back down. You have to give them an "out." Inmates, like most folks, can be like an animal that will lash out when cornered, but if you give them an "out," they'll take it.

I tended to get along with all the ethnicities equally. That is, I didn't treat one any differently than the others. Some of the ABs didn't appreciate how I would laugh and joke around with the Blacks, who they called "Toads" and "Moon Crickets". I asked one of them what he had against blacks, and he answered in verse, stating, "Their hair is nappy, their lips is flappy, and they never knew their pappy." When he saw the look of dismay on my face, he said, "Actually, I got no problem with black folk. Hell, I think everybody should own one!" He also told me that the best way to cut crime rates in America was to require blacks and Mexicans to mate so that the resulting offspring would be "too lazy to steal anything." Just letting you know the attitudes within the Beast, I'm hoping he meant it to be funny.

That same AB explained to a black officer, while I was sitting there, that he was not a white supremacist, he was a white separatist. "It doesn't mean I think I'm better than you, I just don't want to be around you."

On a similar note, a black inmate once told me, "Whites ain't so bad, once you get used to the smell." Their standard put-down for whites was the way we talked, walked, how uptight we are, lack of athletic ability and perpetuating the stereotype of our inequity in reproductive equipment. I guess they consider it a violation of the "Penile code". Most women I know say they prefer guys with the standard White Boy issue anyway, at least that's what they tell us… A female sergeant who happened to be black made a very funny observation to me about us honkeys one time. I had asked her what the blacks made fun of us about. At first, she said she couldn't think of anything but then she thought a minute and said, "Yeah, I got something. When you white folk are out on the dance floor. What are you thinking? Do you really think that off-beat shuffling is workin'?" I have no doubt that we have been the source of much entertainment for black folk watching us do the white-boy sputtering over the centuries. She was a great dancer and showed me how to do "The Shuffle" when we worked in Main Control together. She was surprised when she saw I actually did have some rhythm. I explained that I was half Scottish and half Welsh, so the upper half was Sean Connery and the lower half was Tom Jones.

One day, I was conversing with a black guy and the subject came up of racial equality and whether justice was equally distributed among the different races. We both knew the answer. He told me about a time he was in a holding cell with a group of fellows who had just been arrested in a predominately black part of town for a reason he felt was unjust. He said, "We were looking for justice and that's exactly what we saw in that cell. . . just us!"

Most ethnicities I encountered inside the walls actually didn't have a problem with bigotry; they always respected honesty, and as long as the person was upfront and consistent about how they felt about a specific race, everyone was cool with it. That included staff.

The Bloods and Crips were the main two black gangs and it was always funny to read their outgoing mail. The Bloods would cross out every *C*, and the Crips would cross out all the *B*s. The Bloods referred to Crips as "Crabs" and the Crips' disparaging moniker for Bloods was "Slobs." The word "Crip" came from some of the founding members using walking canes as part of their attempt to look cool, and the name derived from them appearing to be crippled.

Southern Mexicans called Norteños "busters" as a negative reference. It was short for "sod buster," as the Southerners considered those from Sacramento and San Joaquin Valley to be farmers and looked down their noses at them.

In my experience, the Hispanics by far were involved in the most violence. There was some action between the Bloods and Crips, but not too much since the peace treaty years ago when it just got so stupid and out of control in L.A. The whites pretty much keep a low profile unless provoked. They tend to exert their influence in more subtle ways.

When an inmate arrives in a mainline joint, they're going to be pressured into becoming involved with whatever ethnic or geographic group they fall into naturally. He may be able to keep from becoming a validated member, but if something jumps off with his ethnicity or geographical hometown and he doesn't get involved, he's going to get "Booked". I've seen many riots that had been pretty much quelled, with all the convicts on the yard lying on the ground while the primary combatants were being cuffed up and taken to the hole, and you'd see a Northern Mexican jump up and attack a Southerner because he knew he was gonna get booked (assaulted) by his group if he didn't. In an SNY joint, you can do your own time for the most part. It was kind of like hockey fights where a goon roughs up your star player and your goon goes after their goon. The convicts know it's not personal and they don't take it that way, difficult decisions are easy when you don't have a choice.

One of the ways staff becomes aware that a hit is going down is that we notice a bunch of inmates staring in a particular direction, especially if it's happening around a corner or in an area where our view is obstructed, whether on the yard or on the dayroom. After observing the inmates staring in a particular direction we would then check it out and see the attack. So the OG inmates know that if something jumps off, they better not even turn their head in the direction of some work being put in or they might be joining that victim in the morgue.

In addition to gang affiliation, the inmates segregated themselves along racial lines. Each yard had a barber who serviced a specific ethnic group. He would travel to the different housing units on different days to cut the hair of the ethnicity they represented. The barbers were paid a meager amount by the state, and the inmates would also tip them with canteen items or other favors. There were different barbers for Blacks, Hispanics, Whites and "Others". In Ad Seg, a lot of the fellas would cut off all their hair upon arrival in the hole ready to do some hard time. When I was the Seg yard gunner, I had to make sure there was a tub of disinfectant called "Barbicide" available for the one set of clippers to make sure none of the previous user's ethnicity contaminated the next inmate's precious head.

Race and ethnicity was the basis for housing inmates when they arrived at the joint or had to be given a cell move. A few years back, some judge or politicians decided that wasn't the best way to do it. So when the inmates got off the bus they were just plugged into any open bunk. This led to numerous convicts refusing to enter a cell that was inhabited by an ethnicity other than their own. They would prefer to be sent to Ad Seg instead of living with someone of the wrong flavor. Frequently, they knew they would get hit by their own race if they didn't exercise this option. The reality is that they segregate themselves in regard to whom they socialize with or choose to cell up with. I've heard that this behavior doesn't exist as much in the women's joints and they hang out with whomever they want based on likability or commonality as opposed to ethnicity, and interact freely without regard to race. Leave it to women to exercise common sense.

First Watch

ONE NIGHT, I was walking out the gate at 2230 after a third-watch shift and the outside patrol sergeant, who usually is posted up in the entrance building where we showed our ID, came running out to catch me. I was getting out late due to shitty relief and was halfway across the parking lot and she was yelling my name. Like the fish fool I was, I stopped. She said I needed to go to Tower 9 and relieve the officer there, and it would probably be only an hour or so until they could get someone to come in for an overtime shift. I complied and ended up there all night! This was my first taste of "First watch." I had nothing to eat or drink and I was so tired it was painful. I tried everything to sleep, even putting a stack of paper towels on the counter by the window and laying my forehead on it. No chance. This is the problem with getting relieved late. Sometimes the watch office doesn't discover that a position hasn't been filled until all the previous watch staff has left.

After a year or so at the Creek, I was put on regular first-watch assignment, otherwise known as the graveyard shift. It went from 10:30 at night until 6:30 in the morning. Later, it was changed to 10PM. to 6AM. When you go into a new position it starts on a Monday, which meant I had to work third watch Sunday night and go right into my first shift after getting relieved at 10PM, so it started off with a 16 hour double. It was in the control booth for building 14, The floor cop stayed dowstairs all night so not much stimulation, that was a long night. A lot of the officers with some time in loved it because they didn't have to deal with inmates or administration. All you really had to do was count the boys at midnight, 0230, and again at 0430. When you're counting inmates who are usually sleeping, the department wants you to see either skin or some type of movement to make sure the inmate hasn't made a dummy or stuffed pillows under the blanket. Some officers would do a "paper count," meaning if their first count cleared, since no doors had been opened, they'd just call in the same one for the next two counts without actually doing another one, but few really did that. I never tried that once. I figured making sure none of these dudes checked out before their reservations had expired was my primary responsibility to the department and the public. It wasn't that much of a chore. On third watch, the 1630 count is called the "standing count." The inmates are all required to stand up as you walk by to make sure they're alive and not ill or injured. Many would not do it and expect you not to sweat them on it but I always made them comply as I didn't want it to be discovered that one of the ones I counted was expired.

On first watch, I always made sure I saw flesh or movement when I shined my flashlight into the cell windows. If the inmates were all covered up, I'd tap the window with the flashlight and usually they would move an arm or leg and that would be fine, but sometimes they'd let out a string of obscenities at me. If they did that, I would tell them I was concerned about their unusual behavior and thought that perhaps they were suicidal. I told them I'd come back and check on them every 10 minutes or so to make sure they were okay. I'd then return and bang on the door and have the control officer turn on the count lights, which would wake up every con in the building. The inmates in the building didn't like anyone disturbing their slumber, so they would make sure that inmate knew it was in his best interest to comply with my simple expectations for count protocol.

Another tactic I used for the ones that wanted to be idiots during count was to yell up at the control booth officer and exclaim, "Hey! These guys here in No. 137 are double parked!" inferring they were sharing a moment of intimacy. I would always use peer pressure to modify their behavior and it was much more effective than using the CDC disciplinary policies.

Many female officers had problems with inmates deciding to "Spank Hank" or expose themselves just as the flashlight shined in on them during count. Who wouldn't be disturbed after a frightening encounter with a Western one eyed spitting trouser snake? If the officer didn't handle it firmly (no pun intended) the whole building would start doing it. I always advised them to make loud, disparaging observations regarding their equipment such as, "Does that thing come in adult size?" or "How much longer is that thing going to be in the larvae stage?" In later years, if an inmate got written up for "spankin' Hank" during a count, they'd be considered a sex offender and would have to register as one if and when they hit the streets.

While we're on the subject of female staff, let me say that they can have a positive effect on inmates at times and provide a calming influence on them. Some inmates will respect them and feel comfortable talking to them about an issue that, left unresolved, could result in an incident. Others will behave themselves better in their presence. Some female staff members will jump right into the pile and put themselves in harm's way to protect their partner. There are a few I'd rather have in the dog pile with me than some of the males.

I know of several officers who had sex with opposite-gender officers while on first watch. There were a few married couples or just couples who might get put in the same building and could go down in the control booth stairwell to avoid having the inmates see them; the prisoners were always watching for something they could use later as leverage to get something they wanted from the cop or get them in a wreck. Many housing units would assign one con to watch the control booth all night just hoping to catch the guards doing something wrong. The bathroom in the control booth was also a possibility, but inmates could be watching through their cell windows and see the staff entering the bathroom. I knew of a few that did it in the perimeter towers as well.

Humans are not nocturnal animals, and being awake at night and sleeping during the day is not normal. I got used to it up to a point, but it's not healthy. We all need that vitamin D from sunlight. I slept many times on first watch but there were two of us in the building, and as long as one of us was paying attention, we thought it was fine. So we'd take turns napping. You know you're tired when you can sleep on a concrete floor. The control booth officers are required to call into Main Control every 30 minutes to ensure they were awake, but many would just set their watch alarms to help them comply—or, on rare occasions, the Main Control officer would be a friend and put them down on the form as having made their check-in calls.

Many staff would play dominos, cards or chess to pass the time. Some read books but that just put me right to sleep. I liked chess and my partner in the Building 13 control booth and I would play 10 or 12 games a night. Sometimes our relief would be yelling at the door in the morning to let them in as we'd be trying to finish up the last game.

That cop who was my partner in Building 13 was the control-booth cop. I was the floor cop, even though I spent the entire time up there with him playing chess and yucking it up, unless I was conducting one of the three counts or standing on the dayroom floor while he released the kitchen workers after the 0430 count cleared. I had to be down there in case a couple of them decided to start boxing.

One duty of the first-watch control officer is to scan all the outgoing mail before it gets sent up to the mailroom. This is to avoid any orders for someone to do a hit out there from a command inside the walls, planning an escape or set up a dope deal. Inmates would use various codes at times—like if you read every fifth word or so, you would get the intended message. It wasn't that hard to figure those out because the sentences would be rather incoherent. Sometimes one or two of the pages within the letter were intended to be forwarded on to an inmate at another institution. They would also write secret instructions or questions with urine at the bottom of the page or between sentences. It will be invisible when dry but if it is heated up or has a flame held near, it becomes visible.

Sometimes an inmate would be trying to hustle several women on the outside who had no better options than to allow themselves to be manipulated into doing an inmate's bidding. The OG convicts who were doing this were smart enough to send letters to the different women out on different nights but some of the younger, dumb ones would send them all out on the same night. Well, we're just stupid prison guards and can't be expected to remember which letter went in which envelope, can we…? It was always interesting to follow these guys over the next few weeks as they'd keep asking the women why they weren't accepting their phone calls, coming to visit, or sending any money into their accounts. Hey, aren't we supposed to rehabilitate them?

Inmates are not allowed to correspond with each other through the mail unless they have special permission. So, if they want to communicate with an inmate at a different prison or yard, they would put an address that didn't exist on the envelope and the address of the inmate they wanted to reach as the return address. So after the post office tried to deliver it and couldn't, it would be sent to the return address, which is where the inmate intended it to go all along. The whole scam was based on nobody paying attention to the return address, and obviously, that was the case on at least some of the attempts.

I was on first watch two different times during my career for almost two years and was glad once I got enough time in to bid for jobs on second watch, which goes from 6AM to 2PM. At some joints, like Folsom, the "good ol' boy" network was still in place, and if you were a fishin' or huntin' buddy of the assignment LT, you could get hooked up with a second watch and good days off. That also applied to the best softball players, and because the assignment lieutenant was the coach of our team. Well, I eventually got a little second-watch action. I never had weekends off, though, until my last two or three years, when I got off Sundays and Mondays. During the CDC Summer games over the years, I had numerous offers from Associate Wardens or Captains to transfer to their joint with the promise of a great position. Although you were supposed to work crummy shifts and lousy days off in your early years, there were also many who never had to do that—and being a cute girl never hurt in that endeavor. There was some resentment towards those who rose rapidly through the ranks. Some staff members got good shifts and days off because they were identified early in their careers as good, conscientious, hard-working cops. They were resented for being "lucky". It's funny how sometimes the harder you work, the luckier you get. The only place success comes before work is in the dictionary.

Third Watch

MY NEXT JOB was in main control on third watch, which runs from 1400 to 2200 hours. It's the worst shift for most people because you really don't have time to do much during the day before work and you don't get home until around 11 p.m. My former wife, Pam, really needs to be commended for working her job in education at UC Davis, studying for her Ph.D., and doing such a great job giving our kids the best possible opportunities to flourish in this world by constantly providing stimulation, reading and interacting with them. I worked every weekend for 20 years, so she really didn't get much time for herself. By now, my daughter Gina had been born and she is still, along with her brother Sam, the greatest accomplishment of my life, even though Pam's DNA and input are largely responsible for their outstanding traits.

In Main Control, I would issue a lot of equipment, push the buttons operating the Main Control sally port and Alpha and Charley yard gates, check the IDs of everyone who went through there, keep the log of everything that happened on that shift and make all the radio transmissions. With my radio background, I relished that duty and treated every transmission like a broadcast. Calling a "CODE ONE! ALPHA YARD!" over the institution-wide radio needs to be done with dramatic flair, phrasing and good voice quality. The best part about working in the Main Control booth was that it was air-conditioned and was one of the few places that was comfortable in summer.

I remember one night a female officer had worked a double—a 16-hour shift—and as she was passing through the Main Control sally port, she stuck her head in my window and announced, "I need a stiff drink and a stiff dick!" Sorry girl, wait till you get home for at least one of those.

There's a monitor in Main Control that displays the identity of which radio made each transmission so they can all be traced. There was a lieutenant that not too many staff members particularly cared for, and due to his reddish hair and Prince Charles ears, he was known as "Opie," a moniker he really despised. I shouldn't say that about Prince Charles out loud since he can probably hear me, I think he gets every premium channel on those things... Anyway, this lieutenant was walking across the yard one day. It wasn't open at the time because of the 1600 count, so he was alone out there. As he's nearing the yard gate, somebody keyed their mic and starts whistling the *Andy Griffith* theme song. It came through on his radio and he stopped and wheeled around, hoping to see the offender. Opie couldn't detect who it was, so he went to Main Control, checked the monitor and it was revealed that the yard gunner was the guilty party. The gunner received disciplinary action for his rendition of the tune.

The most interesting thing about Main Control is taking the counts. It's very complicated and my sergeant frequently had me setting up and taking all the calls from the various areas with their counts.

The "out counts" were the biggest issue; every inmate who was not in his bunk at count time had to be accounted for wherever he was, and that list had to be turned in about two hours before count time began. Sometimes there'd be a fight, or someone would get hurt and rushed to the infirmary or Ad Seg at the last minute and mess everything up. You might have a housing unit with 197 convicts living there, and you might have eight guys working in the chow hall, five guys on yard crew, two guys working as clerks or porters in the program office, three guys working in different housing units as tier tenders, one guy in a holding cage because he got in a wreck on the yard, two guys in the infirmary, and it all had to add up with staff calling in counts from those areas. With about 3,600 residents, it was not all that uncommon for the count to be off. Maybe whomever was in charge of the out-count list for the chow hall or wherever had screwed up, or whomever made a recent bed move didn't do it right in the computer—or hell, I bungled the count set-up. Regardless, if it was off, you had about 15 minutes to track down where the problem was or start considering the possibility that there had actually been an escape. That's a lot of pressure, and if count hadn't cleared in 15 minutes or so, you had the watch commander and other suits looming over your shoulder anxious for the answer. It was fun really, a good brain exercise, and it felt wonderful to announce over the institution-wide radio, "Count is clear", with...appropriate inflection of course.

In my later years at the Creek, there were institutional radios in each control booth and one of the floor officers would carry one too. Prior to that, the telephone was the only way to reach the officers, and many staff members whiled away the hours gabbing away to friends or lovers around the joint, making it difficult to contact them regarding something important. If somebody needed to reach someone in a housing unit and the phone was busy, they could call Main Control and have them cut in on that phone line, advising that motor-mouth to call whomever was making the request. There were also times when the officer or sergeant working in Main Control was involved in some extramarital shenanigans or perhaps suspected that their lover or spouse who worked there was doing so, and the officer could cut in on the suspected landline and eavesdrop on any conversation that person might be having. I knew of several instances where it occurred and sometimes resulted in a breakup.

Whenever someone picks up a phone inside and doesn't dial within about 30 seconds or so, an "off hook" alarm goes off in Main Control. It's a security feature in case staff was being assaulted and the phone got knocked off the cradle. We then would get on the radio and advise the sergeant on that yard to go to the location and verify that no hijinks were afoot. Some joints call it a "no dial," but not at MCSP.

Third Watch

I worked third watch for many years and had one of my most intense moments during it. I was working as the yard gunner (OBC) on Charley yard. At Mule Creek, there's only one gun tower on each yard and it's a small booth sitting high up on the roof of the gym.

Using the bathroom can be tricky while working a gun post and still being able to protect staff and inmates. In Tower 1 it was especially difficult, because you're operating both the employee and visitor sally port gates *and* issuing keys *and* dealing with staff trying to check their personal weapons in the tower base. There are a couple of cameras pointed at the folks in either visitor or staff sally port so you can see them on monitors in the tower if you're using the toilet, and there is a little sign you can put in the window letting people below that, "Staff is using restroom." Still, some staff and visitors would become impatient if you didn't immediately let them in or out of the sally port. While working in a yard gun post, you had to be aware that if inmates were about to carry out a hit, they would watch the gun booth and if they didn't see you for a minute they could surmise that you were having your morning constitutional and get busy with a good stickin'.

OBC is the name for the yard gun on *C* yard. It stands for Observation Booth on *C* yard. The yard gun post on *A* and *B* yards are called OBA and OBB, respectively. It's a concrete booth with windows on three sides. It does have AC, but it's way in the back of the booth and doesn't put out much cold air anyway. You can't see the yard from back there, so it does get quite hot near the front because it faced south, which was the direction from which the sun was blazing. In later years they put a shade above the window but in the early years your face just got roasted. I got a fan from R&R and put it back near the AC in an attempt to blow some of that cool air towards the front window where I was posted. It wasn't very effective. OBC is responsible for keeping staff and inmates safe while on the yard. It's impossible to see everything that goes on, so you just have to do your best. One thing you always had to be aware of is a helicopter or an ultra-light plane landing on the yard to pick up an inmate or two for the purpose of self parole. The natural instinct is to shoot the pilot, but you can't be sure that he/she wasn't somehow extorted into doing it, so I always planned on aiming for the rotor or any mechanical part that would prevent them from taking off. There is also a warning painted on every building wall stating that any inmate seen running towards a helicopter could be shot.

One of the most important responsibilities of the yard gunner is to call any building where a supervisor or administrator is approaching. It's not like the officers there are going to get caught doing anything especially wrong, but everybody was grateful for the heads-up. Most OG sergeants or lieutenants also appreciated it, because they didn't want to be put in a position of having to discipline officers for a petty offense they'd witnessed, but if the inmates saw them witness such an occurrence and look the other way, the supervisor knew the inmates might rat them out further up the food chain.

It was a long walk along the rooftop from Main Control to all the yard gun booths. The stairs up to the roof of Main Control were very steep (almost like a ladder) and were very slippery when it rained. There was a hatch at the top that had to be unlocked each time there was traffic coming up or down in order to prevent the bad guys from entering Control, which was also a sub-armory. Whenever a yard gunner or cop was returning from the dining gun-post they would tap on the hatch to alert the Main Control cops to unlock the hatch. They had already announced over the radio that they were en route from their post. If no such announcement had been made, that hatch wasn't going to get opened.

You also had to be aware whenever a fight broke out that it wasn't a diversion. Any time I'd see a fight start, I'd quickly check the other end of the yard to see if the scrap might be a rouse to distract me from someone there getting booked. Sometimes all the inmates had to do was start mad dogging—staring—at each other as they walked the track in large groups to get all our attention on them. Usually if our double agents alerted us of something brewing and the inmates were walking the track in large groups, passing by a rival faction, staring them down (a "drive-by"), we'd "pull them over." This meant putting them on the wall and patting them down for weapons. Once we did that, they knew we were focused on them and they'd put off the rumble for another day or shift. Eventually, walking the track in groups of more than four or five was prohibited.

One day when I arrived and relieved the second-watch cop, the yard was out and there were around four or five-hundred criminals enjoying the swings, slides and merry go round on the playground. At 1600, it was yard recall and they'd all go home for count at 1630. Once count cleared, Main Control would usually wait at least a half-hour to announce it so the staff to eat their lunch or dinner. Then we'd start releasing two units at a time to come to the chow hall. The inmates are required to wear full prison blues with their shirts tucked in and are supposed to keep walking (but not running) without stopping. This is all for security, as it's hard to conceal and pull a weapon with your shirt tucked in, and more difficult to get close enough to hit someone without running or stopping. For most of their day, inmates are allowed to wear whatever they have received from catalogues on the outside as long as it complies with the rules, but must wear full prison blues to chow, work/school, and visiting.

Chow went smoothly that evening, and there was a bit of a break until night yard opened. Not all joints have night yard, but Charley and Bravo yards are Level 3 yards, so night yard is normal. Alpha yard is Level 4 and they don't have any yard after 1600, only dayroom activities. Yard usually opens at 7PM as it did on this night, and all seemed cool. We could usually tell if there was any tension between factions because of rats telling us, but also from grouping or mad doggin'. Another way to tell trouble is brewing is if the inmates start stocking up on food from canteen, anticipating a long lockdown, or shaving their heads and coming to yard dressed in state blues and boots, making it harder to identify them once the melee begins. Canteen staff would alert us if they noticed any specific ethnicities stocking up on food items.

All was mellow this night, and at 8 p.m. there was an "unlock," allowing inmates to go inside their unit to get something, drop something off, or stay in. After the 8 p.m. unlock, the units started opening their outer sally port doors to release those who wanted to go back onto the yard.

Within a few minutes of unlock, I noticed the Whites, whose turf was in front of Building 15, had started to increase in numbers. Soon after, the Southern Mexicans started to group up as well, and their turf was also near Building 15. If we noticed it, you can bet the other inmates noticed it too, and before long, each side had about 40 or 50 associates each. I called the yard sergeant and told him he had better get outside because something was brewing. I told the two yard cops who were standing below my gun tower also, and before long, every eye on the yard was watching the scene unfold.

We learned later that a Southern Mexican had sapped a White boy in the head with a sock filled with *D* batteries in the Building 13 sally port as they were going inside for the unlock. This was a frequent weapon of choice, as neither item is contraband and you can't get in a wreck for having them. The White boy came out and told his homies what happened, so *C* yard was on the brink of war.

After both sides had reached full strength, the shot callers from each side walked towards each other and had a little chat. I had enough time in by now to know what this choreography entailed. The White leader had asked the Sureno Jeffe if they were going to take care of the assailant "in house" and the Mexican had replied "No". With that, both leaders returned to their group and within about 10 seconds the groups approached each other from about 30 yards apart and *it was on!*

The brawl was just a sea of swinging arms and legs. I thought someone on the yard would call a "Code 1!" on the radio, but nobody did. I picked up the yard PA mike and yelled for all inmates to GET DOWN! I then grabbed my radio and yelled, "Code 1, Charley Yard!"

Staff was responding from the various housing units and applying their batons, trying to gain compliance. We didn't carry pepper spray back then, and were using the older side-handle batons.

The inmates were not stopping, so I racked a round into the chamber of the Mini 14. I was still a cherry as far as firing any gun other than at the range, and in the flurry of fighting inmates at twilight, when the yard lights aren't that effective, I couldn't see any weapons being used.

It was utterly surreal! I was going to have to intervene with the gun and quite possibly end someone's life if circumstances required it. Experienced staff on the ground know at this point not to get too close to the combatants, to stay out of harm's way, and allow the gunner to handle matters. I continued yelling for them to get down but after they continued to sling blows I finally aimed towards a place just off to the left of the melee and squeezed the trigger. *BOOM!* We always have ear protection on at the range and you don't realize how loud this gun is. Some gunners, when utilizing a warning shot, will fire straight down below them but the inmates can tell by the sound if the barrel is pointing towards them. It's a muffled *thump* sound versus a sharp *crack.*

The inmates all got down at that point, but a few popped back up and resumed fighting. By then, additional staff had arrived from the other yards and were beating them down with their batons. As they were doing that, others would jump up and get busy again.

I was about to bust another cap, but they surely heard the first one, and if I have to shoot again, it's going to be for effect. I had seen no evidence of any weapons nor any inmate getting beaten so badly that "great bodily injury" was imminent, so shooting someone would be hard to justify. I didn't want to anyway.

At that point, all inmates finally lay down and it was over. It had probably lasted only about a minute, but my senses had become so acute it seemed much longer. I became aware of the smell of gunpowder mixed with the scent of the dishwashers from the roof vents above the nearby chow hall. It was quiet other than occasional orders from staff for inmates to comply in some way and the radio traffic. My disbelief of what was happening changed to anger as I thought the inmates must have felt I wasn't going to do anything and felt comfortable in having this riot while I was the gunner. In reality, it was spontaneous, and it wouldn't have mattered who the yard gunner was; they would have gone off regardless.

Staff began identifying all the involved inmates and recalling the yard for those not involved. Someone was sent up to relieve me so I could begin writing my report and could receive some traumatic counseling if I wanted it. I was shook up a bit for sure, but I declined. I think it's a macho thing; you don't want to appear weak to inmates or staff. I was just happy I hadn't disrespected my underwear when it became clear I was going to have to intervene and perhaps utilize deadly force.

The whites and Southerners are allies, so it was unusual for them to have problems, but matters dictated that something had to be done and they were all friends again when they came off lockdown a week or two later. That is, all the ones who weren't in the hole. The only excuse for not being involved would be if they were in their cells or buildings and weren't aware of it or couldn't get out. Anyone on the yard who was affiliated with either faction in any way— geographical, ethnically, or whatever—who *didn't* get into the melee would get booked by their own people later.

I was talking to one officer shortly after the incident. He had transferred in from Folsom, was a Vietnam vet, and had that old-school attitude. He said to me, "If I had been up in OBC, I'd a shot about 10 of those assholes!" I stated that since the departmental policy elements for using deadly force were not present, we would have been that much closer to having them take all the guns out of the prisons, which many politicians are always trying to do.

There was an old lieutenant who had so many hash marks on his shirtsleeve that it looked like you could play piano in several keys on it. Each hash mark related to three years the wearer had been in the department. He was always saying that we didn't need any guns inside. I had several discussions about it with him. His take was that whenever the inmates wanted to hit someone, it would be a quick two or three thrusts, and even if the gunner saw it, the attacker would just throw away the shank and get down on the ground in an act of full compliance, which would eliminate the gunner from intervening. I would retort that the reason the attacker would only use two or three quick thrusts was because of the gunner. If there was no gunner, he would take his sweet time while fileting his target, and even if the attack was detected and staff responded, he would keep whittling meat away until restrained. Who knows which of us was right. I felt a lot better knowing those gunners were there, hopefully paying attention.

Any time there's a shot fired—whether it is a warning shot or someone is actually hit—there must be a shooting review. A few weeks after the described incident, I was summoned to an associate warden's conference room for the shooting review. There about six or seven people in there, including the Captain of the Guards, associate wardens, and various training and union folks. My report was read and an associate warden stated that I was current in my range qualifying with impressive scores. Really, I knew this one was a no-brainer. These review boards can be quite stressful, because you could be subject to discipline like having them take 5 or 10 - percent of your pay for a year, suspension or even termination if it's determined to be a bad shoot. This one was a circumstance where if I *hadn't* shot, I probably would have gotten in a wreck. It was ruled a good shoot.

The next one wasn't so clear-cut.

About three months later, I was still up in OBC. By now, the department had begun implementing its new shooting policy wherein warning shots must meet the same criteria as using deadly force.

It was night yard again, and nothing seemed out of the ordinary. It was later in the year, and even though it was around the same time of day as the first one, it was darker. The yard lights don't provide very good illumination, and that was a factor in this one. I was just observing the yard when I saw two inmates attacking one other guy in front of Building 13. I called the, "Code 1, Charley yard!" on the radio and ordered the yard down on the PA. All the inmates on the yard hit the ground but the assault continued. At this time, I realized there was a second one-on-one boxing match going on in front of Building 14. Some of the combatants were not wearing shirts and one of them had such dark skin, I thought it was Mexicans and blacks going at it. One of the scraps was very close to the Bloods' turf, plus there were multiple altercations. I thought it was about to escalate into an interracial riot, so I popped a cap near the two-on-one in front of Building 13. Grass flew up within about five yards from where they were fighting, and all the penal pugilists dove for the dirt.

Turns out they were all Norteños and they were just doing a little "house cleaning" among their ranks. Apparently, the two inmates were getting tuned up because they weren't as down for the cause as the others felt they needed to be.

In that shooting review board, they grilled the hell out of me and the only thing that saved my ass was that it appeared to be interracial and involved multiple altercations. Because there were no weapons and nobody was getting socked up to the point of being in danger of losing his life, it was an iffy shoot, but it was ruled good.

At one time there was a 10 year gap between shots being fired at Mule Creek and guess who pulled the trigger? Stay tuned.

Another time, I was in OBC and Building 13 activated its alarm. I put the yard down and heard on the radio that medical staff was responding to a "staff down." In that unit. Man, I'm thinking something serious had happened. After a few minutes, they came out of the sally port with an officer on a stretcher. He had blood all over his head area. Geez! What happened? I found out later he had been trying to pass a food tray of the evenings dining offering up to the control officer who was there on OT. During this attempted tray transfer, the floor cop had tried to stand on a chair . . . that had rollers on the legs. During the ensuing ass-over-teakettle flip, he smacked his head on the side of the desk. Apparently, he didn't listen at the academy when they told us eating State food was unwise.

One time the Northern and Southern Mexicans were on the verge of warfare. Seems the Southerners were encroaching on one of the benches on the weight pile that had previously been part of the Northerners' domain. I could see there was grouping and mad-dogging going on, but nothing jumped off. When I got back from my weekend on that Friday, I was working in the watch office. They still hadn't gone off, but our double agents had let us know the situation was still simmering. At around 8 p.m. that night, I was sitting in the watch office and heard the radio crackle, "CODE ONE, CHARLEY YARD!" There it was. My job was to run to the gate on Charley yard, I had a key to the gate and monitor who went in or out, and wait to see if secondary response was needed. There were scraps going on all over the yard, secondary response was called, and staff from other yards came a runnin'. Eventually all the combatants were proned out and being cuffed up and escorted over to the hole, which thankfully is on the same yard. One by one, each housing unit was instructed to stand up and return to their unit. Each time they were walking to their building, it would flare up again. Inside Building 13, a big donnybrook broke out.

Supervisors was afraid that when the inmates residing in the gym were recalled, a fight would break out and be really difficult to control because there are no cells in that dorm setting, and no gun coverage. I was sent back to Main Control, grabbed a rifle, strapped on a handgun (we were required to wear a sidearm any time we transported a weapon on the roof in case an inmate had gained access to the roof and might try to get the rifle), and got the proper keys to get into the gun booth in Charley gym. No one had been up there in years and it took a while for control staff to find the right keys, but I got up there to find three inches of dust on the floor! I threw open the inside windows and all the inmates freaked out when I chambered a round and stuck the barrel out the window. Everything cooled down and it was over. I thought I was going to be up there overnight, but around midnight, somebody that wanted the overtime came up and relieved me. All over *one* weight bench. A few years later, that gym gun post was activated on a permanent basis and there was a gunner up there 24 hours a day.

That central service S&E (search and escort officer) was a great job. You just hung around the watch office and helped out in Main Control during shift changes, either issuing equipment or pushing buttons to open sally port doors or yard gates. There were two S&Es in there, and at some time during the shift, one would do an inner perimeter fence check and the other would do the outer perimeter fence check. It simply involved walking the entire perimeter fence, occasionally tugging on the fence to make sure it was firmly attached to the fence posts. We also had to check the temperature of the water boilers and report it to main control for the shift summary. I loved this job because I could get out of the office and enjoy the outdoors, but it wasn't so fun on those blistering summer days or stormy winter ones, either.

One of the biggest incidents happened when I was in that job, but it happened on my day off. A CDC bus had come into R&R to drop off a few thugs. It was pretty late, so they were going to leave all the ones scheduled to continue on to the next stop by temporarily housing them overnight. In R&R on third watch there was only one officer, and he was a real doozy. The holding cells could hold around 20 and 30 inmates. These guys were headed for Pelican Bay, and were some bad hombres.

A fight broke out in the cell, and this lame C/O opens the grill door to quell it, and oh jeez, it's on! The whole fight had been staged and it was a set-up to get him to open the door. The cop had time to activate his alarm before getting socked up and lumped up with his own baton. As responding staff entered R&R, they were met with about 25 of the highest custody level convicts, intent on tuning up a few officers. The watch sergeant was looking out the window of his office and said he saw one cop run in the door and immediately came flying back out on his ass. The inmates had acquired several batons from responding staff and were swinging at them with ill intent. Eventually, enough staff responded and the event was quelled. Two involved officers resigned shortly after that, both female. It got a little too real that day.

There were times when I was working in Main Control when an inmate was misbehaving down in the main infirmary. The central service S&Es are supposed to be first responders to any issue in the main infirmary or R&R. Perhaps a particular dude was being so unruly that he needed to be put in five-point restraints. This one particular shift, the S&E was a woman. They sent her into Main Control to relieve me so I could go down to the infirmary and subdue this fellow.

There's the sense that one has to act all macho in these situations and get excited about the opportunity to get physical with one of our unruly inhabitants, but I resented it to some degree because I'm thinking, "Am I getting paid more than she is?" No, she actually made more than me because I was still fairly new and had not reached some of the step pay raises. There were many times when I was relieved and sent to do a cell extraction or some other act that would be beneficial to have some beef involved. Some of these guys really wanted to be chosen for it and would get upset if they weren't invited to the party, but most of that was pure theater. It definitely made the inmate who was acting out think twice about his behavior when facing the reality of being rushed by a group of Rhinos. But if you're involved in enough of these situations, you're gonna get hurt eventually, maybe ending your career or even your life. I never needed that kind of validation. Not on third watch or any other.

Second Watch

AFTER A WHILE on third watch I went to second watch, which consists of working from 0600-1400 hours. I wasn't crazy about getting up at 0400 but it is the closest thing CDC has to normal life. I had a perky sergeant who had been on this watch for years and when she saw my sleepy disposition one morning he offered, "Rise & shine, the early bird gets the worm!". I'm thinking, yeah, the early bird may get the worm...but the second mouse gets the cheese. I was working a job as the Plaza officer. The Plaza is the area between the three facilities and is where the main infirmary and R&R are. Inmates from the different yards have appointments every day for some of those places and must be escorted to and from, mainly to try to keep them from having contact with convicts from the other yards. This is partly to avoid enemies from getting into it, but also to cut down on how much information moves from one yard to another.

One day our beloved (hah!) governor, Arnold Schwarzenshriver was coming to the Creek for a photo op in order to take credit for a program that had shown some positive results. Whenever a program was working, everybody wanted to be associated with it. Success has a thousand fathers, but failure is an orphan. Schwarzenshriver didn't endear himself to our brethren when he advocated privatizing the prison system. Do you have any idea how much contraband would be coming into these joints by staff who are making minimum wage? The inmates would be running the place. A lot of grief just so some corporation can make a profit. In order to maximize profit, so many corners would be cut and understaffing would be the norm, which would lead to security issues as well as the endangering the safety of inmates, staff and the community. There would be no attempts to reform anybody, just warehouse them and keep collecting the rent.

That day, he was going to visit several places, but towards the end of his photo op, he decided to walk down the Plaza. The suits decided to shut down all programs and let the females from various offices come out and adore him as he strutted along. They had yellow crime-scene tape along both sides of the sidewalk so the unwashed masses wouldn't rush him.

I was the Plaza cop that day and they told me to wear my Class A uniform, which I didn't mind too much. So here he comes, sashaying along with his orange hair and ostrich-skin cowboy boots. The boots still didn't make him very tall, and I thought I witnessed him whisper to his aides not to let the tall guy (me) stand near him in case any pictures were taken. He would have been someone's trophy punk if he ever got sent to the joint.

While working the Plaza I would encounter that day's parolees lined up by Main Control, waiting to be released back into the wild. They would be processed through and continue out the gate to the van, which would transport them to the bus station. I couldn't resist getting a dig in and would frequently ask them, "How many you guys gonna be back by count time?" One guy actually said he'd be back and this was just a vacation. Out the gate at eight, on the spoon by noon, back again at 10.

I've done that parole van job several times, and it's always interesting.

A few weeks before an inmate would get paroled, his friends or relatives would send his "dress outs" to the prison so he could walk out in street clothes. One time a black guy was paroling. Before he arrived at R&R, we opened the dress-out box and put some rhinestone cowboy-type clothes in it and taped it back up. When he came into R&R to be processed out, we gave him the box and when he saw the clothes, he was like, "Oh, hell no! I ain't going out like this!" After we had our laugh, we gave him his real dress outs, a nice lime green, one-piece velour pimp outfit. We should have kept that one for the next White boy who paroled.

When I took the parolees to the bus station, if they had a ride waiting at the gate, we'd give them their gate money (that's $200 from your taxes) and cut them loose right there. I'd usually tell them that if I ever saw them in here again I wanted their permission to stick my boot up their ass, and most would say that was fine since they didn't plan on being back. We did not carry guns on those parole runs. We counted on them having a rational thought process and being able to conclude that assaulting one of us while being so close to the freedom they'd been dreaming about for years would not be too smart. I heard some interesting conversations in that van between fellas from rival factions discussing events that had occurred and some of the inside decisions of the players involved from the opposing perspectives. It was good to know that some of them at least were already transitioning to the civilian world. So far, I haven't heard of any trouble regarding any parolees attacking the officer setting them free.

One time, there was a wild-looking girl waiting outside the gate for her squeeze in a red Firebird convertible. I gave him his gate money and he jumped in that sled and they took off down the road. I got back into the van and headed down the same road for the bus depot in Stockton. Before we'd gone a mile, a CHP driving towards us made a sharp U-turn. When we got farther along, we saw he had them pulled over and was cuffing dude up! Shortest parole I ever saw. I don't know if they were naked, speeding or flashing booze to draw the focus of that CHP, but natural selection wins out again.

When I first started, we took the parolees to the Sacramento bus station. That was later changed to the one in Stockton. We would just drop them off in front of the station with their money and scram. There were times I'd look back and see them fighting on the sidewalk in the rear-view mirror as I drove away. Not my jurisdiction. There was a liquor store right across the street, and many professional ladies would hang out there, recognizing the state van and the guys in it had gate money and were eager for actual sex other than their cellie's "back pussy." Some never made it out of town and ended up in county jail. Not good if you were a Sureño. Some Norteños told me they would hang around the depot waiting for Mexicans with Sur 13 tattoos to get out of the CDC van and sock them up. In later years, we took them to Stockton and had to sit there with them until every last one was on a bus. Prior to that, sometimes they'd ask me to let them out of the CDC van down the street from the bus station in order to avoid embarrassment, but I'd always pull right up in front, get out and count out their gate money in front of all present, including the bums, gangsters and soiled doves. One last effort to remind them prison is not a nice place and it might reduce their urge to make choices that would likely lead to them returning to the State's fold.

One of the next jobs I had was in the Building 1 control booth on Alpha yard, the Level 4 yard. The control-booth cop opens the doors into the building and into the cells, controls the four inmate phones and is responsible for protecting staff and inmates inside that building. He/she can also help the yard gunner out by keeping an eye on the yard through the back window and providing gun coverage from there. I had to do that very thing from that very window a year or so later...read on.

Control booth in a housing unit. Originally the declaration above office door stated: NO WARNING SHOT. But later the words: "is required" were added. The office was originally where the officers hung out but then podiums were put up off to the right of the frame so we could have a better view of who was coming in or out of the sallyport as well as both corners of the dayroom. Inmate ironing board left of door with a state shirt as the cover.

The Belly of the Beast

When I came to relieve the first-watch cop, they would let me into the building sally port outer door. Once it closed, they would open the outer door of the small control-booth sally port. Once I stepped inside and closed that door, they could look down into that sally port through a window on their floor to make sure it was staff and not an inmate. Then they'd open the inner sally port door so I could enter and climb up the stairs into the booth.

Once there, first-watch staff would convey any pertinent information from his or her shift and I would do a quick inventory of the weapons, keys and other equipment before allowing him or her to leave. If any equipment came up missing, I would be held accountable. We were even expected to count each round in all the magazines. You never wanted to get the reputation of being bad or "straight-up" relief. Straight-up referred to the big hand on the clock and meant you got there at exactly the time your shift was to start. So for the poor previous shift officer that you were relieving, after inventory, exchanging information and time getting out of the building, walking across the yard to the program office, signing out, getting through Main Control and then to the last sally port gate, and to the car in the parking lot, it could be 10 minutes later. Bad news. Plus, if he or she got out late, there was always the chance of getting held over like I was in Tower 9 for first watch years earlier.

Because I was on second watch, it was 0600 and no inmates were out. I would let a few out of their cells, like the clerk and a few tier tenders, so they could begin their various duties such as sweeping and mopping the floor emptying the trash cans, etc.

The control room is the height of a second floor and has a back window that allows the control officer to provide gun coverage on the yard if it's needed or doesn't interfere with the primary job of protecting the inmates and staff within that housing unit. It's about 10 yards square with a bathroom that had one-way windows. You could see out and be aware of what was going on in the dayroom while you were in there. As long as you didn't turn on the lights, no one could see in, but a few female guards found that out the hard way.

There's a panel inside the control room that you would either stand or sit in front of; it shows the layout of the building with buttons for each cell door and the sally port. There is also a microphone that you can use to make announcements inside the dayroom or out onto the yard. Usually, someone would have brought in a radio so you could listen to music, talk radio or sports. This was against the rules because in theory it could hinder our ability to hear something happening in the dayroom, but most sergeants didn't sweat it. The radio would usually be put away in a drawer or otherwise hidden whenever a sergeant came up into the booth so as to not put them on front street. Someone usually also brought in a microwave and refrigerator which was permitted but you were supposed to get written permission.

There was a glass window/hatch on the floor above the office below, which allowed us to communicate or pass paperwork or other things to each other. The first few years I was there, we kept the H&K 9mm carbine in a gun rack just on the right side of the control panel, which was about four feet from the hatch opening. Somebody figured out that it would be easy for an inmate to use a string or rope to lasso the barrel of the gun, pull it towards him, and get it down through the opening. The floor officers were rarely in that office. More often, the inmate clerk was there, typing up building rosters or reports, so it wasn't difficult for any inmate to get into the office. Gaining possession of that carbine would have been a disaster, as you can imagine. The gun rack was later moved to a different, safer place in the booth.

We would conduct the yard release around 0800, and then, around 9 or 10, the dayroom would open. This meant that any inmates who weren't at work, at school or on the yard could come out and shower, use the phones, play table games or watch TV, of which there were two on either side of the dayroom. There were two big convex mirrors hanging outside of the booth near the front corners, so the areas towards the back of the dayroom could be observed without having to take your vision away from the officer's podium, which was directly in front of and below the panel.

At 10AM, we'd have an unlock so inmates could come in off the yard and either stay in the dayroom, go in their house or return to the yard.

Then, at noon, we'd recall the yard for a close custody count. This is the only count second watch does and would give us the chance to eat our lunch and relax a bit before returning to the normal program. If an inmate has a lengthy sentence, perhaps lives in the area or has an escape history, they are considered "Close Custody" and are counted two times daily in addition to the regular counts.

For the most part, I really didn't have to intervene much in any problems. Until one August morning... We had an inmate named Garofalo, who is the cousin of Janeane Garofalo, the actress/political activist. He was a Hells Angels dropout and a solid convict who knew how to behave, was liked and respected by staff as well as residents and never gave us any problems. He once showed me a police report of a shootout he'd had with LAPD and showed me the scars from his bullet wounds. You can google those events. After a while, he moved next door into Building 2 because he told me more of his homeboys lived there. They couldn't just move around freely from bunk to bunk, but if they got the convict they wanted to live with to sign a cell-move slip and floor officers from both affected buildings signed off, it could happen. I knew he must have moved for some legitimate reason because we always got along very well plus, since he was a Hell's Angel, he loved anybody with the last name of Davidson.

Building 2 would go to chow before us, and I would usually be sitting near the back window of my control booth, reading the paper there because it was an August morning and the sun was well up and the light was better.. Frequently, Garofalo would shout some snotty remark up to me as he walked by on the track and I would give an equally smart-ass retort.

A view of building 11 outer sallyport. Building1 was exactly like this one on Charley yard. You can see the inner sallyport door just inside and left of the outer building sallyport door. The window with the bars above the sallyport was where I was sitting when I heard the stickin' on the track. Railing on roof is where the roof hatch is. Intercom is just right of the door. Under the door's hood was where inmates liked to hide while a friend of theirs would talk the control cop into letting him in, once the door opened, the concealed felon would sneak in with him. We couldn't see them from the window. Usually it was just a minor infraction but someone from a different unit could come in to execute a hit too.

On this particular morning, my two partners were up in the booth with me because there were no inmates on the floor other than a few tier tenders. Peter White was playing jazz on the radio and the smell of fresh-brewed coffee and mown grass drifted in through the window I was sitting by. Seagulls screeched and circled above the yard, as they knew the procession to the chow hall meant sack lunch scraps from the inmates once they consumed their Eggs Benedict and Mimosas. We had been on our shift for about 10 minutes when I suddenly heard some yelling coming from out on the track in front of my building. I looked out to see inmate Garofalo on top of another inmate, Bardo, and was stabbing him about the head and neck with a pair of shanks, one in each hand.

I jumped up and told my partners, "It's *on* outside and he's stabbing him!" I grabbed the Mini 14, which was right next to me, and Officer Childress (Chili) jumped to push the buttons on the control console to let the other guy, Officer Chavez (Dirty Roy), down through the sally ports so he could respond to the event. I stuck the barrel of the rifle through the bars in the window and yelled for Garofalo to "GET DOWN!" All the other inmates were hugging asphalt, and yard staff was just then becoming aware of the altercation from their positions across the yard in front of the chow hall. OBA utilized his yard mic and ordered the inmates on the track and in front of the chow hall to "GET DOWN!". OBA knew not to interfere since he was much farther away than I was and he could see that I was in a better situation to conclude what level of force was required. Garofalo was still intent on shedding some sunlight into Bardo's brains, and wasn't stopping. Instantly, I could see the weapons, the wounds, the blood, the continuous stabbing motions and his refusal to comply with my lawful orders. All the criteria was there to utilize deadly force. I chambered a .223 round in the Mini 14, a sound inmates have become conditioned to recognize from hundreds of yards away, and yelled once again for Garofalo to get down. Realizing that if I didn't act, Bardo could be mortally wounded within seconds, but not wanting to take the chance of being fired or disciplined, plus knowing Garofalo was such a solid convict, I gave him another two seconds to live by busting a cap about two yards to the right of him. Looking back, I have no doubt that he had cultivated a relationship with me, hoping I would give him a pass at this moment. I did...but it was only for two seconds.

To my great relief, he dropped his weapons and rolled over onto the grass. Had he not done so, a .223 projectile would have ripped through his chest in another two seconds. Within moments of complying, responding staff cuffed him up and called for medical to respond.

After the area was secured, the yard was recalled and the process of investigation began. A member of the goon squad came in through the hatch in the roof with another Mini 14, because mine would be held until the investigation was finished. Even though the yard had been recalled, the squad member had to go around the back of my unit, climb onto the roof and enter the control booth through the above hatch. This eliminated any possibility of an inmate who may have been being escorted across the yard from rushing him and gaining possession of the rifle. Any time a weapon was moved from the armory to a gun post it was always transported separately from any ammunition. The entire yard and dayroom was shut down, so I didn't need to be relieved, but was instructed to report to the program area and later to the Administration Building.

They sent someone to give me trauma counseling but I was okay, having been through it twice before. Still, it was a bit unsettling because I knew that if Garofalo hadn't ceased, the next round was going to rip through his chest. Corrections Officer J. Beatty had been sent to counsel me and she was a friend of mine and a great cop. Her brother, Cornel, was also helpful in reminding me of various stories for this writing. I wrote my report and the supervisors asked if I wanted to go home. I declined because I wanted to return to my post and show the inmates that the incident hadn't bothered me and I'd do it again in a second if necessary.

By coincidence, I was off for the next five days anyway and had reservations at New Brighton campground in Santa Cruz. I would be taking my trailer there the next day. My wife and kids would join me a few days after that so I was there for two days alone. It was wild sitting there by the campfire, drinking some whiskey, looking up at the starry sky, the Milky Way seeming so close I could smell the caramel, and realizing how close I had come to ending a man's life. Garofalo was well liked among the heavy white boys, and me plugging him would not have gone over too well. Several convicts in later years thanked me for giving him that two-second pass. It's utterly amazing how different the world is just a few feet on the other side of those walls. So beautiful and mellow in Santa Cruz and so wild, primal, dangerous and chaotic inside the Beast. Even as I sipped in this peaceful setting, I knew at that same serene moment prison politics were playing out at the Creek and across the state.

It was amazing to think how the millions of variables caused our lives to intersect at that critical time and place. Both Garafolo and Bardo could have had their lives end right then and there not to mention mine being altered forever. As it turned out, all three of us continued on our paths towards whatever the infinite, unwritten variables determine.

Eventually, what had transpired became clear. I didn't know who Bardo was, but if you remember that TV show, *My Sister Sam,* there was an actress, Rebecca Schaeffer, who costarred in it with Pam Dawber. Robert Bardo was an overzealous, stalking fan who had found out where Schaeffer lived, rung her doorbell and gunned her down when she answered the door. I remembered the incident but wasn't aware that puke was at MCSP. I'm surprised he even got convicted, the D.A. in his trial was Marcia Clark from the O.J. debacle.

Bardo was life-flighted to a hospital and brought back that night with seven stitches in his face. A few days later, he approached my window and thanked me for saving his life. I told him to get lost. He disgusted me, but since I took the oath and cashed the paychecks, I was compelled to save his pathetic ass even though my personal feelings were that he deserved to die. The reality is that, if I hadn't intervened, his family might have sued me for not protecting him.

Garofalo was already a lifer and knew he would simply get a two-year term in the hole. I was over there one day and went to his cell to talk about the incident. I leaned up to the crack of his cell door and said, "Hey, Hermano, you put me in a tough position that day!" He said, "Yeah, Big D, I thought you might enjoy the show. If you'd have killed me you would have been doing me a favor." The weapons he'd used were two broken off broom handles he had sharpened by rubbing them on the concrete floor of his cell. As soon as they hit Bardo's bulbous pumpkin, the points broke off. After that, he was just scratching him up. I asked him why he hadn't used steel, because he surely would have killed him if he had. He replied, "I had steel but when I was sharpening it, my neighbors could hear it, and this being Camp Snoopy, I knew they would tell, so I got rid of it." I think the only reason he stopped the attack was he realized all he was doing was scratching Bardo up, and that wasn't worth dying for.

He told me he had left his building that morning expecting to die and had stopped on the track and was standing on the inside curb and looking back, waiting for Bardo to come along so he could jump on top of him. Bardo apparently sensed the danger and tried to walk behind him out onto the grass field, but got jumped him anyway.

Garofalo was what is known as a "sleeper" and had worked his way to MCSP and laid low for a full year to pull off his plot. He and his cousin knew Ms. Schaeffer and he felt he owed it to her to rid the world of Mr. Bardo. Garofalo doesn't reside at the Creek anymore, and I'm sure he's not upset about it. Once you've displayed any such aggressive behavior, they're not going to let you stay on an SNY yard. He probably wouldn't want to stay on one anyway and be surrounded by Chesters and rats. He didn't have to worry about anyone questioning him about why he was there. As I stated in the introduction, respect is the Beast's ultimate currency, and by that measure, he is a wealthy man.

Recently, after my publisher expressed concern about liability regarding disclosing so many events that might not be appreciated by the subjects, I tracked down both Bardo and Garofalo, wrote them letters with a release form inside which both signed and returned them to me. Garofalo told me he had done the same thing to another felon that he felt deserved it, but that gentleman survived too. He said he must be getting too old, maybe the prison chow. Bardo agreed to allow the story to be told but insisted on receiving a copy of this book. Keep checking your mail, Hoss...

> 3/21/2020
>
> Mr. Big D.
>
> How the Hell are you.
> Of Course i remember you.
> Thank you For Not Shooting Me dead on that very hectic Morning.
> We Were both Just doing our Jobs.
> As For My Name its Vanilis With a I Not a u. And Janeane is My Cousin.
> We use to See Rebecca Schaeffer at a Restaurant Called Canters in Los-Angeles. She was always Nice to My Then 5 year old Son Bobby.
> Janeane and Rebecca Knew Each other through the Entertainment Industry.
> I owed the Schaeffer Family At least a Reckoning of Bardo.
> Dig What i'm Say'n Mr. D.?
>
> Well Thanks For Writing
> I'd be Honored to Sign Your Permission-Slip. Take good Care, Good Luck.
>
> Respectfully
> Vanilis D.

Letter from Janeane Garafolo's cousin, passing along his thoughts and permission to use his name for this story. Solid convict.

The inmate phones are another responsibility of the control-booth cop. There are four phones in each unit, and the receiving party must accept charges for collect calls. There are no incoming calls. The officer is supposed to listen in on the calls to make sure nothing illegal is being said, and all the calls are recorded in the squad office. So, if we hear something that sounds funny, we call the squad and tell them which phone to listen to and what time. It was not unusual to hear a conversation during which you could tell they were trying to get a visitor to bring in some dope. Things like, "Did you get that CD?" In the old days, we had an old, raggedy tape recorder next to our speaker and we would have to press "Record" on it to record anything that sounded wrong.

On many occasions, I would hear an inmate telling a woman he was trying to romance that he would be getting out in the near future. Frequently, I knew this guy was an LWOP (Life without parole), doing all day (life) and I had to keep my mouth shut. I could pick up the receiver and talk to them but never once did so. I simply had to hope that she would find out the truth before he could take too much advantage of her. The majority of the calls would vacillate between, "Oh, baby, I love you so much!" to "I called last night and you didn't answer, who you fuckin?" and then back to the "I love you" angle.

You'd be amazed at the sex calls that transpired on those phones. Usually the inmate would be coaching the person as she pleasured herself. The woman would be moaning and panting as he directs her with commands like, "Faster, now harder!" I have little doubt that the majority of these women were sitting in a chair in the living room, channel surfing through Jerry Springer or soap operas, and faking the whole thing.

I had one guy who was constantly doing this coaching with his wife. One time, according to her anyway, her cat was giving her oral pleasure! Having seen her in visiting as I had, and knowing how grungy she was, I wasn't surprised, the cat probably just thought it was a can of Friskies. I yelled down onto the dayroom floor to the floor cop and told her to call me. When she did, I held the phone near the speaker so she could hear it. This officer also worked in visiting on the weekends and knew both of these people. They were later busted for doing sexual things in the visiting room and the wife was denied the privilege of visiting for a year. I called a buddy on the goon squad and told him to go and listen to the recording of phone No. 3 at 11:41 for the cat incident, and when I was walking out that day, he was standing by Main Control and stated, "Man! I need some post trauma counseling!"

Whenever I heard an inmate yelling and being abusive to his woman, I'd cut the phone off, then turn it right back on again, so all he'd hear would be a click followed by a dial tone. He would think she'd hung up on him and call her back and she'd deny it. Behavior modification.

I talked about the difference between inmates and convicts earlier. Inmates were constantly trying to get special unlocks or things because they wanted them right then. They would come to my back yard door and want to be let in before the next unlock because it was hot or raining outside. Maybe they wanted to drop off a bindle they'd acquired. If they were inside on the dayroom, they'd want to be allowed to go in their cell and get something they had forgotten and couldn't wait until the next unlock. I usually told them that I was required by law to rehabilitate them, and I needed to prepare them for the outside world should they ever get out. The best way to do that was to get them to plan ahead and anticipate what they needed for the day. A convict, on the other hand, would just wait until the next unlock and not whine about being inconvenienced by their own lack of planning.

The ones on the yard trying to get inside would run through a multitude of excuses. It was almost like that old *SNL* skit about the land shark. They would stand by the intercom and say something like, "I just got off work," then if that didn't work, they might try, "I have a ducat to go to a hearing and I need to put on my state blues." I had a list of all ducats issued for that day so I knew if they were legit. They'd try anything that *might* give them a chance to gain entry. I almost expected one of them to utter, "Candygram." I had one old guy who always wanted to get in between unlocks and one time he was going through his whole repertoire and finally he tries, "I'm on heat meds!" Not bad because whenever the outside temp exceeded 90 degrees, we were required to get them inside if they indeed were on heat meds, and we had a list of all those that were. Not bad, except it was *January*.

They were especially desperate to get inside whenever they returned from canteen with one or two laundry bags full of goodies. Usually, they owed some of the fellas on the yard, either to repay a debt or from having borrowed similar goodies with the promise to repay them, and were hoping to gain entry before one of them spotted him with the booty. Many inmates who had debts owed to them would hang around the canteen window waiting to swoop on anyone who owed them. Inmates would stand outside my window and yell up that they were returning from canteen, and I guess there were a few control-booth cops who would let them in. I would advise them that there would be a regularly scheduled unlock at the top of the hour. The common ploy would involve them claiming that they had ice-cream among their haul and it was melting. I'd ask them if they had a freezer in their cell because it was just as hot in there, so I'd advise them to start eating! I wasn't trying to be mean by not letting anybody in, it was simply that any time I opened the sally port. there was a chance of somebody coming in for an illicit act who didn't live there, or another slipping out while on yard restriction.

If an inmate was already on the dayroom and just wanted to go into his house, I would always give the "one way" because it meant one less potential problem I would have to watch on the dayroom floor. If they went into their house and didn't close the door completely, hoping I would get distracted and not notice them sneaking back out, they would get an issue of Big D's stress program.

In each housing unit there were several intercom speakers

around the dayroom on the walls. Inmates could push the button and speak to the control officer to tell them something, like they needed to get into their house because of some legitimate reason, or maybe the hot water wasn't working. Staff could also use them to tell me something without yelling it for the entire unit to hear. There were times when I would see a couple of inmates standing near one having a conversation that appeared to be about something secretive. I could turn on the intercom and eavesdrop on the chat, but frequently, it was something I didn't especially want to hear.

In the control booth, if an inmate approached after working in the chow hall, returning from a visit or if a sergeant had called me to send this guy to his office, I would let them in. Frequently, one or two others would be hiding under the hood of the sally port door and would try to sneak in with him. One of their favorite ploys was to approach the intercom and tell me they needed to take a dump and that I just had to let him in. Since there were three outside crappers on the yard I would offer to toss them some toilet paper out the window so they could complete their evacuation. That usually ended the conversation.

On the subject of TP, let me elaborate. I believe the TP the state uses was probably its most effective tool against any parolee reoffending. It was single ply and was like binder paper. They gave it great sounding names like Rain Breeze, as if it were a combination of a bidet and trade winds. Some staff members would bring in their own stuff since the state brand was so poor. When the inmates would complain about it, I would just tell them to use the poor man's bidet . . . a turkey baster!

Nevertheless, TP was another form of prison currency and it was valued to have a stash of it. Inmates were issued one roll apiece at the beginning of the week and would frequently come around begging for more claiming they'd had the squirts for a few days. I remember asking one inmate what he did if he ever ran out at an inopportune moment, and he held up his index finger and stated, "Sometime you just gotta go digital."

They would also roll out a few feet of it, rub stick deodorant on it, twist it into a tight wick, and burn it to cover up tobacco, pot smoke, or maybe after having their morning constitutional—masking "The Bouquet of the Bootay."

After three years in Building 1 control, I took the job as the Dedicated Patrol Officer (DPO). When they put up the electric fence and closed all the perimeter towers except the two that operate sally port gates, they had to put an officer in a car that just putts around the perimeter fence for 24/7.

The fence has big metal hoops attached to each strand of wire, anything metal is touched, an alarm goes off in Main Control. This is to prevent any escape attempt by spreading the wires and crawling through or over the top. So whenever an alarm goes off, my job would be to race over to the spot where the alarm was located and make sure no escape was underway. The vast majority of alarms were from birds landing on the wire and touching something, which would kill them immediately. They could sit on the wire all day without harm but if they touched anything else, thereby grounding themselves. . . *zot!*

The Belly of the Beast

The Stir Fry fence. You can see that after I retired, there is now mesh screen encompassing the charged wire to protect birds from being nuked. You can see that the wires are closer together near the bottom. There are also small openings in the concrete base, allowing small rodents and birds to get from one side to the other safely. If anything closes the circuit by touching the wires, an alarm goes off in main control, the outside patrol sergeant's truck and the DPO car. The area between the fence and the buildings is called "No man's land" and only a few inmates can go there for clean up with special clearance and supervision. Housing unit 6 in background.

Once a week, we would post gunners on the roof on several housing units, shut down the fence and have to go between the two fences on each side of the stir-fry fence, retrieve the dead birds, bring them back out, identify them, take a picture and log it into a book. I did that task on a numerous occasions. It was kind of intense being so close to a lethal fence that is supposed to be off, but you could never be too sure. One time, when I was working as the Central Service S&E, we went far into the perimeter fence to retrieve a dead bird that was supposed to be on the inner side of the electric strands. When we got to the reported location, we discovered that it was actually on the other side of the wire. It was such a hot day that instead of walking all the way back to Tower 7 and back to get over to the other side, I held my breath, reached through the wires and retrieved the feathered carcass. Not too smart, but laziness has no bounds.

There would be a yellow crime-scene tape tied in the fence, indicating the location where the dead bird was, so we could retrieve it easily. One time, Main Control radioed me: "DPO- Main Control, can you check to see how many ribbons are on the fence?" This was so they could determine if there were enough to warrant posting roof guns for a bird retrieval. I drove around the perimeter to check it out. Obviously, a retrieval run hadn't been made in quite awhile, because there were so many yellow ribbons on the fence. I radioed back and said, "Main Control- DPO. It looks like Tony Orlando has been out here!" I don't think many of them got it. He wasn't a country music star.

I liked the job because it had AC for summer and a heater for winter and I could listen to my radio shows during the shift. I could get out and stretch my legs way around the back of the institution by Tower 4. But, if there were any inmates out and about, such as work crews on the weekdays, the only place I could get out was to pull into the Tower 7 vehicle sally port to use the bathroom. Since I had a shotgun and handgun, I had to be very careful whenever I opened the door or even rolled down the window if I was near any convicts. Getting in there for the bathroom wasn't difficult on the weekends since there were no transportation cars, buses or free staff workers around, but on weekdays it was quite crowded at the vehicle sally port, so it was dicey when the contractions reach 30-second intervals. "Free staff" refers to any employee who not working in a custody role, such as plumbers, carpenters or cooks.

Of course, for me, the radio wasn't entertaining enough. So I had my little handheld TV with a 3-inch LCD color screen, too. I would park near a shady tree on the weekends and watch football, golf or NASCAR. I'd take a quick lap around the perimeter during the commercials. We used many different vehicles during my time, because CDC would use the cars until they reached a certain number of miles and then get rid of them. Whenever a new car would come along, I would bring in a dozen doughnuts for the free-staff guy in the garage, and he would have his inmate workers put a tape deck in it. Then I would go to the county library and check out a bunch of audio books. It sure made the time go by, and even though I might be cruising around the dry, stark perimeter of a prison in Ione, I could escape to the jungles of Borneo or some other exotic locale within that cool car.

There was a really sweet, cute, girl who worked Tower 7 on the weekends. One particularly creepy sergeant frequently would go up into the tower and just hang around up there with her. He had a habit of picking his nose constantly, regardless of who might be present at the time... just buried to the third knuckle doing brain surgery and would extract a hairy meatball while she looked on. It isn't very roomy up there and with his creepiness combined with his skullduggery, it was really unpleasant for her. Of course, she was too sweet to give him any bad vibes so he thought he was doing pretty well with her.

I had a chance to stick it to him one day but let him off the hook. There was a fence alarm, so after I cruised the perimeter, spotted a bird sitting on the wire with a look of shock on its face and reported in which section it was located, he had to come out and reset the alarm. I need to be careful here and not disclose too much about the procedure, but let's just say he had to unlock the cabinet that contained the panel to reset the alarm. The cabinet had a large padlock on it, and after everything was done, I resumed my normal patrol . As I came around to where that cabinet was, I noticed the padlock sitting on top of the cabinet. Can you imagine the depth of this security breach? If an inmate or an associate would have come across the unlocked panel to the electric fence, it could have been a mass self-parole!

I'm licking my chops over the multitude of options at my disposal to throw this lame to the wolves. I grabbed the padlock and resumed my patrol but kept making U-turns in order to keep the cabinet in sight so I could see if anyone got near it. As much as I would have been a hero to most staff *and* administration if I got him in a wreck, I still needed to make sure that the first priority of an officer was intact, preventing escapes. I was going to wait until there was another alarm and watch his reaction when he came to unlock the cabinet. I waited awhile, but there was no alarm activity and I began to feel some pity for him so I radioed him: "OP-DPO, 10-19 Tower 4," and when he arrived I handed him the padlock. I did make sure he knew he owed me a favor.

That sergeant kept going up to that sweet officer's tower and, realizing he was going to keep bugging her, whenever I would see him go up there, I would drive around to the back 40 of the joint and throw rocks and sticks over the outer chain link fence onto the electric wire, which would set off the fence alarm. He would have to come down out of the tower to reset the alarm, and she could relax a bit. She later became a counselor and was the woman I walked out the gate with, arm in arm, on the day I retired (Future chapter).

Thunderdome, the Infirmary, and the Psych Ward.

AFTER THE THREE years as the DPO, I went back inside and took a position in the "Thunderdome!" That was what we called Alpha gym. All three of the gyms had been converted into dormitories when I arrived. This one was a lawless place where assaults, drugs and sexual activity were commonplace. The Level 1 and 2 offenders were housed in the other gyms, but since A yard was Level 4, the Thunderdome had Level 3 inmates... housed in a dorm setting.

There were two floor officers and one cop up in the gun booth. After a year or so as one of the floor cops, I moved up into the gunner position. The gunner had no responsibility to open doors or anything like that, just protect us and the Thunderdome residents. I was in that gun booth job for about a year, and it was wild. With 160 level 3 inmates triple-bunked and tons of blind spots, it was hard to maintain security. I had one assault when I was in the gun booth. I was watching the whole thing unfold, saw it coming, but when the one guy unloaded on the other one, the perp ducked under the bunks, crawled to the other side of the building and changed clothes, making it impossible to ID him. I felt foolish after I pushed my alarm button and staff responded, because I couldn't ID the assailant.

Thunderdome, the Infirmary, and the Psych Ward.

This is not the Thunderdome but is Charley gym. The gun booth in the Thunderdome is less than half this size. I have never seen the gyms like this, there were always 160 inmates triple bunked in here when I was there. Good idea to discontinue housing level 3 felons in a open setting like this. There was an officers podium just below the gun booth. Showers were off to the left and toilets just behind the photographer. The gun booth was entered from a roof hatch after walking along the roof from Main control. Now it's actually a GYM! Dodgeball anyone?

The best thing about that job was I could listen to the radio. It was a small booth but had a new AC unit, and it was *cool* in there. One time, I phoned into an FM talk show on KLOS from my cell phone. I told the call screener, Priva, in dramatic golf announcer style, "I'm calling from a gun booth overlooking one hundred and sixty convicted felons in a state prison housing unit". She exclaimed, "I'm putting you on the air right now!" I told her I couldn't do it because someone might recognize my voice and realize where I was, and even her suggestion of me using a pseudonym wasn't going to be okay. She understood but wanted me to call back when I was in a different location. Maybe I'll get around to that someday.

My clerk in the Thunderdome was a flamboyant queen who had implants and long straight hair. Her Majesty had a full dance card in the Thunderdome! She had her eyebrows tattooed on, but they'd been put on too high, so she walked around with a look of persistent astonishment on her face. She told me that she had performed at a drag queen bar prior to being incarcerated under the name of Dawn Morningwood. She loved getting new tatoos but didn't have money or groceries to pay the artist, so she would let them fondle and kiss her breasts in exchange. A pure example of tit for tat... Every day she would need to get the building roster from me in order to make any changes because of bed moves. She would ask coyly, "Big D, I'd like to have your rooster?". I would correct her but she knew what she was saying and I wouldn't give her the satisfaction of thinking I was embarrassed.

Whenever there is a full-blown queen, I bet you're wondering about showering and strip- outs. Well, she would usually be attached to one specific dude, and if it was a dorm-type shower, like it was in the gym, that dude would post up, stand guard and hold a towel or blanket in his outstretched arms for modesty while her grace tidied up. I personally never had to strip out a queen, and there are varying degrees of royalty.

I did escort one royal inmate over to Ad Seg one time, and after relinquishing custody to the Ad Seg staff, I was completing the transfer paperwork. The inmate was put into a holding cell—it's like a wire-mesh phone booth with an opening in the door for passing things back and forth. Every inmate being admitted into Seg gets stripped out and issued a white jumpsuit. As the floor cop is stripping this individual out, every eye from every inmate in every cell on both tiers of that section was squished against the cell door window and there was lots of whooping and whistling when that T-shirt came off.

There was another time when I was in the Building 1 control booth and we had one of the more, umm, convincing ladylike inmates living in there. Something jumped off on the yard and everybody out there was lying on the ground as the situation was mapped and sorted out.

Thunderdome, the Infirmary, and the Psych Ward.

The incident was serious enough that every inmate on the yard was stripped down to his boxers (or teddy), and after each inmate was completed, he was supposed to proceed to his unit. Our little lassie was around the corner from my viewpoint, but I heard the loud whooping and hollering that preceded this poor individual hustling around the corner, clutching the underclothing to her chest and briskly headed for my sally port with the most rosy-red, blushing cheeks you've ever seen.

Any time an inmate or staff was hanging around an occupied shower, they were said to be "Peter gazin'" or "shower sharkin'". I would frequently get on the PA system in the housing unit if I noticed someone hanging around the showers and declare, "No Peter gazin'!" That would always make the dayroom crack up. There was one guy who did it often and I asked him if that was his name, Peter Gazen. I started referring to him as Inmate Gazen. Even the inmates picked up on it and it became his moniker. Some of them may not have appreciated my sense of humor but what could they do? I had a "captive audience."

Any time there was tension between rival factions, most of the groups would post two guards by the shower whenever one of their own was in there. It didn't matter if it was the gym or a regular housing unit; taking a shower, being naked and washing your hair puts you in a very vulnerable position for a hit. Those soldiers were not considered shower sharks—they would be facing away from the shower and focused on the dayroom floor.

Most inmates hated living in Thunderdome because even though they had lockers with combination locks, things were always getting stolen, there was no privacy, it was loud, and if you had the top bunk it was always too bright to sleep well. They dimmed the lights at night but they still needed to be bright enough for the officers to see what was going on, especially when we had to walk around the bunk area for the counts. Most of the top-bunk guys would tie a towel or T-shirt around their heads to cut the glare. Some convicts would actually misbehave in order to get their custody points up to Level 4 so they could get into a cell and out of the Thunderdome.

In the bathroom, there were twelve toilets lined up side by side with no partitions between them. Can you imagine sitting there for your morning constitutional and your mortal enemy is sitting right next to you? Plus, you must be in full view of staff while pinching off a few German Browns, regardless of the staff's gender. Hope you don't have bashful bowels, and talk about vulnerable. That alone should have cut down on the rate in which these guys reoffend! I don't know which would be worse, sitting with 11 other cons while doing their business or being confined in a small, enclosed cell while your cellie blows up the crapper.

The inmates with lower or middle bunks would hang blankets on each side, giving them peace, dark and privacy, but if we can't see them at all times, it's a security breach. It was a constant battle with them to stop the "tenting."

Another job I had was working weekends in the crisis-bed wing of the infirmary. It had 12 cells, which were pretty barren except for a sink and toilet. They were used mostly for inmates who were either claiming to be suicidal or coming back from surgery, and CDC felt they couldn't protect themselves from any assault until they recovered. The ones coming back from surgery had decent accommodations, like a bed.

Inmates claiming suicidal thoughts would be issued a security suit that looked like a Barney Rubble outfit and, in theory anyway, could not be torn up and used to fashion a noose. Sometimes, if an inmate was really in a severe crisis, he would have no clothing whatsoever and sleep on a bare floor. A concrete floor is about as hard as anything you could sleep on. I had an inmate who had spent some time in there tell me "That floor is as hard as a preacher's cock". I hoped he was just speculating. Frequently a nurse or an officer on overtime would have to sit in a chair outside the door and observe them through the window, making a notation on a form every 15 minutes about what they were doing. This is one thing about the Jeffery Epstein "suicide" that baffles me. I can't believe they didn't have somebody sitting right in front of the cell looking through the window 24 hours a day, like we did. That incident doesn't pass the smell test, but I'm not sure whether the left or the right may have been complicit. Since the righties controlled the White House and Justice department, I'm going to assume that they felt they had more opportunity and incentive to silence him. Just a guess though. I got held over on Christmas day one year for that very job of sitting in front of the cell of an individual who had alerted supervisors that he was having those feelings. It's not unusual to see a spike in such thoughts around the holidays, and if he truly felt that way, he was right to bring it to someone's attention, regardless of the day.

If extremely suicidal or disruptive, the inmate would be put in five-point restraints. When that happened, we'd have to go in every few hours and release one limb at a time so they could move it around, and let them pee in a bedpan. I saw a few just piss all over themselves, so a nurse would have to come in there and wash him up.

There was one guy who was a frequent resident because he seemed determined to end his life. He was a very gregarious individual and very polite. He certainly didn't fit the stereotype of someone despondent, but I watched him through the cell door window one time sitting on the floor next to the wash basin/toilet trying desperately to affix a towel that he had around his neck to a small button that flushed the toilet. He was doing everything in his power to pull himself down in order to get the makeshift noose to cut off his blood and airway. I alerted the doctor and we unlocked the door and took the towel away, I have no idea how that towel ended up in his cell but he was going to have to face another day of life. He finally succeeded in his quest about a year later.

Overall, I think the department does a good job at preventing suicidal inmates from ending their lives, but if someone is determined to accomplish the task, there's really not much more it can do. Through medication, group sessions, one-on-one sessions with doctors, and preventing anyone who has voiced any such intentions from having access to materials that could assist them in accomplishing the task, and having an staff member dedicating to observing him. That's about all that can be done. When one would approach me and reveal they were having these thoughts I would alert his doctor and also say "Regardless of your religious beliefs and conclusions regarding any afterlife, they are really just conjecture and speculation. This life is the only one we know we have. You're gonna be dead for a long time, you will have plenty of time to be dead so why not milk this one for everything you can? Suicide is a permanent result from a temporary problem. There are always better days ahead." A few actually felt this approach had some merit and several told me later when the crisis abated that it helped their outlook.

Every morning, we'd make the rounds with the psych docs, nurses and sometimes a sociologist. The inmate would be cuffed up through the tray slot and brought out to have his vital signs taken and for the psychs to ask them a bunch of questions to evaluate if they were ready to return to their regular housing unit.

We had one guy in the infirmary for the whole time I worked there, and he would vacillate between screaming obscenities at us and being contrite. He definitely had some challenges. He wore diapers, but even then, he and his cell would be somehow completely covered with feces on a daily basis. I think someone was sneaking extra food to him because it was unbelievable the volume of poop that dude generated. Every morning when the door was unlocked to let me into that wing, I was hit in the nostrils with the funk of his food-processing capabilities. Some staff members tried spraying air freshener to mask the funk coming from his trunk, but that just made it just seem like someone had taken a dump under a pine tree. The nurses would have to go in and wipe down the walls, his bed and him pretty much every day. He thought it was funny. I guess there's nothing wrong with a little "self-defecating humor." Because it was practically impossible to keep up with his evacuation pace, he would sometimes sit with a dirty diaper for hours and as a result of that, the nurses would have to apply medication to his rash. He would stand there after getting out of the shower with a nurse sitting in a chair behind him applying the lotion. And just about every time, while her face was a foot away from his exhaust pipe . . . *FRAAAAAPPP!* He would bust some noxious gas in her face.

These expulsions were so vile I'm surprised they didn't set off the radon gas detectors. I was ready to take a page out of the old coal miners manuel and insist on having a canary in a cage nearby so if the bird keeled over we could all run for our lives.

He was also diabetic and was taken out a few times to have a toe or two amputated. I think he was actually trying to escape, piece by piece.

The last jobs I had were in Building 6, which is the psych unit on Bravo yard. When the state decided to close the mental hospitals. they simply dumped all the patients into the prison system. When I first went to Building 6, I was one of the escort officers, which involve escorting the inmates who were on orientation to various places and appointments. When an inmate arrives at the institution, they are on orientation status until the counselors can review their file to determine if they have enemies on that yard, what is the best job or schooling they should have and what custody level they should be assigned. They are locked down except for an hour several times a week when we close the dayroom floor to other inmates so they can shower and watch TV or play games. Usually they make a beeline for the phones, but we didn't allow fish to make phone calls. Sometimes the control booth cop would forget to turn off the phones for the orientation program and the inmate would get over on them. I also sat in on the committee that took those inmates off orientation after the usual 10- to 14-day period.

Those committee sessions occurred twice a week and were interesting. The state description of a crazy inmate is an EOP, which stands for Enhanced Out Patient. Sounds better than crazy I guess. If they have genuine issues they absolutely should be in the best program for them to flourish. The reality is that maybe about half of them actually have mental challenges. Every one of us is loco in some capacity but most of us manage to avoid committing violent felonies in spite of it. The ones that are actually "normal" are just hiding in the program for the free state dope, the opportunity to prey on the actual "nutters," and to hide from anybody questioning them about what their incarcerating offense was. They also have much greater access to female staff and *any* inmate who paroles while in the EOP program gets put on SSI, which is basically welfare and free taxpayer income. The inmates all know exactly what to say to get into the EOP program, and many of the psychs are too scared of any legal repercussion to weed them out. I've heard there are actually cheat sheets circulating among the inmates detailing what to say and do in order to get into or stay in the EOP program.

I was responsible for rounding up all the inmates scheduled for committee that day and keeping them in the building until it was their turn to go before the group. I would sit behind the inmate as long as he was being civil, but if he started acting a little mouthy or unstable, I would get up and loom behind him, which would usually result in him reconsidering his options.

If the psych wanted to take a faking inmate out of the program, he would simply claim he needed more time and would harm himself if removed from EOP. I remember one guy in committee going on and on about how he was making such progress but needed more time in the program, but this psych was adamant about getting him out. He left the meeting, and the counselors and I looked at each other and were speculating on how long it would be before he was in his unit and threatening to harm himself. Within about two minutes, we heard on the radio that an inmate had climbed the fence surrounding the water boiler on the yard and was lying unresponsive on the concrete floor inside the fence. He had scaled the chain link fence, climbed partially down the other side, dropped the remaining two feet to the ground, and was lying there all crumpled up in a heap. It was a pathetic performance, The suits peed and put him back in the program.

One of the more unique moments I witnessed in committee involved an inhabitant of my housing unit. We all were aware that he had come to the conclusion that drinking urine had benefits. We would frequently pull him over to search him on the yard and usually would find a tumbler of whizz in his coat. Always a good idea to glove up anytime you had interaction with him. So I'm in committee for his quarterly EOP hearing and the counselors and doctors are questioning him about this practice. He was unapologetic and touted his research about it being fairly common practice in other countries, including India. He admitted it wasn't just his own urine he drank but experimented with other brands available on the yard. He was bisexual and enjoyed taking it right from the tap at times. Whether it was actually beneficial to him or not, I guess he just enjoyed curling up in his bunk after breakfast with a good book and a warm cuppa piss. Nobody had to tell HIM about things that would guarantee his reservations being extended in the EOP program.

Some of the psych staff can be a bit naïve and too trusting when it comes to the fellas. There was one inmate who convinced a doctor that he suffered from such claustrophobia that the doc wrote an order stating that whenever this inmate went on his frequent medical transports, he was to be allowed to ride in the front seat with the window down and no seat belt on. That got shot down pretty quickly.

I remember one time I overheard two psychiatrists having a heated discussion about differing diagnoses of a particular inmate. It was getting quite volatile and I thought they were about to start slingin'. The hostility eventually dissipated but for a minute I thought it was about to become the gunfight at the I'm OK-You're OK corral.

The inmates meet with the psychs alone, often in private rooms, and talk about deep feelings. I think the prevailing attitude among the psychs is that custody staff are a bunch of knuckle-dragging goons, and that all these inmates are misunderstood and need all the sympathy and understanding they can get. Sometimes they're right, it's hard to know when it's true. The inmates know they can go in there and complain about how we are mistreating them and it will get traction with the suits. If it's a female psych (or occasionally a male), there's always the chance of exploiting that opportunity and getting one of them to cross the line, which happens way too often.

There are a bunch of psych techs also. They conduct some of the group meetings the EOPs are required to attend, and they also hand out the State dope. You can imagine that the fellas try real hard to get close to these employees, most of whom are female. The vast majority of them are responsible and clean, but a few have strayed across the median. It always made me nervous when I saw one with gang tattoos visible on their neck.

I stayed in Building 6, but became a floor officer. I bid that job mainly because it had Sundays/Mondays off, and I liked that just fine. I still didn't have enough time in for Saturday/Sunday, but I liked the idea of being able to stay up late on Saturday night, having Sunday off for day trips and still having a weekday for golf, outings and other things less crowded and easier on this Scotsman's purse. It was the last job I would have in my career.

The main headaches were doing bed moves, conducting counts, running unlocks, breaking up fights and observing the med line.

The inmates always want bed moves because their cellies are assholes, which isn't surprising. Main Control doesn't like bed moves because it's a lot of work and it can screw up counts, so Saturday was bed-move day. It could be a real pain ,and they weren't supposed to get a bed move unless they had been in that bunk for at least 90 days. It was also hard because so many of them had been granted a lower bunk or lower-tier "chrono" by their shrink. A chrono is an order usually written by a shrink, doctor or administrator allowing the convict some special exception to have certain items or certain behavior. They could get a single-cell chrono, too. Sometimes we would have to move them on days other than Saturday if there was a cell fight or if one inmate told the sergeant that he would either harm himself or sock the dude up. If there was a cute queen in the building, they'd all try to cell up with her. I remember one inmate telling a sergeant that his cellie was trying to pressure him into sex and the sergeant told him, "Well, you can either fight or fuck!" That was long ago and is not the norm these days for a sergeant's attitude.

Every morning around 0700 we would run the med line. There is a small office inside the unit where all the meds are kept, and my partner and I would stand on either side as the inmates lined up for their pills. The control cop would release them steadily so that there was always around 15 or 20 in each of the two lines. As each one approached the window, he would show his ID card. The psych techs would have already put each guy's meds in a little paper cup.

The inmate would toss the cupful of "Skittles" into his mouth and hopefully swallow them. The psych techs would have them open their mouths and show that they hadn't "cheeked" the dope. Then I would make them do it again for us and we'd shine our flashlights in there and have them lift their tongues to ensure compliance. In spite of all this, they were quite skilled in cheeking, palming or swallowing for regurgitating later. Some can even take it all the way down to their Adam's apple and still be able to bring it back up after returning to their casa.

Looking inside some of these mouths was disgusting because many were a funky, diseased hole full of snags and breath that would make a buzzard puke! This was the main reason why so many of them wanted to be an EOP, and no matter how hard we made it for them, they were still successful in saving these meds for later. Once back in their house, they would crush them and snort them, producing a big high. When conducting cell searches I would always keep an eye out for a small rock they picked up on the yard for crushing pills and any mirror with residue on it. They were allowed to have mirrors, but they were made of plastic, not glass.

They would even sell the pills they'd had in their mouths to other convicts. You gotta be pretty horny for dope to ingest something like that. It was easy for the "sane" guys to pressure real EOPs into cheeking and giving the dope to them.

Mostly we were standing there to ensure compliance from the

convicts, but also to make sure the staff wasn't supplementing anybody's prescription. This did happen on occasion. Our rats knew that it was going on and would tell us. I'll go into that later when I address dirty staff.

There really weren't very many fights in that unit while I was in there, but there were a few, so I had to use a little "baton therapy" a few times. CDC considers the baton and pepper spray to be equal in the level of discipline, meaning that we could choose either depending on our preference or the circumstance. Most officers like the pepper spray because you didn't have to be especially close to the inmate to use it, but I preferred the stick. Pepper spray is very effective on inmates, but it doesn't discriminate on whom it effects. If you sprayed somebody, most likely you were gonna get an issue of it yourself. Many times, when responding to an alarm, I ran into a housing unit and the whole dayroom was a cloud of pepper spray. It can be quite incapacitating. The baton allowed me to focus the penalty on the guilty party. I never once used my pepper spray. When I first arrived at the Creek, we used the side-handle baton, but later went to the telescoping type sometimes called an "Asp." It was smaller and straight but you could just flick your wrist as you were running to an alarm to extend it. The old-school side handle had some retention and defensive advantages for blocking blows, but if you were running to an alarm it would be flopping around in the ring holder, banging against your legs, and sometimes would fall out as you were running. Not good. It was also a pain to sit down in a chair with one; kind of like wearing a sword.

Whenever an inmate got pepper-sprayed, the protocol was to take them to one of the three or four decontamination stations on the yard. These were mesh cages like phone booths that had a water nozzle shower head inside. The remedy for pepper spray is flushing with copious amounts of water, fresh air and time. Once I was working on the yard and a fight broke out in Building 8. I responded, and after the combatants were cuffed up, I took the one I was escorting to the decontamination booth. He stood in there rinsing the pepper off, and then I took him inside the program office and put him in a holding

Thunderdome, the Infirmary, and the Psych Ward.

cage while the sergeant made arrangements for him to relocate in Ad Seg. The inmate called out to me and said his skin was still on fire. I asked if he wanted to go back to the decontamination station, and he said yes. I took him back out there, put him in the cage. He was just wearing boxers and had the cold water running over him. It was a very cold, rainy night and it happened around chow time, so all these inmates were walking on the track by the booth on their way back to their unit. They saw this guy in there shivering in his boxers and a few of them said, "You're one cold cop, Davidson!" I didn't bother to enlighten them that it was his idea; let them think I was a bit ruthless.

On that note, sometimes I would tell inmates that were on my shit list that I always carried a "planter bag," meaning some dope I had gotten from a gooner, with me so I could plant it in his cell while conducting a search in order to get him in a wreck. Sometimes when I was in a gun position, I might tell an inmate that I kept a "throw-away shank" up there so I could shoot him and toss the shank down near him to justify my actions. None of these were true, and I think they all knew I was just being playful but, as I said, sometimes it's not a bad thing if they think you're a little unhinged. If they only knew about the DDT spray in Japan...

I've had to put the wood (baton) to a few along the way, and most of them don't take it personally. The next day or so I may run across that guy and he'll say, "That's okay, Big D, you had to do your job." Of course, they would also expect me to not take it personally if one of them opened me up!

In the last couple of years I was at the Creek, the higher-ups created this stupid method of keeping track of how the EOPs were spending their day. It required writing down everything they did like: showering, sleeping, eating or socializing and document it in a binder. It was a waste of time because they changed how they wanted us to do it every day. And it was a distraction from us doing our jobs, which was keeping the guests from sticking each other, doing drug deals or performing other nefarious deeds. I refused to do it.

Every once in a while, they'd send some representative from

headquarters to see if we were doing the book right. Hell, even they didn't know what the "right way" was, because they changed it every day. Whenever a rep was headed our way, we'd get a head's-up from the yard gunner. My control-booth cop would alert me when they were approaching the sally port and I'd head for a cell, have the door opened, and begin a cell search. When the rep would tell me to come over to our podium and go over the book, I'd say I just got some information about a weapon being in this cell and I was in this job to maintain security, protect everybody in the unit and prevent escapes, which took priority. They would eventually get discouraged, leave… and would only come in on my days off.

Speaking of higher-ups, some of you may be wondering why I never promoted to sergeant. The truth is, I never even took the sergeant's test and had no interest in becoming one. I was much more concerned about being a father and being home with my kids than having a few more bucks in my pocket or strutting around with chevrons on my sleeve. By now, I had a little time in, and when you promote, you go right back down to the bottom of the seniority list. That means going back to first watch, then third watch, crummy days off, and being the first one to get held over if they needed a body for the next shift. And God knew I wasn't going back to Thunderdome.

CDC has implemented some really good programs that are beneficial not only to the inmates but to the community as well. They now have a Service dog training program where inmates are training dogs to be utilized in the community for various services. The dogs are allowed to stay in the cell with their trainer while undergoing training. Great idea. I hear Canteen is having difficulty keeping peanut butter in stock these days though…probably just a coincidence..

Discipline

I WANT TO state here that there are valid reasons at times for convicts to do things that they get in trouble for, and also that they should expect to be treated fairly within CDC guidelines, without bias or malice. There are also occasions and certain inmates that these CDC rules do not achieve their goals. I can't vouch for other staff, but when I used my own brand of discipline, it was intended to get them to adhere to the rules such as not violating other felons/staff safety, rights or property, and not because I enjoyed it or wanting to stick it to someone I didn't like...well, maybe for a few Chesters.

CDC has its own philosophy about how to keep inmates from establishing chaos and misbehaving completely. They call it progressive discipline. I'm not disclosing anything here that the guests don't already know, but if one of them is misbehaving, you start with verbal counseling, which means you talk to him about it and tell him if it continues there will be further consequences. If that doesn't work, you can go to writing him up, starting with a CDC 128, also called a counseling chrono. It doesn't really carry any punishment, but shows you're following the progressive protocol, and the write-up stays in his central file. If that doesn't modify his actions, you can go to writing a CDC 115, which carries a bit of bite in that the inmate can catch some extra time in, lose some privileges and his points will go up. That means he may be lifted to another level and could be transferred to another yard or joint. A lieutenant will hear the case and decide if it warrants a loss of yard, loss of phone, loss of dayroom, or maybe even extend his reservations at the Mule Creek Inn.

The reality is that way too many lieutenants will either dismiss the 115 or bust it down to a 128, making the whole process a bit of a joke, and the inmates know it. If an inmate goes a year without any write-ups, his points will go down and he could go to a softer yard and get more privileges.

If two inmates are fighting, it's considered "mutual combat," but if one guy gets jumped, it can be "assault with battery." In my early days, any fight would land both of them in the hole and they'd both probably catch some more time. Now, if they both agree not to have any more tiffs, the whole thing is basically just "let go." They have to sign a form of non-aggression we call a "Barney" chrono. You know, Barney, as in the purple dinosaur who professes the "I love you, you love me" approach.

I rarely wrote anyone up and preferred my own style of getting their attention. I used peer pressure and my stress program. What good is it going to do to write up an inmate who is already a Level 4 and has three consecutive life sentences? NONE!

For instance, when I was in Building 1, we would usually allow our inmate porters and clerk to use the phones before dayroom opened. If someone in the unit pissed me off, I'd stop that privilege for all and make sure my workers knew why. They'd go to that inmate and let him know they didn't appreciate his choices, and that inmate would come to me with his hat in hand, apologizing and telling me it wouldn't happen again. If any one of them acted the fool, I'd start enforcing the rules to the letter, and everybody in the unit would threaten or convince him to get right with me. When in a control booth, I could turn off the breaker switch to the dayroom TV if someone drew my ire. I would just tell them that it was an electrical problem and I'd put in a work order to fix it. That always got the offender's attention, and he would be swift in trying to get right with me.

Discipline

Usually, while conducting a routine cell search, I would try to be somewhat respectful and leave it in about the same condition it was in, but if one inmate was disruptive, I'd tear up his house and throw all his and his cellie's stuff on the floor. His cellie would then make the problem child aware he didn't appreciate having to ride HIS beef, usually resulting in compliance.

They're not allowed to lend anything to one another, so if I found an appliance like a fan or a CD player in a cell who's resident who was interfering in the smooth operation of the unit and that appliance had another inmate's name scribed on it, I would confiscate it, causing tension between him and whoever lent it to him. I didn't do these things to be mean and I didn't derive any pleasure from it. I just concluded it was just the best way to maintain security and keep any supervisor heat away from me because the CDC version wasn't effective.

There was a practice known as "dropping the belt," and that meant going into an area that had relative privacy with a convict you had a problem with, dropping your belt, and settling it with your dukes. I never personally knew of anybody doing it while I was at the Creek but I know it happened in older times and perhaps still does at some rockin' pens. At the Creek, there are too many rats and you'd never be able to pull it off without it becoming known to the suits. I always thought it couldn't be done because there are really no places you can go without being seen by somebody, but also because one or both of you were going to get marked up in the scrap and you didn't want to sign out in the program office with a black eye that you didn't have at the start of the shift. One of the convict OGs told me the understanding was, "No head shots, no paperwork." That meant you couldn't punch or kick anybody above the shoulders and there would be no paperwork about it. A gentleman's agreement. The prison version of the Marquess of Queensberry rules.

When I was the yard gunner on *C* yard and the inmates were on the track headed for the chow hall, they were not supposed to stop at any time during the process. It seemed like the blacks were the ones that were most commonly stopping along the route to wait for their homies, and I was writing a lot of them up for it. It occurred to me that some lieutenant might notice that I seemed to be inflicting my ire along racial lines. so after I realized that, any time a white would even slow down, hesitate or not have his shirt completely tucked in, I would slap paper on him. Profiling at its best.

Inmates are not allowed to "sag," which means wearing pants down below their ass cheeks. If an inmate tried to do it in my unit I'd call them over and ask, "Why are you in a room with 200 horny convicts, trying to get all of them to focus on your ass? Are you soliciting for prostitution or are you displaying gang affiliation?" I would also tell them that I didn't appreciate them putting me on front street like that. If a supervisor walked in and saw him with his Pampers hanging out they might jack me up about why I was allowing this to happen.

I'd tell them, "Active gang members are not allowed on an SNY yard so if that's what it is, then let's get you transferred to a main line joint where you can be all active. If you're soliciting, then I'll book you for that and you'll have to register as a sex offender when you hit the streets. Which is it? If I see you walking around with your Kimbies showing like that again, we'll do one or the other." That would usually get their attention. Speaking of suburban white boys trying to be all gangsta, I have seen these punks walking around outside the joint with T-shirts saying, "Snitches get stitches!" If any one of these dorks were put in a situation where they had to ride someone else's beef, they'd be singing like a canary!

In addition to "sagging," some of the fellas tried to display their gang affiliation by "flaggin'." On the streets, this is the act of hanging a handkerchief out of their back pocket that matched their gang colors. Many of the convicts whose gang affiliation used blue as their color of choice would rip up a piece of the blue chambray shirt or jeans and have it hanging out of their back pocket. This was also unfair to the Bloods and Norteños, since there wasn't any red cloth they had access to on the yard. Most staff didn't notice, care, or thought it was just something that happened to be partially visible from the pocket, but I always jacked them up for it and took it away from them. I gave them

Discipline

the same speech about transferring them to an active prison if they wanted to display their affiliation. I'd tell them you can't have it both ways, hiding on an SNY yard and trying to be active.

While working in the main infirmary one day, we had an inmate in one of the holding cages prior to him seeing one of the doctors. He was spewing all sorts of venom at everyone that walked by, particularly the female nurses who came by the cage that's about the size of a phone booth. He was saying very personal and lewd things to them and wouldn't shut up. Eventually, we were going to have to open that door and deal with him, so I went into the break room and got a bunch of salt-and-pepper packets. I opened the packets and started sprinkling them on the floor in front of the door to the cage. He stopped his verbal abuse for a minute and asked what I was doing. I advised him I just wanted the floor to have some flavor because if he didn't shut up, he was going to be eating it as soon as that door opened. He surmised that even well-seasoned concrete didn't sound all that appetizing and that ended his vile diatribe.

When an inmate swears at one of the newer officers, the cop sometimes will feel compelled to write them up for "Disrespect." Even though there is such a provision in the *Title 15 Book of Rules,* it almost never gets upheld by the hearing lieutenant and is just a waste of time. It is a much better avenue to discourage such behavior by writing them up for "Inciting" and trying to convey that the aggressive behavior of the inmate cussing you out was having an inciteful effect on the other inmates in the area. This can affect security and will likely cause the lieutenant to consider applying some teeth to the disciplinary result. That's all assuming you didn't deserve the cuss out…

Sometimes in R&R, an inmate arriving on a bus or getting transferred to another pen would get mouthy or disruptive. Whenever an inmate transfers, their property is boxed up. When they arrive at their destination, they won't see the boxes as they're being processed off the bus, and the possessions in it won't be issued back to them until they come off orientation in about 10 days. I've only heard about this tactic, and can't be sure it actually happens but . . . one *could* let the transportation sergeant on the bus know that this one particular gent had been giving R&R staff a lot of trouble, or maybe the inmate had been a major problem child for the bus team already, and his property boxes just might get left on the bus at the next destination. The property boxes might even take a tour of all the prisons up and down the state. Eventually, the inmate would have to file a grievance with R&R staff. The process to locate his property would begin, but it could take months to remedy, or so I've heard...

Many housing-unit cops would try to move the assholes out of their unit to another building but that just dumps your headache on another guard. I tried not to do that. I always made sure I kept two or three of the smelliest, most disgusting, ugly, creepy, annoying, filthy losers in my unit. I would utilize them by moving anybody who got on my fecal list into a cell with them. The inmates all knew it, and it really got their attention. Then the problem inmate would either comply with the bed move or refuse, which they're not allowed to do, so he would go to the hole. Either way, it got the attention of every other inmate in the building.

Any time an inmate was not supposed to be let out of his house for any number of reasons, those little Monopoly game houses and hotels were used to cover up the button that opened the door so it couldn't be accidently pushed or opened by a cop that wasn't aware of the situation. The little green houses would cover the one button and could mean he's confined for some disciplinary action and the red hotels usually meant they were on orientation status. All 15 housing units had enough of these items to address any circumstance but not one of them is Park Place...

One time a new inmate came from off the bus and a counselor told me he had shot up a schoolyard full of kids in San Diego, apparently intent on thinning the herd of yuppie fledglings. When he walked into my unit I called him over and told him, "The state of California has determined you're entitled to three meals a day, a shower every few days, yard, dayroom, a toothbrush, TP, medical and dental coverage. Don't ever ask me for *one* other thing because that's all you're gonna get from me!"

Much more effective.

Inmates have an avenue to grieve any staff behavior with a 602 form. Some use it as a form of harassment and are always threatening to write us up if they don't get their way. I had many say they were going to "602" me, and I always told them, "Please do! You'll be doing me a favor by letting my sergeant know I'm doing my job."

I'd offer to write my name down so they wouldn't misspell it, because I couldn't buy that kind of publicity. That always changed their minds, I got 602ed one time in 25 years.

Prison Rape

EVERY CONVICTED FELON has the right to expect that during his incarceration he will be protected from any type of assault by inmates or staff. There have been times, however, when I knew of a Chester who had committed some horrible atrocities on a child, maybe him being subjected to some turnabout wasn't such a bad thing, but it was not my place to make that determination.

Whenever anybody finds out I worked in a prison, their mind always goes to rape. In reality, it doesn't happen that much anymore, mainly because, unless he's your cellie, you just won't have the opportunity. With better designs and procedures, it's rare that an inmate would be in a situation that provided the chance to be able to sexually assault anyone without being seen. In the older joints, there were blind spots everywhere, but not anymore. There have been times I was working as the chow hall gunner—which is in a little booth, accessed from the roof, and you tried to find a little privacy. There's *no* bathroom in the booth and you can be up there for three hours sometimes. I've had to bleed off some liquid pressure and would go up the ladder onto the roof between meal runs to handle it, but no matter where I went, I was always within somebody's vision. I guess that's the whole idea in a prison.

There are also plenty of queens around more than willing to take care of the other inmates, so rape simply isn't that common anymore. The whole idea for the rapist is not to get laid however, it's to hurt or inflict power over the victim. Consensual sex is not what turns them on.

Sometimes you would see an inmate in his cell with his boxers on backwards, with the fly in the back for easy admittance, but that would usually be for consensual lovin'. When rape does happen or is alleged to have happened, there are very specific new procedures to follow, and I'm so happy I've never had an inmate approach me in later years claiming to have been raped. The protocol has changed quite a lot recently, and whomever is told by the inmate he's been raped takes control and stays with the inmate through the entire process from the first disclosure to the hospital.

The only time I ever had an inmate come to me and claim he had been raped was well before this policy was introduced, so I just called for an S&E to report to my unit and escort him to the infirmary. I also had another cop come to escort the suspect to the sergeant's office. The suspect was an old *B* number, indicating he had been locked up for a very long time. Years later, I was at a local post office getting my passport and I spotted him there. I don't think he saw me or was just trying to hope I wouldn't notice him, but I knew he was a "lifer." So I was surprised and a bit alarmed to see him on the street. I considered confronting him and holding him until I could confirm that he hadn't escaped, but decided I would have heard about it if he indeed had. A few months later, I saw him again at a local store and approached him and asked him if his name was _____. He confirmed that it was and remembered me. I told him I thought he was an LWOP. He said he "was." LWOP refers to being sentenced to "Life without Parole." He told me the department had let him out for some reason that I don't recall. It was concerning to me that this guy was obviously living in my neighborhood, especially because he was apparently a sex offender. It's been many years since that incident and I haven't seen him again, so he either moved on or reoffended. Sex offenders almost never stop their predatory behavior, so most likely he got busted for trying to mate with someone who didn't share the attraction.

We did have one inmate from Oakland who was famous for raping every cellie he ever had, and he is an *A* number, meaning he's been in prison for a looong time. I can only remember running across six *A* numbers during my career. I won't use his name but he was known by a name similar to "Randy the Beast." Any guard with any time in knows who I'm referencing. He was a true Rump Ranger and had done time in just about every joint in the state. He hated being transferred however because, he just hated having to leave his cellies' behind...

He was skilled at martial arts, and the White boys sent a few torpedoes after him over the years but nobody has been able to take him out. He was in my unit for a while and was always respectful to me. Maybe he just liked the effect all those lunges I'd been doing at the gym were having on my glutes. Whenever a new, young cookie would come on the yard, Randy would start charming him in order to convince him to be his cellie and hoping to reach fifth base with him. It got to the point where we would have to get such fish to sign a release form stating that they understood there was high likelihood of being impaled by Randy and were going into that cell willingly, otherwise they could sue us, claiming we set him up.

I heard one story about him from another joint many years ago. I can't vouch for the authenticity of the story, but I'll pass it along anyway.

Seems Randy had a fresh young fish cupcake assigned to his cell and the floor officer was watching his window and saw Randy standing there, shuffling around with his ball cap pulled down over his eyes, looking out the window smoking a cigarette. The kid came down during the first unlock and told the floor staff he'd been raped. The cop told him it was impossible because he had seen Randy in the window smoking the whole time. The kid went back into the cell but came down for the next unlock claiming he'd been raped again. This time the floor cop had been watching the window intently, and all he saw was Randy still hanging there looking out the window while smoking, and sent the kid back a third time. Sure enough, the kid comes down saying it happened yet again! The cop refused to believe him and thought it was some sort of manipulation to get a cell move so he sent him up there again. This time the cop snuck around the tier and peeked into the cell. There was Randy, hat on sideways and a cigarette hanging out of his ear while longboning the poor kid he had bent over the toilet. Very resourceful. I must say that such behavior from the floor cop was unlike anything I witnessed during my career and was not the prevailing attitude within my sphere of awareness.

As I said, the vast majority of sex in prison is consensual. I had an older fellow who I'll call Marsala. He used to run the boxing program at Folsom many years earlier. He didn't have one tooth in his mouth, was taking hormone shots so was sporting a decent bust line, and I think he could put his lips around the exhaust pipe and suckstart a Harley Davidson on a January morning. He also would go through cellies at a rapid rate and would sometimes complain about not liking the cellie he had and always wanted a better one. I'd say, "Marsala, you got tits and no teeth, you're the perfect cellie! What's the problem?" He'd usually reply with, "I want you as my cellie, Big D." Actually he was a pretty interesting guy on the occasion when I'd have a conversation about his experiences in the old rockin' joints like Quentin and Folsom. He wanted a full sex change operation and, on several occasions, tried to cut his male plumbing off, or at least make the suits think he tried to so the State would recommend funding his transition to female. I used to tease the ones that wanted to be females and threaten to transfer them to a woman's prison and tell them they'd be miserable there because there would be *no men!* They'd usually complain to me whenever new royalty moved into the unit and say, "Too many bitches in the house ruin everything!"

Marsala had been a big part of the boxing program they had at Old Folsom. You should never assume that because they identify as female they can't fight. I witnessed several ass whippings administered by royalty on some dudes who had previously been considered tough. There was one guy who strutted around like he was some sort of badass, but got pummeled one day by a queen. He tried to downplay it by saying he only got hit two ways, unfortunately those two were hard and frequently. The boxing program at Folsom was unique. Not only did they have classes and competition; if you had a beef with another inmate you could put the gloves on and bomb away at each other with no repercussions. Not from staff, anyway. The ring was right out there on the yard. When I had gone in there to play softball I saw a few good bouts taking place.

I had a white boy once volunteer a story about how he and a couple of his homies had not appreciated the trash a new arrival on fish row was spewing at them from behind his locked door. They informed him that they were going to rape him as soon as he came off orientation and placed among the general population. This story is a bit disturbing, so feel free to skip down a couple paragraphs, this will be graphic. I'll try to clean it up a bit.

This was at Soledad, which is one of the oldest joints in the state and has many blind spots. Sure enough, the day he came off orientation they rushed his cell and all three proceeded to take turns obtaining his core temperature. Proving once and for all that North American convicted felons will mate in captivity. He then told me they forced him to take a dump to eliminate the DNA evidence.

I told him I understood that what they did was intended to be punitive in nature but still . . . how do you get turned on enough to reach climax in a man's nappy doughnut? He replied that they had laid *Playboys* on his back and apparently that was enough to detach themselves from the reality and complete the fantasy.

To this day, whenever I see an inmate with tattoos of nude woman on the small of his back, I know what time it is with him.

Escapes

THE OTHER THING people are curious about is escapes. In my 25 years at the Creek, we probably had about 20 to 25 escapes. All but one were from the Level 1 minimum custody dorms, which only have a 6-foot chain-link fence, and no razor wire. Inmates are not in cells, so they can pretty much leave any time it seems like a good idea to them. There are also no guns out there, at least none that we had. If you have any history of escape, even if it was in YA or county jail, are a sex offender, have more than two years to do, or have any arson history, you're not supposed to be outside the secure perimeter in the dorms. These guys are not especially dangerous and whenever they escape, it's not really much of a danger to the community, they just want to get out, frequently because of a problem on the home front they felt needed to be addressed personally.

I've talked about the Level 1 dorms a bit and I want to expand on some stories about them. The first time I worked out there it was hard to relax and not be too strict with the inhabitants. Unlike inside, when they go to the chow hall, they can sit wherever they want and can leave whenever they feel like it. There are two dorms with one cop in each; a sergeant and an S&E. No gun coverage whatsoever. The officer in a dorm can leave and go to the other dorm, out onto the yard, or to the program office at any time, except count time. The inmates are for the most part left to be trusted to behave within the expected parameters.

Most of them work in the warehouse, the Administration Building, the Elegant Mule snack bar, or maintain all the areas outside the perimeter fence. Eight live in the firehouse and they will respond to car wrecks, fires or emergencies within a few miles of the prison. Some inmates have been responsible for saving lives on some of these calls.

There is also an "outgrounds" crew that goes into the community and cleans up parks and things like that, similar to the county work project you see sometimes; and also a group that goes to the academy every weekday to do various jobs like clean-up, maintenance and work in the kitchen preparing meals for the cadets. One of the jobs of the first-watch staff is to review the tapes from cameras set up all around the academy grounds. Apparently, some friends and family members of these inmates would come by in the middle of the night and leave dope in the mailboxes of homes across the street from the academy grounds. When some of the inmates arrived at the academy early in the morning, well before the mail came, they retrieved the stash from the mailboxes and were identified on the tapes. Neither rain, sleet or snow kept them from their appointed rounds, or being busted and moved inside the security perimeter.

When the crew would return to MCSP, they would get stripped out before entering the minimum perimeter. Usually they would just pull their boxers down around their knees, then do the squat and cough exercise. Officer K.T. Smith worked out there for years and told me he noticed a large bulge in the undies of two of them so he told them to take them off. Upon further examination, he discovered that they had sewn pockets into their state boxers. Inside one of the pouches was about 200 sugar packets acquired from the academy kitchen and no doubt intended to become the main ingredient in a batch of a fine wine with a sweet finish. The other guy had 35 sausages in his pouch. Talk about compensating; must have been a White boy.

Although there are signs up and down the highway in front of the prison warning all motorists that stopping anywhere along the road is forbidden, there have been many instances where associates have stopped briefly and thrown or hidden dope, tobacco, booze or even weapons near the fence line. Since the perimeter fence around the minimum facility is only a 6-foot, chain-link fence with no razor wire, it's not hard for the fellas to excuse themselves for a quick jaunt to the fence by the highway to retrieve the care package. They could go out and be back in about 10 to 15 minutes.

One time, the guy who had been my buddy's roommate at Chico State was the outside patrol sergeant and was cruising around the outskirts of the minimum facility. He spotted a guy, covered in mud, walking around. He yelled at him to stop and tried to question him when the dude took off running. An emergency count was conducted and no one was missing, so the Amador County cops were alerted. They discovered him at a laundromat in Ione washing his muddy clothes. Turns out he was recently paroled from the Creek and came back to drop off some sundries for his old homies. Welcome to time inside the walls of the Beast, Homie.

As I mentioned earlier, some of the Level 1 inmates work maintaining the grounds around the prison and it was not unusual to see one of them driving around a tractor or a truck. During one escape, the squad was searching the area outside the dorm fence and the outer perimeter and came upon a pretty sophisticated pot-growing operation. Factoring in that Mule Creek comprised about 400 acres of land, it wasn't that hard to find a place that could be fairly inconspicuous. The operation was being done by one of the inmates who was cleared to drive a tractor. He had taken it out on the back 40, plowed up some rich foothill soil and sowed his crop. He even put a fence around it to keep the deer away and had rigged up a drip irrigation system. Such wasted ingenuity. Maybe the state should have embraced these growers; the budget crisis would be eliminated.

I worked some graveyard shifts out in the dorms and you have extra counts that don't happen inside. On that shift, those extra count times are varied every day and are known only to Main Control, the watch office and dorms. It's kind of eerie, walking into those bays with a bunch of convicted felons lying in bunks, unconfined, and having to get up close to a lot of them to see because it's pretty dark. If one or more of them decided to jump you, it would go unnoticed until the minimum Search &Escort officer came by to pick up the count slip and that cop could get jumped, too. In that case, it would go undetected until Main Control alerted the dorm sergeant that one of the dorms hadn't called in their count. Usually, the S&E would try to get there and post up in an area where they could see all the bays at the same time while you were conducting the count to prevent an inmate from bunk-jumping. That means that after being counted in one bay, they could sneak into a different bay and slip into the bunk of someone they knew had hopped the fence and self-paroled, to be counted there and delay the discovery of the escape. I also tried to minimize the likelihood of bunk-jumping by varying the sequence I would use to count the different bays. Once count had been called and a red "count" light had been turned on, they were not allowed to get off their bunks for any reason, including to take a whizz.

Dayroom in the dorms. Eight bays surround the dayroom, officers office off camera to the right. You can get an idea of how inmates can bunk jump in order to throw off the count if a buddy had escaped. The dorm S&E would come and sit there watching during count to prevent bunk jumping. If you counted a felon in the bay top right, proceeded to the left to count the other top tier bays before working your way through the bottom tier bays, he could slip down to the bay below and get under the blankets in the bunk on the bottom bay. Four I/M phones visible center frame. There were enclosed TV rooms off to the right so the noise wouldn't bother inmates trying to sleep.

Sometimes, if your count was off, which wasn't rare out there, it could take a while to track down where the discrepancy was, and if their bladders were full it could lead to confrontations.

We've caught, I think, all but about two escapees— and those guys most likely had someone waiting close by in a car to pick them up and were in Mexico within 12 hours.

I'll try to walk the fine line here by not disclosing any secrets about how we deal with escapes, but I'll speak in generalities about what is already known to the inmates.

When we discover one of our clients has left before his reservation has expired, we call a "Code Blue" and all those procedures go into effect. A bright blue light is turned on at the top of the Preston Castle, Tower 1 and Tower 7 at the Creek, alerting the locals and arriving staff of the situation. Many officers go out in CDC cars and cover specific assigned areas, while others are busy inside calling all the folks on the phone list that live within the area, alerting them of what's transpired. The goon squad will be notified and hurry in to interview inmate friends or others in the unit to see if they can glean any information about the escapees. They'll also go back and review the phone tapes in their dorm from the last day or two and see if they offer any clues. The squad or local PD will be watching the houses of all relatives and friends to see if they'll show up.

The outer gate was not manned when I was there so upon suspicion of an escape, a couple of C/Os would be sent out there to search our vehicles as we were leaving. That gate is posted around the clock now since I retired. If you've just completed a double shift, you'd usually be excused from escape detail.

In the old days, we would be taken out to some remote field and just leave us there with a shotgun, a .38 revolver, and a radio. Of course, Amador County is very hilly, and because the radios only work on line of sight, they're useless. They have cell phones now but the reception is spotty at best. All they'd tell us was they'd be back when they could to have someone relieve us. It could be a few hours or many hours and sometimes it was freezing! Even if you caught the guy you might have to sit on him for hours until relief came.

CDC used to have someone driving around to the various posts towing an outhouse for people to use while sitting at their assigned area. One time, the guy who was driving it was making a U-turn and hit a telephone pole, causing an injury to a female officer who had been in the Academy with me. She was riding in the vehicle, not the outhouse. She was being evacuated, not evacuating. She left on a medical retirement.

There were numbers attached to fences around Amador County to identify the posts to which different officers had been assigned to occupy. I'm sure local residents never realized the meaning of those numbers.

Now we have better equipment and procedures.

Almost always, we'll find the escapee a few miles away. Most escapes were not planned out very well and were spontaneous, perhaps just a drunken, spur-of-the-moment decision. Often they involved a wife/girlfriend giving them the boot, his woman were being bothered by somebody or maybe one of his kids acting out. If an escape goes on for a while (and I remember one that went on for four or five days), the inmate is pretty much ready to come home. He'll be dehydrated, discouraged, hungry, sore, exhausted and scratched up from briars, and most have severe poison oak. Coyotes also add to their stress. They could forget about any more dorm life or getting out on the EPRD (Earliest possible release date) they had been assigned, they would be inside the secure perimeter for the rest of their extended stay.

At the Level 1 minimum dorms at Mule Creek, the gun range was pretty close by and many times we were out there using tear gas. If the wind was right, it would blow over to the dorms and give them all watering eyes and runny noses. The sewage treatment plant was right behind the dorms, too, and when the wind direction was right, the stench would envelope the dorms. During hot summer days and nights, the funk would drift inside the secure perimeter to the yards and permeate the whole joint. It was hard to have much of an appetite on those days, the tear gas was less objectionable.

I remember a time when some supervisor decided that an inmate who was living in the minimum dorms needed to be housed inside the perimeter for some reason involving security. The dorm officer was called and advised about the situation and was told to have the inmate roll up all his property so he could move inside. The proper protocol would be to stay and observe him while he rolled up his stuff, but this C/O gave him the news, and then went about her business. Next thing she knew, homie wasn't around

The Belly of the Beast

anymore. He'd hopped the fence and was beating it on down the road. As usual, he was apprehended shortly. That officer got an earful from the captain.

I loved escape detail unless I got stuck sitting in a car overnight with some lame. It was exciting, and I always wanted to be the one to catch the prisoner, but never got to. If you didn't have enough to eat or drink it wasn't much fun either, but it would usually be overtime, and I rarely minded being sent out. It was OK to pop into a fast-food drive through and grab some grub, there weren't a lot of those around Ione but there was a "Stop & Rob" in town.

The one time we had an escape from inside was very interesting. This guy was hanging on the undercarriage of the laundry truck as it left the back dock and entered the vehicle sally port at Tower 7. There was an officer working there to search all vehicles going out, and the inmate later described that the officer squatted down to look under the truck and looked right at him but apparently didn't see him. He told the tower cop to open the gate and out they went. At some point when they got out to the highway and into the sprawling metropolis of Ione, he dropped off the truck and approached a woman who was near her car and tried to get her to take him to Jackson, which is about 20 minutes away. She threw her car keys into a field and ran away.

He then entered a home in Ione telling the elderly couple inside that he was an escaped convict but wouldn't hurt them if they would drive him to Jackson. They complied and dropped him off there, but being a black man in Amador County, circa 1987, made him a bit conspicuous and he was apprehended shortly thereafter.

Even though he didn't threaten the couple, the judge ruled that identifying himself as an escaped convict was enough for the couple to feel threatened and he caught another dime to do out of it. A few years later, the officer working the sally port that day ended his life

I often would put myself in the inmate's place and think of how I'd escape. My favorite book was *Papillon*, by Henri Charrier. He was an escape artist, so I was always looking for ways to beat the defense. The easiest way, of course, is to walk right out the gate. It's not that far-fetched, really. Years ago, we had a dry-cleaning place in Charley yard vocations where we could bring in uniforms or any clothing to be dry-cleaned by inmates for cheap. We didn't have any electronics at the entrance gate to scan ID cards like we do now. You just held up your ID as you walked through with the rest of the crowd. So how hard would it be to get a uniform and anything that could pass for an ID and walk right out with the crowd during shift change? There were always so many new cops coming in, I was constantly seeing officers I had no memory of ever seeing before.

There was an escape attempt from Alcatraz involving this exact tactic. All the laundry from the staff members living on the island was taken to San Francisco by boat, where it was cleaned and returned the same way. An inmate who worked the dock area there stole articles of clothing from the bags until he had a full outfit. On the day he chose to scram, he wore the civilian clothes under his prison garb until the boat was ready to depart for the city. He then ditched his outer layer and walked onto the boat. He made it to land, becoming the only know escapee from the Rock to make it to freedom. But a head count had been done on the dock after the boat left, revealing the discrepancy, and he was captured as soon as the boat docked. It is for this reason that we now conduct a head count prior to allowing any truck to leave a vocation or kitchen area and headed for the vehicle sally port.

When I was working first watch, after the midnight count cleared, I'd take seven or eight inmates in with me to clean the visiting rooms. I was always on alert, because I realized how easy it would have been for them to conk me over the head with a mop, take my keys, ID and uniform, and walk right out the gate. The visiting rooms are very close to the front sally port gate, and back then there was nobody working overnight in that entrance building checking IDs. You just had to hope that the cop in Tower 1 who operated the sally port wouldn't think anything of it and let you out. I would intentionally choose short, skinny workers for that assignment, so that if one tried to walk out in my uniform he'd look so ridiculous that the tower cop would become suspicious. I also brought this scenario up to my sergeants and they started to clean those areas during the day. Now they have an officer working in the entrance building 24 hours a day. There is a device that scans the magnetic strip on IDs, bringing up a photo on a screen they're watching. Years ago, they tried using a fingerprint scanner. It rarely worked, so there was a long back-up, resulting in officers getting relieved late.

There were many rubber trash cans around the institution, and it wouldn't be out of the question to cut the bottom out of one, cut through the chain-link fence on both sides of the electric fence, stick the insulating rubber trash can between the wires and crawl through. It would set off the fence alarm when the metal hoops on the fence contacted another wire, but you'd have a few minutes before anybody got there to check on it.

In many third-world countries, most escapes are accomplished by having inside help from a staff member. This can be accomplished by bribery or threats. We all heard about the one in New York recently involving a female vocational instructor getting romantically involved with an inmate and bringing in tools for him and his buddy to cut themselves out. If someone were able to compromise the outside patrol sergeant, they could have him "forget" to reset the alarm to the electric fence at a certain time, allowing felons to cut through it and bust out.

There is an area between the yard fence and the perimeter fence called "No mans land". Sometimes supervised inmate workers who have been approval to work there and have no escape history, are there doing maintenance and cleaning. One time at a different joint, a crew was working in the area and the supervisor left a large truck running and a impulsive felon hopped in and crashed it through the perimeter fence. He did bust through the inner and outer perimeter fences as well as safely making it through the electric wires but...the concrete barrier ripped out the oil pan of the truck and the engine seized up within a few hundred yards. The impact also injured his legs so he was apprehended immediately. Hey, opportunity knocked...

Years ago, we had a program where we'd take in old bicycles and refurbish them to distribute to kids around Ione who couldn't afford them. That is, until one Level 1 inmate grabbed one and pedaled his ass down the road. He was caught within an hour, must have been a Huffy...

Another escape idea? I heard some inmates speculating about kidnapping a Chester, throwing him on the fence and crawling over him. Interesting thought and I like one part of it, but they'd still get zapped.

One inmate had plans to somehow get onto the roof of a housing unit, use a makeshift bow and arrow, shoot a cable over the fence into one of the telephone poles, and shimmy from the rooftop and over the fence. Good luck on that one, Robin.

Obviously keys are an important aspect of security. Every position we worked had a specific key ring assigned to it and it could include anywhere from 2 to 25 keys. The ring was welded closed to prevent a key coming off by and falling into the wrong hands.

When we were relieved during shift change, we never set the key ring on anything like a desk or table, we always put it in the hands of our relief.

There are a few keys that are so critical to security that they are kept up in the control booth and only temporarily passed down to floor staff for a specific purpose. For instance, the bar box key, which is used after the last count of the day at 2130. The bar box is located at the end of each tier and has a handle inside that can be cranked to three settings. One allows the control cop to open a cell door by pushing a button, one opens all the doors as soon as you crank the handle to that spot, and Deadlock, the spot used after the final count locked all the doors, rendering the buttons in the control booth useless until the box was opened and the setting changed. This is to prevent a button being accidently pushed or touched overnight and letting a felon out.

We never called that key by the number, we just asked the control cop to pass down the bar box key. We didn't want the convicts to know which key unlocks which gate or door. Time could be critical if a convict were to obtain a key ring and it could be the difference between a successful escape and failure if they had to try 20 keys before finding the right one. I even tried not to let them get too good of a look at them. If they can make a weapon out of anything, the can make a key just from memorizing what they see.

Chewing gum was not sold in canteen or allowed in packages to avoid being used to make an impression of a key. It could also be stuffed into a keyhole, preventing that door or gate from bring opened. Staff was not supposed to have it either because convicts could fish a wad out of a garbage can or off the ground to use.

We always had to keep very close control over ladders that were needed by maintenance staff. Anyone whose appearance radically changed was also suspect. If one of them gained or lost a lot of weight, grew a beard, shaved it off, or grew out their hair, we would bring them back into R&R for a new ID picture. This was so that if they did escape, the picture circulated would be accurate and he would be more easily recognized.

Probably one of the most dangerous tasks CDC undertakes is a transport—an opportunity that presents one of the easiest ways to escape. Transports could be medical, legal or transferring to a new neighborhood, but all involve leaving the walls of the prison and allow a convict his best opportunity to grant himself a pardon.

All prisons have a transport team, but almost every day there are emergency transports that require the watch office to put together staff to facilitate the movement of an inmate from the prison to his destination. Sometimes it's sickness, injury or overdose. There are also several CDC transportation bus teams that move inmates all around the state, usually for the purpose of changing their residence. The buses have a driver and two gunners who sit in cages, one in front and one in the back. The inmates are shackled in waist chains and leg irons and could be in those restraints for the entire day. I still see these buses driving around, but I'm sure most citizens have no idea that they're CDC vehicles.

The most common type of transport is due to an inmate being injured in a fight, but it can also be due to an illness or chest pains. The watch office will call C/Os to volunteer for the transport, and if they can't get the required number, usually three, they'll order officers over to do it. One officer will go to Tower 7 and get the chase car and his weapons while another goes to the Admin Building to get the inmate's file. The third will get the paperwork ready. One of those will get a jumpsuit from R&R, strip the inmate out thoroughly (if it's not a complete emergency), give him the new jumpsuit and apply the restraints. Regardless of how critical he is, some sorts of restraints are going on him. Sometimes the inmate will be fat or claim to have a shoulder injury and want us to connect two sets of cuffs together so there isn't as much tension. Some inmates have a two cuff chrono in their file. On transports we used waist chains, which allowed us to secure the inmate's hands alongside his waist. Usually an ambulance would arrive and stabilize the inmate.

Once they'd done all that, they proceeded towards the Tower 7 sally port, where the third cop is waiting in the chase car. The other officers will get weapons from the armory nearby, and once the OP sergeant or sally port officer have cleared the transporting party to Main Control, they'll head out for the hospital. One cop will be in the ambulance with the inmate and they will not be carrying their weapon due to having such close contact with the inmate. The chase officer will radio Main Control alerting them of their departure, but will not transmit their destination over the air. They will also vary the route they take and try to make sure to stay up tight to the ambulance to ensure that no car gets between the two transporting vehicles.

Transportation van exiting vehicle sallyport. Gates were all operated by the officer in Tower 7 after being commanded to do so by the sallyport officer. It was from here that Mule Creek's only escape from inside the security perimeter originated.

We would usually go to the ER in Stockton, where we'd get the inmate into a bed and attach one of his leg irons to the bed frame. One cop would stay close to the inmate for unhooking cuffs for the various tests the doctors need to do, and that cop would not be armed. Another officer would be packing heat but would keep his distance from the inmate for security reasons.

These are extremely dangerous times; the possibility of a friend of the inmate getting on the phone and alerting their homies that this guy will be at that hospital within two hours or so is very real. They could then show up with their automatic weapons and decide to spring him and put us in the morgue. The whole time I was at MCSP, we only had .38 revolvers with two speed loaders. I'm told that now CDC has upgraded to .40 automatic handguns. It's a great move, because we would likely be outgunned in any confrontation that might occur.

We had to be very wary of anyone who came into the room. Only a few whom I knew were hospital staff got near the inmate's room, and I checked their IDs before letting them in the first time. I was especially alert when we were sending guys out for weekly physical therapy. Any friends wishing to bust out their buddy knew he'd be at a certain place at the same time every week. Too easy!

Those transports that went to a specific place at the same time every week were really dangerous. There was an incident involving the Sacramento county sheriff wherein an inmate was sent out from county jail for a doctor's appointment. He was able to get the information to a buddy on the street, and when the deputy was inside the doctor's office with the inmate, the buddy came along and sliced one of the tires on the transport van. When the deputy came back outside and put the inmate in the van, the co-conspirator brought the cop's attention to the flat tire and offered to change it because he was simply a good citizen. As the situation was being discussed, the prick drew a gun and shot the cop (he survived) and the two criminals scrammed in a getaway car. The two apparently got into some disagreement later on and went their separate ways. A couple of days later, I saw the accomplice on TV, lying face down on the street with a 12-gauge shotgun pressing his head to the asphalt. The other escapee was caught shortly afterward.

We had a weekly transport that would take some of the psych patients out to a psychiatrist in Stockton. We called it the "Bipolar Express."

The cop who was getting the inmate ready to go out had a lot of pressure on him. First, when stripping him out, he had to be very thorough to make sure the inmate didn't have a cuff key or anything like a bobby pin in his hair or in his mouth or other cavity. I've known of inmates who got a cuff key, tied it to dental floss, and tied the other end around a molar. He'd then swallow the key but could pull it up when he was ready to grant himself a pardon, so you had to look really carefully in his mouth with a flashlight.

The cop also had to make sure that the restraints were applied effectively. Inmates would puff out their stomachs so the officer would put the waist chains on snugly, but after they were applied, the felon would relax and the restraints would be loose. There were ones who could slip the chains over their feet, and then you really had trouble. Remember what happened in that scene early on in "No Country for old men"?

When putting on leg irons, I'd have the inmate kneel on something and put the irons on from behind. If you did them from the front while he was sitting down, you might get a mouth full of state boot. The buddy who helped me get into CDC, C/O K. Henderson worked R&R at New Folsom and had to process serial killer Charles Ng out to court every day. Each day, Ng would intently watch as the restraints were put on, just waiting for one cop to make a mistake. By the way, Wilseyville, where those crimes took place, is not that far from Ione, and I talked to many staff members who remember seeing Leonard Lake, Ng's partner in crime, walking around town before he got busted.

I've had to change into scrubs and be in the operating room while an inmate was in surgery. Most of the operations I witnessed involved broken bones, usually in their hands. The inmate would most often claim it happened when they were working out with the heavy punching bag on the yard and accidently hit the hard bottom part. Most likely it was from a fight that went undetected. It's kind of amazing and a little unsettling to observe how violent doctors are when inserting pins or rods into the bone. I got woozy. When in surgery, I would attach the leg restraint to the operating table. Sometimes the doctor would tell us we had to remove the restraints, resulting in a conflict. I never allowed it because you can't be sure that the doctor or anesthesiologist weren't in on some escape attempt. Perhaps they were even being blackmailed, bribed or extorted into being involved. If an inmate's got to have an MRI, it gets real tricky. There can't be any metal in there, so we had to switch to some plastic restraints and make sure we didn't have any credit cards or cell phones on our person because they would be rendered useless by the extreme magnetic exposure.

Any inmate knows he can walk up to one of us, say they're having chest pains, and the doctors will call for an ambulance to take him to the hospital. Some do it about once a week! It means they get a nurse fussing over them at MCSP, and more when the EMTs arrive, and even more nurses touching them all up when they get to the ER. Plus, they get a nice drive through the countryside and a good chance to check it out for an escape. Not to mention each time this happens, it costs the state around $15,000, minimum.

I went on a legal transport to the Amador County Courthouse one time, and I was extremely alarmed at how lax the security was. My partner was with the inmate, so he had given me his six-shooter to hold while he was in close proximity to the prisoner. I had no place to put it, so I just held it in my hand. One of the attorneys became alarmed by me standing near the door with a pistol drawn and another in the holster. He approached me and asked, "Are you expecting trouble?" I informed him that the situation was strictly based on policy about not having anybody armed near the inmate. I watched, amazed, as people strolled past me in the front door with briefcases and boxes. There was no metal detector and all these people were just coming right in off the street without having to show any ID or be checked out by security. They could have had any type of weapon inside those boxes or briefcases.

If I was getting ready to go on a transport, I'd check the inmate's file to see if he had any escape history, or if he was a local. If he was, he might have a lot of friends around ready to help him, plus he would be familiar with the area. I'd also find out how much time he had left to do. These facts would determine how much of an escape risk he was. I'd tell them within minutes of leaving the institution, "I'm fine with conversing with you and having a good time but understand this: "If anything goes down or anybody tries to assist you in escaping, the first thing that's going to happen is I'm going to shoot you!" I wanted him to understand that no matter what, he wasn't getting out. I also wanted him to put the word out on the yard that anybody going out on a transport with me could expect the same promise. Even though I might not survive, neither would they.

I'm amazed we haven't seen disaster in these areas with our antiquated weapons and medical people being so urgent about treating these guys without realizing that our primary objective is to protect the public. You get a 19-year-old kid with three consecutive life sentences outside the secure perimeter, what has he got to lose? Medical staff will tell us we need to do this or that and we need to decide if that will be a security breach or not. It's just a matter of time in my opinion before disaster strikes on one of these transports.

All in all though, I'd say that CDC has done a pretty good job of having policies that work in preventing escapes. The fact that we've only had one from inside, and you really don't hear about them happening anywhere else in the state, bears that out. The one we had wasn't the fault of the department, just one guy who wasn't in any condition to facilitate the policy. A policy is only as good as the humans executing it.

There have been times when some state blue clothing would be discovered on a back dock, or someone would call into the prison saying they had seen a man walking on the highway near the joint wearing a blue shirt and jeans, and we'd immediately do an institutional recall, lock them down, and do an emergency count. Whenever we did an emergency count there were no outcounts, everybody had to be in their bunk. It would take a while to get all of them out of the vocation areas because they all had to be stripped out before leaving a place with so much weapon stock available.

Whenever the fog rolled in there would be a fog count, because it is so much easier to escape when you can't see more than 100 feet. Many times, I'd drive all the way in, creeping along in dense fog, and once I got within a mile of the joint, it would be crystal clear! I would be especially bummed if I was working in one of the yard gunner posts that day because there would be no yard. When fog conditions were called, officers would be stationed along the track during chow releases because the gunner couldn't see across the space. If anything jumped off, it would be up to the nearest control booth cop providing gun coverage to intervene from his back window.

In my early years there we'd do what they called a fog line. That meant we'd send officers outside, arm them with pistols, and they'd just walk back and forth between two towers. The tower officers were supposed to open all windows and silence everything inside the tower, including the heater, so they could hear better. I loved fog line and would always volunteer for it. Most cops hated it because it involved walking back and forth for hours in that damp, penetrating cold, but I loved it because it broke up the monotony. The inmates always accused us of having fog machines in the fields nearby and that we could make it roll in whenever we wanted. It would always start in the fields across the street from Alpha yard then sweep in and across to the other yards. When the zapper fence was installed, the need for fog line was eliminated.

A buddy of mine who started at San Quentin, north of San Francisco, told me that whenever they did fog line, which was frequently, they would give an officer a metal folding chair and a blanket and station him between two towers for eight hours. He said he did that one time and it was the longest night of his life.

Besides fog or escapes, there were a few other times we'd go on institutional lockdown. Sometimes there would be a power outage. Even though there was a big generator out by Tower 7, it was only connected to what was deemed the critical loop, which meant mostly doors. There were battery-powered lights in every unit plugged in to keep the batteries charged; these would come on automatically whenever the power went out. Sometimes they worked, but not always. On New Year's Eve 2000, we locked them down because, if you remember, there were all sorts of concerns about cyber issues or kooks pulling some stupid stuff. We also locked everybody up when Crips founder Tookie Williams was executed at San Quentin, apparently to remove the temptation to act out in some destructive manner.

New Year's Eve seemed to be commonly a difficult night and would often end up in a lockdown. The year before I got there, a total blackout occurred and all hell broke loose. Inmates were starting fires in trash cans and trying to break windows. You could still, even years later, see numerous windows with wire mesh reinforcement covering a web of cracks. Of course, the first place they tried to gain admittance to was the pharmacy. There really wasn't much damage or major problem during this incident, but I heard about a cop who was in the yard gun (OBA) using the hand-held spotlight up there to illuminate some officers down below, thinking that would protect them. All it ended up doing was showing the inmates where staff was, and they were pelted with rocks.

My first year at the Creek on New Year's Eve was also eventful. I was working the control booth in Building 3 on A yard and we were running the 2000 unlock. I had the sally port gates open, and inmates were filing in. I heard what sounded like the *popping* sound of somebody stomping on a paper cup. The floor cop, C/O Gandy, yelled for me to close the sally port door and we proceeded to lock up all the felons on the dayroom floor. I looked out the back window and it became clear that the North/South tension had boiled over. OBA had popped several rounds. Nobody was shot or seriously injured in the melee, although they found a dozen or more shanks on the yard. I was sitting by the back window with the Mini 14 while the incident was all mapped out and everybody identified. There were Hispanics lying all over the yard and, being December 31, it was freezing!

They held me over and sent me out to the Level 1 dorms after I got relieved because they thought the dorm inmates might go off at midnight. My wife was waiting at home with Champagne and a slinky negligee. Sorry, Sweetie. I was instead sitting out there among inmates tipsy on pruno, in a dorm setting, wondering exactly what I was supposed to do if they did decide to go off. There are no guns out in Level 1, and we didn't carry pepper spray back then. I'm guessing my verbal admonishments were not going to discourage their behavior. If a code is called out at the dorms, especially in the middle of the night when staff numbers are much lower, it's gonna be a while before the cavalry arrives. Any staff responding would have to leave their yard, pass through the checkpoints, and then procure a vehicle to drive the two-minute trip out to the dorms. By then you'd be in bad shape. That night the inmates had heard the traffic over the PA system indicating a code had taken place on *A* yard and, the fact that I was in the dorm with some additional staff indicated that something serious had transpired. The fact that they didn't know which ethnicities were rumbling lead to an edgy atmosphere in the dorm. For all they knew, their set was at war! They didn't go off, and my bosses let me go around four in the morning. The Champagne was warm, the negligee had been replaced by flannel jammies but they still worked. Maybe it was just all that testosterone I had been enveloped in all night.

I asked a Hispanic inmate later why it seemed like every New Year's Eve something jumped off. He said both sides wanted to kick the other's ass so they could say they ended the year on top.

Famous Characters

DURING THE TIME I worked at the Creek, I met and interacted with many famous and unusual individuals. Probably the most well-known would be Tex Watson, Lyle Menendez, Rick Stevenson, Andrew Luster and Suge Knight.

Tex may be the most notorious, and he was the guy who did most of the killings for the Manson gang. Manson never actually killed anyone during the Tate/LaBianca murders, it was Tex and the girls who did the actual murders. Manson was condemned to death along with the others, but his sentence was commuted to life after the state supreme court ruled all executions illegal.

I mentioned in the opening chapter that I recently got a signed, written release from him to use his name and the stories we shared. It was a lengthy process. I had gotten a post-office box just so the mail I got from the three gentleman (Watson, Bardo and Garofolo) wouldn't disclose my home address. Unlike some other felons I tell stories about, being able to use their actual names makes the stories much more compelling due to so many people being familiar with their names and the crimes they're associated with.

I tracked Watson down to the prison in San Diego where he now resides and contacted a lieutenant there who gave me his housing information in order for me to send the letter. A few weeks later I still hadn't heard back, even though I had included a stamped, return-address envelope along with the release form. I had told him back when I worked near him that I intended to write this book, and he gave me verbal permission to include our encounters. I wondered if maybe he was out to court or out to medical and hadn't received the letter, so I tracked down his counselor and called his office, which was in Tex's housing unit. After explaining to him who I was and what had transpired, he got Mr. Watson from his cell, brought him into the office and put him on the phone. We had a nice chat and he said he had received the letter but thought it was from a former inmate who was writing a book and he threw it away, no doubt after removing the stamp for his own use. After explaining my intent and refreshing his memory (he remembered me and recognized my voice), he gave me verbal permission again and I said I'd send him another release letter and he said he would sign it. A week or so later I got his letter back but now he said he was having "second thoughts" and wanted to see the excerpts pertaining to him before he signed off on it. I sent him most of the parts relating to him and he sent them back with comments on them saying that this part was inaccurate or that part needed to be moved here or there and adding his own personal feelings and clarifying various stories. He wanted to see everything that included him and did not sign the release. I sent him all the parts he was mentioned in (except this part and some later additions) but also told him I wasn't going to do this back and forth with him while he wrote the entire chapter himself. I reminded him that he had given me verbal permission twice and I felt that every man should be true to his word, especially if he wanted to declare himself a "Christian." I also told him I wasn't talking to him as staff to inmate but, "man to man". I informed him that if he didn't sign the release, I was going to write him out of the book or just refer to him in some generic manner so that his identity would not be obvious. He then sent the parts back again, with more editing, but DID sign the release. Whew! I was so relieved because the stories are so much more compelling when you know they actually came from the mouth of this well-known and infamous murderer.

Amazingly, Tex actually gets parole hearings. He's had several since I've known him. I once escorted Patti Tate, Sharon's sister, from the front gate into the hearing room so she could voice her opinion on his lack of admirable traits. All of those convicted in the murders have been denied parole at the time of this writing, and Susan Atkins recently died in prison after being denied a chance to expire at home because of her terminal cancer.

Tex prefers being called Charley but I always called him Tex. I remembered that crime very well and was frequently asking him questions about it once we became acquainted. If you lined up every inmate at the Creek and were told to pick out the mass murderer, he'd be the last one you'd consider. He's a skinny, meek, mild, polite jailhouse Christian and doesn't look or seem the least bit dangerous. To my knowledge, he's never been in any fights or even written up since he's been at the Creek. I think his points are actually at zero, so in theory he could be housed in the Level 1 minimum custody dorms. He is kept on a Level 3 override due to his notoriety and lifer status. Could you imagine the public outcry if he were to walk away from the dorms? I still don't think they will or should let him out. If you're going to murder someone, make sure none of them is named Abigail Folger, the heir to the Folgers coffee fortune. Interestingly enough, the coffee crystals they get at canteen is Folgers, and I used to tease him that the family was somehow going to poison him.

One time I was pestering him about events he was involved in during those days and he told me, "You know, Big D, if you really want to know these things, you should read my book." I didn't know he had written a book, but he said it was called *Will You Die for Me?* I looked around various used bookstores but never found it. I had read *Helter Skelter* and also Susan Atkins's book called *Child of Satan, Child of God*, but couldn't find his. One night a while later, I was working graveyard in a control booth and I had my little handheld TV with me and was scanning through the channels when I see Tex being interviewed on one of those Christian ministry channels. It was recorded in a visiting room at another joint and it was not especially interesting to me since it was mostly about faith and not his crime. When it ended, I turned off my TV and walked away from the window, because that was where I could get decent reception. As I turned around, there was the book sitting on my desk! I'm not particularly spiritual and believe most of these type of things are just coincidental, but that was pretty weird. I read the book during the rest of my shift but it was a little too religious for me and I didn't glean much from it.

During our numerous discussions on the subject of those infamous murders, Tex disclosed many things about Manson and those murders that I didn't know and he shed a lot of light on how Charley manipulated his followers. He told me the true motive behind the Tate/LaBianca murders. This is my understanding of what happened, based partially on my conversations with Tex, as well as with other research I did.

First of all, Manson never really told them what to think and feel but according to Tex `He had a way of planting a thought impulse in your mind and convincing you to feel like it was your idea. He would also mix some deep, true observations in along with his pyscho babble and it resonated with a lot of the tribe. It was kind of like what Father Merrit says in "The Exorcist" that the Devil will mix truth in with lies. It was especially effective when they were tripping on LSD. As P.T. Barnum said, "There's a sucker born every minute". Many of the "Family" had come from less than ideal family situations which made them ripe for manipulation. When you combine the desire for inclusion with the fear of rejection, you can get people to do whatever you want. Tex was the quarterback on his high school football team in Denton Texas and Leslie Van Houton was the homecoming queen at hers.

Although it was partially true that he hoped to create a race war between the Whites and Blacks, allowing himself to rise as the leader of the Blacks, whom he felt would win the race war. There were, however, other more pressing reasons for attempting to make the Tate/LaBianca murders appear to have been committed by Blacks. Tex was very forthcoming to me and has no reason to lie about anything since he knows he will probably never see the gate. He disagrees with some of what I'm writing here but I believe this is close to accurate.

The Belly of the Beast

   This part about the dope deal was not told to me by Watson, but was gleaned from other "sources". It all started with him trying to make some money on a dope deal where he was going to buy 25 kilos of weed for $2,500 from a dealer he knew who had a vending-machine business as a cover for his dealing. He then intended to sell 22 of those kilos to a gent named Crowe who was affiliated with the Black Panthers for $2,750 and keep the profit and remaining weed for himself. His dealer friend fronted him the kilos and he went to see Crowe, intending to get him to front him the money. Tex did not tell me this part about the girlfriend but other research revealed that he did take a female with him. If Crowe would front him the money, he could get away with both the money and the dope for free. Crowe was wary about letting Watson leave with the money and no dope so Tex left his girlfriend behind as collateral. He then burned all three of them by taking the money and dope and leaving his girlfriend there to fend for herself. Once Crowe realized he's been burned, he bound and gagged the woman and called Manson at the Spahn Ranch where the cult was then living and threatened to come out there, burn the place to the ground and rape all the women. Manson instead went to Crowe's place and things got a little heated, so Manson shot him. Crowe survived, but Manson didn't know that and was worried that the Black Panthers were going to come out to the ranch for revenge. Realizing there weren't enough men at the ranch to thwart the attack he believed was imminent, he recruited a local biker gang known as the Straight Satans for protection. I wonder why they felt the need to specify their sexual affiliation in their name…He lured them to provide the protection by promising that they'd be able to have all the sex they wanted from the girls who lived there. While the Satans were staying there, they wanted to get some mescaline, an LSD-like drug. A member of the Manson gang, Bobby Beausoleil (Bo Sa Lay) got some from a friend of the family, a musician named Gary Hinman.
   The Satans claimed the dope was bad and demanded their money back, so Beausoleil went to Hinman's house in an attempt to get the money back and satisfy the bikers. Hinman refused and Manson came

later and sliced off his ear with a sword. They convinced Hinman to sign over a couple of old raggedy cars he had, which they thought they could sell to repay the Satans. Bobby then killed Hinman (at least he was convicted of doing so) and wrote things on the wall in blood, intending to convince the cops it had been committed by Blacks. Two days later, he was arrested while driving one of the cars. Manson was worried about being charged with shooting Crowe, who he still didn't realize was alive, and also was concerned that Bobby would rat him out for it if he were charged with the Hinman murder. Manson felt Tex was responsible for this whole mess because of the drug-deal debacle so he sent Tex and three girls to the house, owned by Doris Days' son Terry Melcher, whom Charley thought still occupied it. Manson felt Melcher had slighted him by not signing him to a record deal a couple of years earlier. If any of you remember a song called "Summer Means Fun" from the early 1960s surf era, it was done by a duo called Bruce and Terry. The Terry was Terry Melcher and the Bruce was Bruce Johnson who later became one of the Beach Boys, mostly noted for writing and singing their hit, "Sail on Sailor".

The cult killed five people at the Tate house, wrote words on the walls in blood intended to shift blame to the Blacks and convince the cops that it was the Blacks who had killed Hinman, so Beausoleil would not be charged with murder. The next night they went to Leno LaBianca's house and murdered him and his wife, Rosemary. It was commonly believed that this house was randomly selected, but in actuality, a year or so earlier, some members of the cult were living in a bus parked outside of the house of a friend of the cult next door to the LaBianca's. Leno LaBianca had called the cops about it and Manson held that grudge against him. Manson took a wallet from them and left Tex and the girls to finish the killings. They again wrote words in blood and carved other words into their bodies, intending to make it look like the crimes had been committed by Blacks.

Charley then left for the coast to the Straight Satan's clubhouse in Venice Beach to pay them the money he had taken from the LaBiancas, insuring protection from the bikers against the Black Panthers. On the way there, Manson put the wallet, relieved of its' cash in a fast-food bathroom in a neighborhood he incorrectly believed was a predominantly Black area, believing it would be found by Blacks and they would get busted after using the credit cards.

So the killings were mostly to draw suspicion away from Bobby Beasoleil, get the Black Panthers preoccupied with defending themselves from the police instead focusing on getting revenge on Manson, as well as settling a few grudges Charley had held for a few years. The main reason for the whole thing from Manson's perspective, however, was to protect himself from being charging in the Crowe shooting.

Another interesting aspect of the various connections among all of those events is that in 1967, two years prior to the murders, Bobby Beasoleil had a small part in a movie called "Mondo Hollywood". The movie was about social, political and cultural changes occurring in California around that time and also included another gentleman in a small part named Jay Sebring, whose body was found lying next to Sharon Tate's.

The DA who was prosecuting the case against the Manson family didn't bring any of this convoluted story up during the trial, and Tex believed if he had, it would have been so complex and confusing that reasonable doubt would have crept in and he would have risked losing the guilty verdict, so the DA only focused on the race war angle. I cannot vouch for any of this being true, it's just the information I gleaned from some research and the way it was described to me.

Tex was a jailhouse Christian before he got to Mule Creek, and I guess he ended up marrying the daughter of the minister who got him into religion. They had four kids conceived in the Boneyard. She moved nearby and came to visiting every day it was open. Nice enough lady and she always dressed very conservatively in long dresses like she was Amish or something. You're required to dress conservatively in visiting anyway but she took it to another level.

After the rules were changed about lifers and sex offenders being unable to go to the boneyard, they divorced, but I can't say that was the reason.

A lot of inmates will go the Christian route while inside because it looks good on a parole report. Each religious branch has a guy who is paid by the state to come inside and conduct their rituals. The inmates will try to get them to write what we call a "good-guy chrono" for the parole board, pointing out all their virtues, and they will sometimes do it. I think the prevailing attitude among guards is that these religious representatives, while providing a sincere service to those inmates who really want to change, are a bit of a security breach. They may be a bit gullible and think these guys just made a mistake and have seen the error of their ways. The inmate may try to get them to take a letter out for mailing to circumvent our screening of such letters. Most of these inmates check their Bible at the gate when they parole.

Tex later became Bravo yard's hazmat guy, meaning whenever there was blood, feces, vomit or sex serum around, he would suit up and clean it up. One time when I was in Building 6 towards the end of my career, we had a guy get all carved up in his cell and there was blood all over the floor and bunk. Tex suited up, and as he was walking towards that cell, I yelled at him, "Hey Tex, try not to write anything on the walls! And by the way, there's no *A* in Helter!" Everybody in the day room cracked up including him.

Lyle Menendez is the younger of the two brothers that murdered their parents to get the money, which they concluded was not going to be theirs soon enough. I told Lyle that it never looks good when the bereaved offspring goes out and buys a few Ferraris and Porsches within days of their folks' demise. The older brother, Erik, was at Folsom, and they keep them apart because some escape paraphernalia has been found in their cells. They tried the old, "Daddy screwed me so I shotgunned him and Mommy to death" defense but it didn't work.

I heard the grandmother got all the money and she was making sure both boys had everything they needed. Lyle married a girl and she visits him regularly. He was always friendly, polite, and became the MAC chairman on Bravo yard. MAC stands for Men's Advisory Council and is a device for inmates to try to make changes in inmate programs or grieve something they consider unjust.

Rick Stevenson was the singer for Tower of Power and was in

for about 37 years for a little double murder up in the Santa Cruz Mountains. He went by Rick Stevens when he was in the band, but CDC calls everybody by their real name. He told me that a dope dealer had socked up his brother and he went over there to set things straight. Maybe he shouldn't have taken that gun with him, because things got a little heated and he ended up giving him and another bloke some lead poisoning.

He said he had been pulled over by a cop on Highway 17, near Summit Road, before the murders, and he had guns, dope and booze in the car but the cop let him go. He said, "If that cop would have done his job I wouldn't be here!"

Rick was always cheery, and we had many good talks about his days in the band and all the decadence that accompanied those times. He said "Sparkling in the Sand" was his big moment during a gig for him to get on his knees and work the girls in the front row for the after-party depravity.

The *only* time I ever brought anything in for an inmate to use was one time I had a music tape I'd made and Rick was my clerk at the time. I handed him some paperwork I needed him to work on with the tape inside it. I had to be careful even though it really wasn't any sort of security breach, but if another inmate had seen it, he would have had some leverage on me. I didn't bring it in *for* him, I just let him borrow it for an hour or two and he gave it back, hidden in some paperwork. There was a song on the tape called "Memphis Soul Stew" by King Curtis. It was recorded live at the Filmore back in 1971, and Rick informed me that Tower of Power had played on that bill, which was headlined by Aretha Franklin. Ray Charles did a cameo with her for a few songs and you may have heard one of them, also recorded that night called "Spirit in the Dark".

Once or twice a year on a Saturday, some electricity would be run out onto the yard and microphones and amplifiers would be brought out so the musically inclined inmates could show off their skills and entertain their fellow criminals. With a member of Survivor (Eye of the Tiger), a well-known member of a well-known Bay area band, along with Ricky, it was a pretty darn good show. We stole the name from all those great concerts at the Oakland Coliseum and it was always called, "Day on the Green." It was fun to see all the queens out there being groupies.

Rick actually paroled just before I did and was living in nearby Roseville. I would have loved to run into him and be able to interact without the boundaries of correctional propriety, and I even sent him a friend request on Facebook. I was upset when he never accepted it, but I later learned that sadly, he had passed away. I'm happy that at least he got to die free and I hope he was able to enjoy the five years he had on the streets before dying. There was a funeral in San Francisco and a memorial in Redwood City afterwards, which I considered attending, but I decided most of the people there would prefer not to be reminded of that chapter of his life. I'm guessing there were some CDC staff members there because he was universally seen as a good, solid guy.

I didn't get a release from this individual and I won't use his name or the Bay area band he was in. Although all the information I use about him is a matter of public record, I got the details of the crime he was convicted of and admitted to by utilizing Google, so don't blame me for defamation. I knew him and interacted with him regularly. He has been out for a while and, as far as I know, has behaved himself. Apparently, he didn't know where the line was regarding being affectionate towards children. According to the story I found on the internet, he admitted molesting a six- and seven-year-old brother and sister duo whose parents had a swimming pool he was working on in an East Bay town. The man of the house found out about it, beat the hell out of him with a crowbar and doused him with gasoline. The man then brandished a Bic lighter at him but didn't torch him. I chatted a bit with him about the good old days of the Bay Area music scene but not too much, due to the nature of his conviction. Again, I won't disclose which Bay area band he played in but hopefully, he has changed his "Evil Ways".

Marion "Suge" Knight was the rap-record mogul suspected of

being involved in the Tupac Shakur murder. He was there twice, I think, and was on Charley yard. I remember him breaking his leg while playing basketball, and it took about eight of us to get him on the stretcher and carry him to the infirmary. Suge needed to back off the groceries a bit. He was always very polite and talkative to me, but when I was driving the car around as the DPO for fence patrol, his people would come to visit him in a limo most weekends and would try to park it near the visiting process building. I had to be very careful since I had a shotgun and handgun as well as some other weapons in the car, but I would roll the window down just far enough to tell them the visiting parking lot was behind the staff lot and they weren't any different from all of the other visitors. I just saw that Suge has been sentenced to 28 years in state prison for a hit-and-run death near the set of *Straight Outta Compton*. I think it's likely he will do that time at Mule Creek: he's been there before and because he was allegedly involved in the hit on Tupac, he has plenty of enemies and needs to be on a sensitive needs yard.

Andrew Luster was the Max Factor heir who was "date raping" a bunch of women and videotaping it. He was caught in Mexico and brought back, and we got the privilege of housing him. Can you imagine having all that money and the only way you can get off is to drug women and record yourself raping them? Most of the inmates and staff didn't have much use for him and he kept a fairly low profile. If he was on fire, nobody would have even pissed on him.

Remember that guy who showed up at all those sporting events back in the seventies wearing the rainbow wig and flashing the John 3:16 sign? Well, that gentleman was one of our guests. Seemed he was at a hotel near LAX and decided to kidnap and hold a maid hostage for a few days. He also threatened to shoot down the planes taking off and landing there. His mind is pretty much toast and he spends most of his days sitting on the curb on the track holding a sign alerting us that "God is love." I talked to him several times about those days and sometimes (rarely) he was lucid enough to have a decent conversation about them. He was literally a sun worshipper and felt it gave people special powers. He once told me how fortunate I was because my height meant I was closer to it and blessed with extra special powers. He told me that in a previous incarnation he had been Helios, the Greek God of the Sun. I couldn't resist the opportunity to insert a little levity so I informed him in my previous life I had been the Greek God, Testiclees. The look on his face told me the only Greek God he thought I may have been was Rectumus... I'm guessing he had a friend who worked in the kitchen who was able to smuggle some tin foil out for him so he could make himself a nice hat with good reception. I resisted the impulse to nuke him with my Gamma ray vision...

Elmer "Geronimo" Pratt was with us for a while. He was the "Minister of Defense" for the Black Panthers and was convicted of killing a woman. He was also Tupac's godfather. Fortunately he got out before Suge Knight arrived at the Creek so there were no conflicts. I frequently talked to him about my experiences with my brother in Berkeley during the sixties and how I remembered reading their Black Panther newspaper. They did a lot of positive things like handing out sacks of groceries in the hood, but their newsletter mostly just encouraged its' readers to "kill pigs". I even wore a "Free Huey" button back then regarding Huey Newton, whom the Panthers felt was unjustly imprisoned. Huey eventually did see the streets but was killed walking down one in Oakland a while back.

Local folks around the Sacramento area will remember Luis Rodriguez. He was convicted of murdering two CHP officers out near the Yolo Causeway between Sacramento and Davis back in the early seventies. You can still see the sign noting that the stretch is called the Blecher/Freeman Memorial Freeway, named after those two officers. Luis told me that his girlfriend had busted him screwing around and concocted the murder story in anger. He later was in poor health and was always being sent out for medical transports. He'd get there, then refuse treatment. Any idea how much each of those transports and doctor appointments cost the state? He was mostly interested in scoping out the opportunities for an escape. He had to wear diapers and a back brace, and one of the last times he was going out, a strip search revealed a cuff key hidden in his back brace.

Damien Williams was at the Creek too. He was that guy we all saw hitting that trucker over the head with a cinder block at the corner of Florence and Normandie during the Rodney King riots in L.A. He was a punk nobody liked, but the Crips protected him. He only did a couple years for that and got out.

I rarely engaged in any levity with rapists but one guy freely admitted to his crimes of sexual assault. Astonishing as it sounds, he told me that several women actually fell for his line when he asked them, "Excuse me, can you tell me if this rag smells like Chloroform?" I'm hoping he's still doing time and some rump ranger cellie has taken advantage of his gullibility.

I obtained a really amazing photo from a member of the goon squad that I really wanted to include in this memoir but...potential legal ramifications, it's extremely disturbing content as well along with the advice from my publisher, I left it out. I will describe it here to illustrate just what can happen if you're locked up in a small cell with someone who believes he is justified in acting out on what makes sense to him. This incident did not happen at Mule Creek but it shows the body of a gentleman's cellie propped up against the shelves...sans head, which is sitting on the shelf. He also cut out his heart for good measure and it is visible on a stick on the shelf too. There is a bunch of rambling babble scribbled on the walls in blood (He didn't try to spell Helter) allowing us a peek into what was spinning around inside his brain. I have no idea what instrument he used to accomplish this procedure but it must have been sharp and strong. Sorry but it really is probably too disturbing for most of the reading public.

We also had inmate Nunez whose father, Fabian Nunez, was the speaker for the California State Senate. Junior got in a wreck for being involved in the killing of a guy in San Diego. I would always see him playing handball against the wall outside my unit. His cellie was a guy named Vellanoweth who was convicted of killing four young black girls when his car careened into theirs while doing 70 mph on a rain-soaked neighborhood street while he was twice the legal limit for DUI. Vellanoweth was a "Schwartzenshriver" political appointee and unapologetic about his deed. He claimed he told the bartender to make his drinks "virgin" and didn't know there was booze in them. I was told that he only drinks martinis! How do you make a virgin martini?

In a pure sleaze move, Arnie cut Nunez's sentence in half on his last day in office but left Vellanoweth to twist in the wind.

I suspected that Daddy Nunez had told sonny boy Nunez to find out who the shot callers were on Bravo yard and let them know there would be mucho rent coming in for them if they guaranteed his safety, and that suspicion was confirmed later by one of my double agents (allegedly). The Beast contains quite a menagerie of characters, some good and bad, but always interesting and entertaining.

And Just Some Interesting Ones...

SOME GUYS WERE not famous but were fascinating anyway. Had one clean-cut White guy who told me he'd obtained some sort of badge and identification and would go to bank managers posing as a security analyst with the promise of making their bank more secure. The manager would take him in the back and show him the vault and, oops, the gun would come out and the money would go away, proving that the bank was truly in need of a security upgrade, beginning with the gullible manager. He had friends that were in the real security business and passed the banks name along to them as a lead.

Then there was Ebony. Ebony was a black queen and told me she had one of those lock-box keys that real-estate agents use to get into houses that are for sale. She would take prospective clients to see the house, maybe offer a little oral pleasure to them, collect a nice down payment from them and scram. Clever. Ebony was very charming, and it was fun to listen to her stories. I could see how some of the home seekers would be "sucked into" the scam. Ebony was renowned for superior sexual skills and was known for leaving her subject with his toes braided in ecstasy.

I don't mean to offend anybody by using this word but there was a homosexual who was alleged to be particularly "blessed" in the endowment department. Another convict, after getting verification upon observing him in the shower stated, "Man, talk about your low hanging fruit!"

I remember a black man, probably at least 75 years old, who had become acquainted with a woman through one of those pen-pal opportunities. She was coming to visit and had never seen him. He had lied to her about his age, so on the day of the big meeting he asked an officer who I frequently carpooled with if he could borrow the black felt pen she had. She let him use it and watched as he proceeded to give himself a Grecian Formula treatment as he covered the gray hair on his head, beard, and eyebrows. Trouble was, it was July and swelteringly hot that day, and the marker's black color ran down his face. The streaks would not wipe off, so by the time he had walked through the plaza from Bravo yard to Bravo visiting, he looked like a black Alice Cooper. I think Rudy Giuliani recently hired him as a campaign consultant.

There was one guy who, judging by his name, was probably of Iranian or Iraqi descent. During the Gulf Wars, he figured it wasn't necessarily in his best interest to be identified as such, so he claimed his swarthy complexion was due mostly to a Mexican heritage. I called him Osama Piñata and accused him of being affiliated with the "Al Queso" network.

There was a fellow from the Susanville area where they're not crazy about homosexuals or blacks, of which he happened to be both. He claimed he only had sex with White Boys but we all knew he'd had more Black dicks in him than a urinal at the Apollo Theater in Harlem. He told me that his aunt took him to her church so that he could be "cured" of his preference affliction. The pastor took him into the church session where several other folks were congregating, handed this gentleman a hymnal and told him to "pick out a couple hymns". He noticed a couple of attractive males sitting in the pews and told the pastor, "Okay, I'll take him and him." Being in a men's prison was like being on cloud nine to some homosexuals and this one was grinning like the butcher's dog every day he was in there.

There were many residents who participated in a gay lifestyle while incarcerated but left that preference behind when they paroled. Sometimes when they got home to their wife or girlfriend, they had trouble differentiating between the dong hole and the wrong hole… Many were ambisexterous. Forgive the raw verbiage here and I hope it doesn't offend any of my friends who find their own gender more attractive but to illustrate the prevailing attitude of the felons they had a saying, "Queer in here, straight at the gate".

I never stopped appreciating the creative monikers the inmates would go by in the joint. There were hundreds of inmates called Sleepy, Joker, Flacco, Boxer, Capone and many others, so if I heard one that was different I always liked it. One guy had the best nickname I ever heard in prison. This guy had a face that was all lumpy and fleshy and had these huge ears, nose, and lips. He was called Bee Sting. Perfect!

Speaking of great prison monikers, there was one guy who had rickets or some disease as a child that caused his legs to have an extreme bow to them; he was known on the yard as "Parenthesis."

An old con had been stuck seventy-something times in various assaults over the years and was known as "Pin Cushion." He had taken more hits than Willie Nelson.

One inmate was known by a moniker that also happened to be his going price for a hummer. Everybody knew him as "Two Soups."

There was a guy in my unit for a few years with one of the great prison names ever: Archie Shanks! He was from West Sacramento and used to box at Memorial Auditorium under the name of Irish Artie Shanks. I was at many of those fights but don't remember him. He had actually been in prison for murder before, got out and caught a new beef at a pool joint on Stockton Boulevard. He said he beat some guys out of their money in pool and they felt they were candidates for a refund so he put a blade into one of them. He had a pleasant, outgoing personality but later got brain cancer, and it understandably changed

And Just Some Interesting Ones . . .

his persona. He got kind of mean and died fairly soon after. His son was also doing all day (life) on the same yard.

I have to acknowledge ingenuity whenever I hear it, and this guy really was clever. He told me of a time he was driving home from the store after buying some of those helium balloons for his daughter's birthday party. He was pulled over by a cop on the way home and had a bag of weed in the car. While the cop was running his license plate, this guy tied the bag of green to the helium balloons and let them go out the window. Bye, bye evidence, gone with the wind! This was back before the patrol cars had dash cameras but even if they did, there would be no proof that it was an illegal substance.

Another example of determination to accomplish the goal of acquiring loot during a robbery was displayed by a chap who's file I read in main control. Seems he had entered a convenience store with the intent to relive the establishment of their cash burden. Upon seeing the meager booty in the till, he tied up the clerk, locked him in the back room, put on the company shirt. He then worked the register for several hours in order to augment the take of this caper. After taking in enough profit, he grabbed a 12 pack of Falstaff and went home to unwind after a tough shift.

As I mentioned earlier, I loved to pick the brains of the felons for helpful information to avoid being a victim myself but also to get some entertaining stories from them. A gentleman from up near Redding told me of being put into a police lineup for a stick up he was not involved in. He was standing there in the line when the cop running the lineup stated to all the participants on stage, "When I call your number, I want you to step forward and say, "Put your hands up and give me your wallet!" As the storyteller was waiting for the chance to recite his line, another fellow off to his left blurted out, "That's NOT what I said!". Darwinism wins again.

While I was in Building 1, we had a guy named Joel Radovcich who was convicted of helping a guy named Dana Ewell murder his parents and sister in Fresno for their abundant wealth. We called him Mad Rad. You may have seen the story on one of those true crime TV shows. I have. Joel had the same cellie for years until one day he saw a TV story about his housemate. Apparently, the story the cellie had told him about the reason he was in prison wasn't quite accurate. Seems he had raped a girl and, while out on bail, tracked her down and murdered her so she couldn't testify about what happened. Even though those two remained in the same unit, they no longer celled up together. The reason rape is considered more objectionable than murder is that sometimes murder might seem justified in a case where perhaps the victim had it coming because of a transgression. But there is never any justification for rape.

Another man from my time in Building 1 was a guy known as Rocky. This man was an older Hispanic and he epitomized what a convict—and for that matter, what a man—should stand for. He was rather short but was in incredible shape and just went about his highly structured daily business without bothering a soul. He had been down for at least 30 years, but I recently heard he had gotten paroled, and that makes me happy. I'm confident he won't ever get in trouble again. He told me he had gone to a drive-in movie in the neighboring town of Merced when he was 17 or 18 and was chatting up some local girls and a few of the local boys didn't appreciate it. One thing led to another, and at least one of the disgruntled locals got stuck and died. Rocky made no excuses other than he was young, dumb and full of cum. He ran some kind of diversionary program in the joint to try to help gangsters get their priorities in order, and he has the respect of every inmate and the vast majority of staff. A true gentleman.

When I worked in Building 13, there was a guy I had some conversations with about his days working in Las Vegas for some of the casinos. He was the one responsible for making sure the high rollers had everything they could possible want. Regardless of whether it was women or boys of varying age, ethnicity, size or skill, he would make it happen. Drugs, booze, whatever they wanted, he would acquire it. He also confirmed to me that if a player was winning too much in blackjack, they'd bring in a "Mechanic" to deal them a bunch of crummy

And Just Some Interesting Ones...

hands to return their winnings to the casino. He also confirmed that casinos will also use someone called a "cooler" who will come to a crap table or blackjack table and act drunk, obnoxious and just be annoying to distract and drive off anybody who's winning too much. He even saw employees and customers who had been caught cheating end up down in the bowels of the place getting tuned up by Knuckles and Rocco.

Loneliness affects everybody at some time and one day I saw one of my tier tenders seemingly feeling a bit of it one day. He was standing in the dayroom, leaning on a broom with a forlorn, distant look on his face. He was usually gregarious and personable so I asked him what was on his mind. With his expression unchanged he offered, "I either need a woman, or a really good lookin' man."

Back around the early 2000s, a felon named Chad was rumored to possess a real blunderbuss between his legs. This was around the time of the controversy involving the Bush Jr. election and of course, he was known around the yard as "The hanging Chad".

We had a fellow who considered himself quite the latin lover type. He was telling us one time about picking up a woman and described it as "Vidi, Vici, Vini". I informed him he had the sequence of that phrase wrong and he smiled and retorted, "No, I saw, I conquered, I came".

Since I had been a waiter during my college years, I understood what this fellow was talking about. It's disgusting but hey, you got this book to know what type of individuals reside in prison. I got this information by reading his C file. Seems this gentleman was also a waiter and one time he got the honor of serving a female celebrity in L.A. He couldn't resist the urge to have what, in his mind anyway, was some sort of intimate contact with her so...he took her dish into the bathroom right before putting the plate in front of her and rubbed his scrotum on the quiche. Apparently he thought she had ordered a "Sack lunch". Every female star in L.A. is probably gargling with Lysol right now but I won't disclose her name. I have heard about various versions of waiters giving a rude customer the "House dressing" or some variation of it but this dude was warped. I never knew previously of any waiter actually doing it but word to the wise...never insult your server until the food is on the table.

In prison, when an inmate is getting close to parole he is said to be "short to the house." Sometimes an inmate might say, "I got 45 days and a wake up!" Sometimes they will just say, "I'm short." A lot of them tried to keep it quiet that they were about to depart in order to welch on debts they may have run up during their stay. It wasn't unusual to hear a staff member nearing retirement use the same expression.

One of the inmate clerks I had in Building 9 was a real OG and had done time in just about every pen in the state. Towards the end of my career, he got sick and was being transported out frequently for treatment of a terminal disease. Whenever I would see him and ask him how he was doing, he'd reply, "I'm short." Since I knew he was an LWOP, I knew exactly what he was telling me. It was sad because even though he was a true OG and had to follow the unwritten rules of maintaining the barrier between staff and inmates, I saw him as a human being and always enjoyed our interaction and the stories he shared with me. He was the one who told me about inmates speaking in a very loud voice whenever they were having a conversation with an officer in order to convince any other inmates within earshot that they weren't a rat.

Department Waste

CDC IS A very wasteful part of our state government. Here in Sacramento, our local newspaper (which no self respecting fish would allow itself to be wrapped up in.) is always trying to stir up public outrage for how much money CDC is costing the state and have done a pretty good job of convincing the public that it's all going into those knuckle-draggin' guards' pockets. We do get paid pretty well, but our salaries are tied into the top five agencies in the State. So if they want to stop giving us raises, then stop giving them to San Diego PD, LAPD, and CHP!

Our salaries are just a miniscule part of the budget and pale in comparison to the money going out to inmate medical, psychological, surgical, dietary, optical, dental and transportation privileges. Not to mention all the lawsuits, not just from inmates but also from staff.

If you or I had to have a hip replacement, it would have to be redone in about 10 years, but if an inmate has one, they use titanium steel and it'll never have to be replaced. They get name-brand medication, not the generic meds you and I have to use. It's the "Drugs for Thugs" program. The cost for one housing unit for just one day is staggering. I've seen so many inmates get elective operations like back surgery, knee surgery, hip replacements, even circumcision! They're even sending inmates out for sleep study. Hey, here's my diagnosis:

lay off the booger sugar and when you get tired enough, you'll sleep.

I have met senior citizens inside who have committed felonies with the intention of being caught because it's the only option they have to get a roof over their head and the life sustaining meds they can't afford. In this case, the meds the State spends extra money on is well spent, but it's a sad commentary on our world today.

As I mentioned earlier, any inmate knows he can walk up to one of us and say he's having chest pains and we'll have them taken to the infirmary and send them out to a local hospital in an ambulance with three staff members, probably on overtime, for a bunch of tests and possible admission. If they actually are in distress they should notify us but too often it's a manipulative ploy. CDC has a policy about life-flighting *any* inmate with a head wound to a trauma center. I've seen it happen to guys with very superficial wounds that could have been stitched up in a few minutes at the infirmary. The CDC is afraid of being sued by an inmate's family and thinks the judge will side with the inmate.

In the olden days, you ate what was for dinner that night or went without. The State is required to prepare enough food for every inmate for every meal even though many do not go to the chow hall. Those either have a stash of canteen food, don't care for that night's bill of fare, or their cellie works in the chow hall and brings home plenty of groceries. So the State ends up throwing away lots of food after every meal. Years ago, a local farmer had an agreement to take those leftovers and fed it to his pigs. Some of them got sick and died, he sued the State and soon it was back to throwing it all away. It's probably due to it being spoiled and not a commentary on State food, which I think they do a pretty good job of preparing balanced, nutritious meals.

Now some judges have ruled that we must provide vegetarian meals, kosher meals and other special-diet meals at a cost of about five times what the original meal does. The Baptists with Dixie roots want cornbread with every meal which is fine with me but where I grew up, it was known as Arkansas wedding cake. When the Muslims observe Ramadan every year, we have to provide special consideration for them, too. When the sun sets, we have to release them to go get their meals. When I was in the yard gun, I'd get on the radio and alert the kitchen staff, "The Romulans are ready to eat." My sergeant gave me a halfhearted berating for unprofessional radio conduct, but he loved it. Don't worry, I was universally insulting to all religions.

I always tried to do my part in keeping costs down. For instance, in "normal" housing units, inmates can buy razors from the canteen. In the psych units, they aren't allowed to have them in their cells, so we keep them in a cabinet where they are kept on a hook designating which bunk that razor is assigned to, mostly because of HIV and Hep C. Inmates in the psych units are given one razor a week, and most housing units allow them to do a one-for-one exchange whenever they want. So basically, they use it one time and swap it out for a new one. Granted, these razors are not top-notch quality, but I've been in situations where I didn't shave that day or maybe even several days and something came up suddenly like an after-work date and I would get a State razor, go into the bathroom and shave using soap and cold water. These inmates were shaving not only their faces but also their heads, backs and who knows what else. I don't need the image of a Bravo yard Brazilian. So I would issue them one a week and that was it. They'd complain about and I would just ask them who said they were required to shave every day? Even though they were crummy razors, imagine the cost, extrapolated out over a year, with every joint in the state of giving each inmate a new one every day!

The state is paying huge sums for lawsuits, as well. Tons of inmates and their families are suing CDC for a multitude of reasons. It can be because of some service they're not getting or because they feel damaged by something a staff member did or because they feel entitled to something prevented by CDC policy.

I had one guy in Building 9 who had dozens of lawsuits going and fancied himself a legal expert. He was so convinced that he or his family was going to be rich! Most of his complaints involved promises he felt CDC had made to him in exchange for him disclosing what he did as the main weapon-maker for the Aryan Brotherhood. He agreed to make a video on how he made various shanks, arrow, and spears out of materials that are readily available inside the walls. We've all seen the video as part of our annual training, and it can be helpful. Of course, any department should keep their word, and if the State promised to protect him from the ABs who would surely hit him if provided the opportunity, they should do so. But any officer who made a comment he felt he could twist into some sort of disrespect or put him in danger was added to his list. He never got me though; I shooed him away any time he came near and let him know I didn't appreciate being a pawn in his personal vendetta against the department. Whether he or his family sees any money is still in doubt but either way, the department is having to pay lawyers to deal with his avalanche of suits.

He was one of the inmates who liked to spend his day hanging around the officers and are known as "podium pals." I rarely allowed them to hang around unless they had interesting stories to tell.

Here's one that will piss all of you off, even though it wasn't the CDC's fault. Everyone knows there are jailhouse lawyers. But there are also jailhouse CPAs. Inmates could get IRS forms in the library, fill them out saying they are self-employed as a janitor or something like that and that they only made a little bit of money that year. They could use the "earned income credit" and were getting thousands of dollars in some cases. Now there is a box on the IRS form that asks if they are currently incarcerated. That stopped the scam but not before costing taxpayers a lot of money.

At one time the state considered handing out condoms to the fellas in an effort to curtail the spread of HIV and Hep C. I'm agnostic on the matter, perhaps it's a good idea. Previously, if a prisoner was having sex with an infected inmate, They just used the plastic wrap for the sandwiches they got with their lunches. I'm not sure if they have ribbed Saran wrap for mutual pleasure...but they might.

I also think the state wastes money with the Native Americans and their sweat lodges. It's really not much money, and the Native Americans have been so taken advantage of over the centuries I shouldn't be concerned about it. A sweat lodge is a place where the indigenous Americans can go on Saturday mornings and enter into a small hut, filled with hot rocks and sweat out whatever it is they think is impure. Each yard has an area, fenced in and off limits to other inmates. These lodges have all sorts of Indian-type décor and symbolic stuff, as well as a lashed-together, wooden-framed, igloo-looking structure, which they cover with State blankets to make the sweat lodge. The State provides all the firewood for this ritual, and every Saturday morning, at the beginning of second watch (0600) the Indians are released from their housing units and start the fire. It is huge, and they put all these rocks around it and get them hot then take them inside the hut and sweat and do all sorts of other things. They used to let them smoke some kinds of stuff, like sage, but I think that got squashed and I'm pretty sure that privilege was abused with weed and later tobacco. They do this regardless of the time of year and it doesn't matter if it's sweltering heat or pouring rain and freezing; they're out there doing their ceremony. I did hear some staff members actually speculate that because all three yards, along with the minimum dorms, had their huge fires going at the same time every Saturday morning, that the Native Americans might be communicating with the other yards by utilizing smoke signals... Hmmmm...

I have absolutely no issue with them practicing their ceremonial heritage but I don't think they need to be let out before yard opens or chow has been run. Too many of them are just out cruising the yard and hooking up deals with other ethnicities while they're supposed to be at the lodge. Many are actually Hispanics who have convinced the administration they have Indian bloodlines somewhere in their distant ancestry (not out of the question) and whenever there's tension between the Norteños and Sureños, being out on the yard early can be a good opportunity to acquire weapons and being in position to jump their adversaries the moment they exit their unit when yard opens. If the Hispanics are on lockdown from an incident, these Native Americans are able to pass food, drugs and information to those locked down in their cells. I'm sure the opposite has occurred as well when different factions have smoked the peace pipe in there and averted an incident. Other than maintaining the area, Native Americans are not supposed to be in there except for Saturday mornings but most of them hang out there all the time. Plus, the state opened up a can of worms when they allowed one ethnicity to have their own little area on the yard that they don't have to share with anybody else. Before long, all these other groups wanted the same privileges, based on their religious beliefs. So now you have the Odinists and Wiccans wanting to be let out early and have their own private area on the yard too. I'm sure the Satanists, Muslims, Buddhists and Jews will be wanting theirs' soon. The State accommodated them as I was nearing retirement and I don't know what the status is now, but there is much abuse going on. For the most part, the Native Americans don't give us any problems and are rarely on the warpath, but I have seen tensions and conflict arise from the ones that are serious about the ancestral rites and those perceived to be abusing the privilege.

At one point, the Odonists did want a fenced-in area, and due to limited space, they wanted it to butt up against the Native Americans' sweat lodge fence. The Indians didn't like that so they filed a grievance against it and won, so the Odonists had to move their spot about ten feet away. The White man is always encroaching on their territory.

I'm not sure if they let the Indians smoke the sage and tobacco that's part of their religious traditions, but what is CDC going to do when the Rastafarians want to observe their religious smoking rights? Marijuana is part of that belief.

One early Saturday morning I was working on *C* yard and was standing outside the chow hall as breakfast was being served. The sweat lodge on that yard is not too far from the chow hall. As I was standing there with a few other cops, we all started smelling something that had a familiar aroma, like a BBQ. Turns out that because *C* yard is where the meat cutting vocation is located, some inmates had smuggled some beef into the laundry area, where the inmates working there stuffed it into the felons' laundry bags. Each laundry bag has the inmate's cell and bunk written on it so they knew which bags to put the meat into. Although every convict that departs the vocational area gets stripped out, they could encounter inmates from meat cutting and laundry while still inside the hallways of the vocational area without being stripped out. The strip-out cops can't go through the thousand or so laundry bags, so those were taken to the housing units. Those Native Americans were cooking up the steaks on the fire used to heat up the sweat lodge rocks. Love the resourcefulness.

Just a few instances where the State could be a little more efficient about distributing their money but also it's just me whining. The parts about the Native Americans aren't really an example of waste, I just thought it provided an interesting aspect of prison life from a different ethnicities perspective.

Capital Punishment

OPPONENTS OF THE death penalty will tell you that it's too costly, that innocent people can be executed, that it is not a deterrent, it's not applied uniformly across socio-economic lines, that forcing inmates to live the rest of their lives behind bars is worse, it's not humane, and that the state shouldn't be killing people.

I disagree with some of those arguments. The death penalty definitely hasn't been applied equally over socio-economic lines, and that needs to stop. How much money the defendant has, what ethnicity he/she is, their gender, their spot within social stratification, their degree of fame should have zero bearing on their sentence. In my opinion, only those in which there is **NO** doubt about their guilt should be sentenced to death. There are plenty on death row who fit that criteria.

Let's address the cost. Yes, it's *way* too expensive, but that's entirely due to the joke that the appeal process has become. These lawyers are making a fortune dragging out all these appeals, both for the defense and prosecution. Why does it take a year for each little step of the appeal? If they can't get the information and come up with their angle sooner than that, we need to find better lawyers. In California at this time, if you are given the death sentence, you will die of old age on Death Row while the state spends a fortune fending off an endless assault of frivolous, minute details about the trial, the lawyers and the jury. Not to mention their housing, clothing, medication, doctor, dental and psych costs, which are usually exorbitant. Right now, the courts are arguing over the exact chemicals used in carrying out the sentence. This has been going on for many *years* now and is just another way that judges are legislating from the bench. For instance, one judge has ruled that only a very specific chemical can be used in an execution and it just so happens the only company that makes it won't sell it to the state because they are morally opposed to the death penalty. The judges know this and are impeding the will of the people by intentionally throwing up roadblocks and incurring huge costs to the taxpayer due to their personal agenda.

Innocent people could feasibly be executed, that is a fact. Innocent people are being killed on the streets every day by guys who have committed murders and have been released. Let me tell a story related to this matter. Authorities came into Building 6 one day and took away an inmate on a cold DNA hit for rape and murder. This guy had actually been strapped into the chair in the gas chamber years earlier at San Quentin for another rape and murder. But back then, some judge issued a stay. After a series of legal maneuverings, his sentence was commuted to life without parole. Then this happens and that happens, and next thing you know, he's back on the streets, where he rapes and murders again. Coincidently, the crime involved a young girl delivering newspapers for a Sacramento rag, and a female officer I frequently carpooled with was also a delivery person for the same rag at this same time and knew the girl. That girl would be alive today if the courts hadn't been so determined to find a way to let this monster out.

I believe that death sentences should only be applied to those cases in which there is *no doubt* that this is the person who did it and that he had no compelling reason to do so—for instance, a parent walking in and seeing someone sodomizing their child and killing the attacker. I know if that ever happened in my house, they'd never find that body. There are plenty of cases where guilt and motivation are not in question. I think many of those opposed to capital punishment would be inclined to carry out an execution right there if confronted with such a scenario.

Some will say that DNA is not foolproof. It gets better all the time, but what's better? Eyewitness accounts? Circumstantial evidence? Fingerprints? Turning state's evidence and ratting someone out? Former cellmate or acquaintance testimony? DNA is the best way by far.

As far as inhumane goes, how much easier could it be than to drift off to sleep? If they experience a few seconds of mild discomfort before drifting off, poor baby. Their victims experienced far worse than that. If the judges are concerned about botched executions, bring back the guillotine. It's fast and no one has ever survived having their heads removed that I know of. It's not a botched execution if the condemned person is put to death. Give them an overdose of pure heroin,. Hell, they'd probably volunteer for that.

The state is not killing people. It's the *people* who are killing this person because they have spoken on this matter. In spite of opponents' constant attempts to drive up the costs associated with the death penalty and the length of the process, it was still affirmed in a recent election. The people want it, and it's not the judge's position to find ways to circumvent the will of the people. If the people decided they didn't want it, although I would disagree with their opinion, I would go along with it because, in spite of some recent actions, this is supposed to be a country where the majority rules and voting matters.

It's hard to say for sure whether it's a deterrent or not to anybody with a rational thought process considering committing a murder but why do so many defendants plead guilty in order to avoid being executed? Who can say whether or not a dude casing out of a 7-11 prepared to do whatever he needs to for the loot or a guy stalking a woman/child with rape/murder on his mind takes being executed into consideration. I think at least some do. These days they don't, because the prospect of actually being executed is so remote. It's certainly a deterrent in the fact that THIS loser will never kill again.

The longer they can delay being put down is another day they could be closer to finding an angle to raise in an appeal, or even abolition of capital punishment. How many cases that might have gone unsolved were resolved because someone ratted out someone else or admitted to the murder themselves in order to remain alive? How many families were able to have some closure because the murderer revealed where the body was in order to avoid the death penalty? It's called "Bones for time".

I hear people say that it's worse for the criminal to have to exist every day in prison, living with what they did. The reality is that these guys lie in their bunks and relive the crime, and usually derive great pleasure from doing so. They can experience joy, human interaction with family members, staff, pen pals and other inmates. They can watch their favorite sport teams, movies and TV programs they love, listen to music they love, enjoy food, the splendor of a beautiful day and sexual activities. Their victims cannot, and the families don't have as much closure in such cases.

Another factor also involves the victim's family. If the criminal is sentenced to life, they still get parole hearings, which opens up all those old wounds when the family has to go to the parole hearings to testify against the inmate being granted parole. If he's not alive, the family doesn't have to deal with having to face the murderer and listen to him ramble on about what a great guy he is, how much "progress" he's made and why he should be released into society.

There really is *no* such thing as life in prison without the possibility of parole. One can be sentenced to it, but all it takes is one determined judge, a witness who testified against the defendant was either being threatened or felt guilty about having contributed to his sentence, and an effective lawyer, and any of them could get a new trial and end up on the streets.

Actually, the vast majority of inmates are in favor of the death penalty. I remember when Robert Alton Harris was about to be the first convict executed in California after a 30-something-year hiatus in the gas chamber at San Quentin. He'd been popped for murdering two San Diego teens and scarfing down their McDonald's food afterward. In the gas chamber, there is a bucket of acid under the mesh chair.

Cyanide pellets are suspended underneath so that when the order is given, the pellets drop into the acid, creating the poisonous gas. The day of the execution, I heard an inmate singing, "Plop, plop, fizz, fizz, oh, what a relief it is!" Harris's last words were, "You can be a king or a street sweeper but everybody has to dance with the grim reaper." I think it should have been, "You can be a nobody or a big deal and still get executed for a Happy Meal."

    Just my opinion

Inmate Hijinks

INMATES HAVE LITTLE else to do but dream up tactics and ploys to accomplish getting things they desire. They're usually ready to open up a can of "get over" on us.

One of their main challenges and goals is how to get or stay high, whether it is alcohol or dope. Pruno (alcohol) is a nasty, disgusting concoction that one must really be desperate in order to drink. However, I've drunk some bottom-shelf, rot-gut whiskey that probably wasn't as smooth as the product some of these masters brew. Pruno can be best described as fruity, with a nice, sweaty T-shirt finish. Some officers could walk down the tier and smell it, but I never could. They had 20/20 sense of smell, I didn't. I wouldn't go out of my way to find it, I would simply try to prevent them from getting the required components to make it. I held to the belief that if they could drink it without us being able to tell, then it wasn't really a problem. If they come out of their house snot slingin' drunk, loud and obnoxious, well now they're putting me on front street and I've got to intervene. I've always felt that I don't care what people do, as long as they can handle it.

It smelled and no doubt tasted horrible, but if you're an alcoholic or just want to keep your senses blurred throughout your stay, it did the job. After drinking Red Mountain Vin Rose, Thunderchicken, or

Mad Dog Plum Supreme on the street, Pruno was almost on a par with that swill.

Inmates would need a large plastic garbage bag, some sort of sugar ingredient and water. If they could get their hands on some yeast from the bakery, that was a bonus. The only place that had yeast was the main kitchen on C yard, but all the inmates needed was some bread from their sack lunches (they got four slices every day), which worked almost as well. They could get the plastic bag if they had a buddy who worked as a tier tender or a friend who had recently moved to a new bunk. We would give them the bag to put all their property in to accomplish the move. I would always use my ballpoint pen or three-hole punch and cut a bunch of holes in it so it would hold property, but not water.

Fruit was the easiest item used for the sugar. We gave them a piece of fruit every day, at breakfast and in their sack lunch. They would sneak it back to their house, and other inmates would give theirs' to the best vintners on the yard. Inmates also started using hard candy or the jelly and ketchup packets they got in their sack lunches, and I kept an eye out for anybody hoarding those items.

The color and flavor of the product would vary depending on the ingredients used. Sometimes when a convict would ask me what was for dinner that night, I would advise them "Chicken patties, which calls for a nice apple blanc pruno…".

Water was not a problem and could be acquired even when locked in their cells.

They would combine the ingredients and then need a heat source. It wasn't required, but it would speed up the process to three days instead of a week or so. They then needed a place to hide it until it fermented. If they could conceal it on top of a machine, like an oven in the kitchen or an ice machine in a housing unit or near a heat vent in the winter months, that would be helpful.

After it was "cooked", they would strain it with a T-shirt to remove the solids, then hide it somewhere. After straining, the mash could be used again and was called "Kicker." Pruno could be sold to inmates a tumbler at a time, or maybe in larger portions. We knew who the winemakers were, and those cells were frequently searched, so it had to be kept elsewhere. A great place was at the bottom of a trash can under the plastic bag with trash in it. If they could hide it in a common area, like the dayroom or yard, it was almost impossible to get busted. There were always carts in the dayroom for laundry, and hiding the bag of wine under a bunch of dirty clothes was another favorite tactic.

Usually, right before New Year's Eve or the Super Bowl, we'd do a wine sweep and all staff would report to a specific housing unit and search every cell for bags of Pruno. The inmates all knew that wine sweeps were going to happen on these occasions, so they would have to hide it somewhere else until the sweep was complete.

Any time we were doing a yard release many would take their tumbler out with them. I would always take a sniff. I saw many pick-up football games out on the yard that started out friendly and fun, that turned into drunken brawls. At the Creek, with all the snitches we had, an inmate would frequently alert us that this guy or that guy was drunk.

Most of the inmates bought a plastic tumbler from canteen to use for the Kool-Aid that was included in the sack lunch they got each morning after breakfast. Many would have something tattooed on it, like their moniker, a team logo for identification, or just decoration.

One trick they employed was to use a razor blade to slice off the top part of the tumbler, maybe about a quarter of an inch from the rim, giving them a plastic ring. The ring would be flexible and they could tie some dope in a watertight bag to the plastic ring with dental floss and attach more floss to it for retrieval, then push it down their toilet. It would expand to fit snugly inside the bowl and remain there, still allowing for waste to pass through it, out of sight, until they wanted to retrieve it by pulling on the floss.

One time I had an inmate tell me a few of the residents in my housing unit were drunk out on the yard. When one of them came in for the noon count I had a conversation with him and he copped to being pickled, which I appreciated, so I just told him to go to his house and lock up, which he did. When his cellie came in a few minutes later, sober, he headed up to the house as well, but in a minute or two I heard banging (no, not that kind) and yelling coming from their second-tier cell.

I ran up the stairs with my partner behind me. There was a lot of thumping and yelling still going on, so I hollered for the control cop to pop the door. When it opened, the drunk guy had his cellie on the floor near the door and was choking him. In a situation like this, we're not supposed to open the door but wait until more cops respond. A sergeant is also supposed to be present. I made an executive decision to handle it immediately due to the fact that the victim was starting to turn blue in the face. The control cop had pushed his alarm and the cavalry was en route, but I knew I needed to stop the assault right then. The drunk wasn't responding to my verbal commands to cease and desist, so I proceeded to apply some baton therapy across his back. He didn't feel any of it. I was really bringing the wood, but nothing. I was actually giving him the benefit of not using the tip of the baton, which would focus the energy, but was instead laying the shaft across his back. If I'd used the tip, it probably would have cracked off, but also broken his ribs and punctured a lung. My partner, who was behind me, finally grabbed his legs and dragged him out onto the tier, where responding staff dog piled him and allowed the victim to draw a much needed breath.

They cuffed him up and he was taken to the infirmary to assess his injuries, which, due to my laying the shaft of the stick on him, were just a bunch of welts. As it turned out, the aggressor was convinced that his cellie was the one who had ratted him out for being pickled, but that was not the case. After a little vacation in the hole, the reformed drunk was back in my unit and said he didn't hold any resentment towards me for lumping him up. He knew he'd put himself in that position and rode the beef for it. All the inmates in the unit had been watching through their windows, and those who couldn't see because of where their house was could certainly hear the impact of the blows. Some voiced their opinion to me about feeling my actions were excessive, but when I explained to them the urgency of the situation, they mostly understood. Some of the cells could see me putting the wood to him and they all could hear the blows, but none could see the victim's face turning blue. They also understood that being the recipient of my baton therapy was something they would choose to avoid.

A whole lot of our "clients" were junkies, so they had to obtain syringes in order to sustain their habits. Usually, they would have to rely on lazy, distracted or dirty medical employees not being careful or aware of where the "sharps" container was kept. This was the red box where the used syringes were put after use. The boxes are supposed to keep the needles from being pulled out, but the inmates could reach inside and extract them if no one was watching or the one that was watching was dirty. If you already have HIV and Hep C, the prospect of being pierced by a used dirty needle doesn't seem so dangerous. They would then cut the barrel and plunger down to about one third of its original length so it could be easier to conceal, sometimes up their ass.

There was a guy on *A* yard who specialized in making "rigs" or "outfits." He sold them on the yard, and they were consider the "Cadillac" of rigs. He would use the barrel of an ink pen and the small rubber grommet inside a disposable lighter, which worked perfectly for sealing the plunger. There are 10 to 15 diabetics in each housing unit, and they take their insulin shots every morning. They administer the shots to themselves. Some would stick the needle into their belly, snap it off inside the skin and drop the syringe into the sharps container. They could then return to their cell and fish out the needle to either use on themselves or sell on the yard. If they could get their hands on an eye dropper, it was easy to attach a needle to it with rubber bands. Many felons had access to them for medical purposes.

There is also a little flap on the fly of state boxers where the seam could be separated. That was another good place to hide a needle.

People are always intrigued and disgusted by inmates using their poop chute as a storage option. It's referred to as "Keystering", in "the trunk", the "Inmate wallet" or in "The safe". If you're willing to do it, it certainly can be an effective hiding place, because we don't want to or weren't allowed to do cavity searches. Only medical staff can do that. Drugs, weapons, money, kites, cuff keys, gang codes or a hype kit (rig) can be hidden there. I've known of some inmates who use things like those round stick deodorant containers to stretch out the storage space to increase their capacity so they could mule in more dope. It's amazing that someone can keep a shank up there without getting all tore up, but they do. I've even heard of inmates being escorted across the yard in restraints and squeezing a shank out while walking and having it fall out of their pant leg. I heard that Richard Ramirez, the Night Stalker, was X-rayed before being transported from San Francisco jail to death row at Quentin and had a rig and cuff key in the trunk. I've even heard of a Derringer being discovered in a dude's "safe." They can "take it to the hoop" in an amazingly quick move.

In the book *Papillon,* the author describes a relatively small, cylindrical metal capsule in which he kept money. He called it a "Plan." I think Nazi war criminals like Hermann Goering and Heinrich Himmler used one to hide the cyanide capsule they used to cheat the hangman. It's been around a long time and is very effective if you are really that determined to hide something.

Most of the time, heroin would come in through visiting, which was open on Friday through Sunday. The "mules" would get it in on the weekend, and on Sunday or Monday it would be of decent quality. Each day after that it would be "stepped on" with some inert substance like baby powder to stretch it out. By Thursday, it would have been cut so many times it didn't give the relief the junkies needed. If it was tar heroin, they would cut it with toner from a copy machine.

There was a clever scheme to get dope in a few years back. The level 1 inmates were the ones who cleaned the administration building and it was basically open to the public. The outer gate was not manned back then and people were coming in and stashing goodies in the bottom of a specific garbage can in a restroom. The cleaners knew which one contained the contraband and easily retrieved it. As they walked back to the dorms after work, they tossed the treasure over the fence to a buddy prior to being stripped out upon reentering the minimum facility. That gate is now posted around the clock and other measures have been implemented to eliminate this scheme.

Back when we used steel spoons in the chow hall, it was easier to cook the dope. After we went to the plastic spoons, they started using the bottom of a soft drink can for cooking. It wasn't hard for them to get cotton balls for straining the smack when they drew it into the rig, and when the really got desperate and were feeling "dope sick," they would wet down the cotton balls to try to extract the little bit of smack residue left to get a bit of relief from "Jonesing."

If an inmate was suspected of using dope, he could be part of random or routine pee tests at any time. Usually the goon squad would perform these tests and take them someplace with relative privacy for the task. They weren't allowed to go into a stall alone to fill up the jar; the squad had to see dick in jar and piss flowing into the cup. This would prevent them from bringing a bag of a clean friend's urine with them and transferring it for the sample. Most often, if they were dirty, they'd claim they couldn't produce a sample and the squad would tell them to come back in 30 minutes. During that time frame, they would put some bleach or other cleaner under their fingernails and hands. They could get it from staff under the guise of cleaning their cell, and then, while providing their sample, sprinkle it into the jar, which would contaminate the urinalysis and render it useless.

I even heard from an inmate one time about a tactic used by a desperate and resourceful inmate to beat a test. This absolutely grosses me out and makes me cringe to even think about, so you might want to skip down a paragraph if you get woozy about this sort of thing. According to this convict, he knew of another inmate who, just before providing a sample, got some clean piss from a buddy and, utilizing a catheter, injected it through his urethra into his bladder. It makes me weak to even think about it and I can't vouch for the story's validity, but I suppose it's possible if you're that desperate.

Inmates also can refuse to take the test, and although it would eliminate them from being able to work in PIA, usually all that would happen is they'd lose 30 days of privileges like yard, dayroom, phones, conjugal visits or quarterly packages. PIA is Prison Industry Authority and refers to various vocational programs like meat cutting, coffee roasting, or fiberglass work. All those lifeguard towers you see on California's State beaches were made by convicts at the Creek's fiberglass shop on Alpha yard. We had to keep a close eye on those so no felons could make a small compartment in one to do a self-parole. They were heavily scrutinized in the vehicle sally port before being allowed to leave.

I also heard of an inmate that got ahold of some rubber tubing and he would get some clean pee from another inmate, fill up a small plastic bottle like ones for eye drops or nasal spray. When he went in for his UA, he would hold the bottle under his arm pit, run the tubing down his sleeve, squeeze the bottle with his upper arm then let it drain into the specimen bottle. This is why most of us doing a UA would make them roll up their sleeves prior to playing "Jar Wars."

Now, I can kind of understand the fellas wanting to smoke a little herb, slam a little smack, or huff a little of the Devil's dandruff, but I never understood the ones that liked meth. If you got sentenced to a 10-year jolt, with any luck you can sleep through close to half of it, but if you like crank, you're gonna end up doing *all* of your time.

I mentioned earlier about the best places the convicts hid contraband in their cells. They would keep things in rolled up pairs of socks, cut a slit in their mattress or pillow, but one of the best places was behind the light switch cover. It's the plastic plate that covers the switch, but in prison, it's not held in place with simple screws but a specific type of screw to which only maintenance staff has access to the corresponding tool. Convicts, being the resourceful rascals that they are, figured out that if they heated up some plastic, like a toothbrush, with a stinger, they could insert the hot, soft, pliable plastic into the screw hole and mold it into a tool that would open the fixture. Since the floor officers did not have the tool, it was the best place in a cell to hide an outfit (syringe) or dope.

A stinger is a device they make; basically a tool with two wires they can insert into a wall socket. Another set of prongs is at the other end. Some are very basic, but I've seen some really elaborate ones, too. At some other joints you can buy them at canteen but we didn't allow them, mainly because inmates could nuke themselves with it or cause damage to the electric circuit in the building. You could tell if they had one because the wall socket would be all black with burn marks around the wall plug. Occasionally, an inmate would approach us saying there was no power in his house and we would have to go into the electrical room inside the building sally port and reset the circuit. It could happen for a variety of reasons, but I would usually go in their domicile, check for marks on the socket, and search for a stinger. The OGs, however, would clean the cover plate regularly with the cleansers they could get from us or the tier tenders to avoid detection.

Betting on sports and poker is an everyday thing and can result in debt and violence, so I usually frown on it. Poker games are one activity that keeps some of them from going crazy or assaulting us. It wasn't much of a secret when it was going on, mainly due to the bed sheet covering the table they played on. I still don't know how they did it, but there was always at least one that knew some secret way of stretching the sheet really tight over the table so it resembled a felt card table. They would use another set of cards, cut in half, for poker chips, and one player would be in charge of keeping the ledger of who owed how much to whom.

I usually didn't make a big deal out of their gambling as long as they knew to pull the sheet off the table whenever a sergeant entered. It wasn't hard to know which inmate was running the sports book either, by who was frequenting their cell door. As another form of behavior modification, they all knew if they pissed me off for any reason, I would confiscate the ledger sheet. That would set off a lot of tension, because they would disagree about who owed how much to whom.

A group of Aryan Brotherhood types were playing cards at a dayroom table one day and I approached them to see if they would panic and start scrambling to hide the ledger and chips. I asked, "What kind of poker are you guys playing? Texas Hold 'em, draw, or stud?" One of them came back with, "We're playing Rodney King poker." I wanted to hear this so I asked, "Okay, what's that?" He stated, "Four clubs beats one king." In prison, nobody is politically correct.

Another way inmates settled debts was to loan out or give an appliance, like a TV, music player, fan or reading light. They are allowed three appliances and must decide which three are most important to them. It's so hot in there during the summer that a fan is a must. These items must be bought and sent in from an approved vendor, and must be written onto the property card each of them has that's kept in R&R. It will also be inscribed with their name and CDC number. Whenever I do a cell search, I check the scribe on the appliances to make sure they don't belong to someone else. If it's not theirs, I confiscated it. If someone loaned it to them and now it's gone, someone's not going to be happy. I've had friends who knew someone who was about to enter prison and asked me for advice on how that person could be safe. I told them the most important thing was not to get into debt. I didn't really care about anybody loaning appliances to others but it was just another thing that could put me on front street and get me in a wreck if my supervisors were made aware of it being commonplace in my unit.

If an inmate refuses to work or go to school, he is placed on *C* status. This means he can't go to yard on weekends and a few other restrictions, but also means he can't have *any* appliances. Usually, when they were in committee being placed on *C* status, their counselor would call us before the inmate got back into the housing unit to let us know about the status change in order to allow us to go to his cell and collect all his appliances. Almost always, he would know he was about to go on *C* status and would have already loaned or sold them to his buddies prior to going to committee. We could go to R&R and make a copy of his property card and quiz him on the whereabouts of his TV, fan, and Walkman which his card revealed they were still in his possession. He would invariably claim the items had been stolen during an unlock. I usually knew the boys he ran with, so I would go to those cells and check the name and CDC number scribed on all the appliances in there and could confiscate them if they fell into that category. I would take them up to R&R, where items like this were kept and sometimes used by the R&R sergeant to settle grievances by other inmates.

Property cards were devices used to discourage inmates from using their belongings to settle debts. Frequently, an inmate would approach me to claim his running shoes, watch, music player or other items had been stolen and wanted me to call R&R and have them take that item off their property card so they could have a replacement sent in from a vendor. I never did because it was almost always a ploy to obscure the fact that those things had been used to settle a drug or sports wager. Inmates would usually approach a fish cop who wasn't yet hip to inmate tactics with the request. If an inmate actually had stolen a pair of shoes or something else, they would be spotted while wearing them on the yard. What were they going to do, just wear them in the cell? As I said early in this book, there are no secrets inside the belly, somebody always knows and at some point, they will tell.

When I first got to the Creek, inmates could have a TV or radio sent in from someone outside and we would scribe their name and CDC number on it. We would also fill in all the screw holes with hot glue to prevent them from opening up the case to hide contraband. Later on, TVs could only be sent in from an approved vendor and the cabinet had to be clear plastic, making it very hard to hide anything inside.

It's true that the variety of things like shoes and other items are limited to what the approved vendors offer within the CDC-allowed products. Inmates can have sweatpants, sweatshirts, or shorts sent in, but they can only be gray with no logos or writing on them. Shoes could not have any blue or red trim or writing visible on them. There was a brand of tennis shoes called BK (British Knight) that were disallowed because the Crips wore them to depict themselves as a "Blood Killer."

There is part of R&R called the package room where the package officer works. If an inmate is on A1A status, meaning he either works or goes to school, he is allowed to receive a quarterly package every three months. In my early years at the Creek, it was sent by a friend or relative and would usually contain shoes, shorts, long underwear, shampoo and deodorant, but mostly food. It could weigh up to 30 pounds, and there was a very specific list of things that were and were not allowed in it. These items could only be packaged a certain way. Usually it contained candy and frequently it was not a type on the list or wasn't packaged exactly the way that was required. When this happened, the officer would give them the option to either donate it or send it back home. Sending it home required them to have money on their books to mail it out, so they would usually select donation, which meant it would be sent to some local charity. The biggest charity around was usually C/Os working overtime who didn't bring in enough food for a 16-hour shift. Since there was no record of these items, it was common practice to head over to the package room and sort through the donation box for goodies if you were working a double shift and got hungry. Sometimes a family member or friend would send in an item loaded with dope that they knew would be confiscated and put into the donation box. The inmate workers in R&R would know who was receiving that package, and when he was there to receive the box would try to go into the package room and fish it out without being noticed or ask the officer if he could have the candy bar or whatever it was and tote it back to the yard.

There were many times when candy bars or some type of food had been steamed open by the sender, who then put some dope inside and glued it back together. Because of this and other ways inmates used to introduce contraband, eventually a rule was instated that packages could no longer be sent in from friends or family. Instead, there were two or three approved vendors that outside people could order a variety of items from. These would be sent directly from the vendor without family or friends ever getting near them. Apparently, even these approved vendors became infiltrated by friends and family members of convicts residing in the Beast. These folks begin working for the vendor, and once they know the order number that one of these felons had sent in, would put dope inside the TV, radio, food or clothing.

Let me address the cell-phone issue, because it was a very real threat to the security of the institution and the public. Years back, almost all of us officers would bring our cell phones in, even knowing it was against the rules. I stopped doing it several years back because they really started cracking down on it, and the punishment got more severe. I understand the concern, and I was okay with not bringing it in any more. More than once, someone would forget to turn off the ringer and it would go off at an inopportune moment while supervisors were around. The inmates would also rat you out if they heard or saw you using one.

Inmates were getting cell phones in, and it became an epidemic. Most likely they're coming in through dirty staff because due to their size, it would be hard to get them from visiting, plus without the charger, they're basically useless. If an inmate could have a conversation with anyone on the outside without concern of being monitored—telling someone to do a hit or bring some contraband in—that affected the safety of staff as well as inmates or their families. I've seen videos taken through cell windows and transmitted to the outside, and I know women who have been called by inmates from inside the walls. Some of them even have Facebook accounts and are on dating sites. Warning, if their profile picture has a number at the bottom of it you probably won't be doing any of those romantic evening walks that all the men on those sites claim to love.

They now have some sort of jamming device or one that can detect and locate the signal, and that's really a good thing. I believed it should have been priority No. 1 for CDC, and congratulations to them for getting on top of that. Of course, it's like doping athletes: they're always a few steps ahead of the testers, so I believe inmates will figure some way to beat it if they haven't already.

One of the ways inmates were getting the phones and chargers into the joint was pretty complex and clever. Seems a friend or family would get ahold of a shipping label from anywhere; it didn't matter what company it was from. They would then ship a box to Mule Creek with "ATTN:" and put the name of a staff member out at the warehouse who never had anything shipped in or maybe didn't even exist. An inmate worker on the shipping dock would check the item off the manifest as it arrived, but because it would not have a PO number or be on any list of things that had been ordered, nobody would notice the extra shipment. After the phones were retrieved from the box, the inmate worker would have to operate in concert with other Level 1 inmates who worked on the garbage truck that would go inside the perimeter daily to empty the dumpsters. The workers would put it in the opening where the forks of the garbage truck would enter to lift the bin to be retrieved by kitchen workers and routed to the buyer on that yard. Lots of logistics; some good planning talent being wasted in the Beast.

In my early days at the Creek, the boys could get naughty magazines like *Playboy* and all the others mailed to them. They would have various centerfolds from the latest issue of *Tits & Clits* taped to the walls and ceilings of their cells until some of the female staff members voiced their displeasure about having to be subjected to them during cell searches. They were no longer allowed to have them after that, but we would frequently find copies of them, obviously made by one of our clerks utilizing the copy machines in the program office or education areas. They weren't of particularly good quality, but after being locked up for so many years, a grainy picture of Kate Smith would get the old flagpole to full staff!

They also had been allowed to have pictures sent in by girls they knew on the street in various stages of undress and unladylike poses. Keep in mind that all incoming mail is looked over by the staff in the mailroom before being allowed in, so these women were really dedicated to keeping their men focused on what they had waiting for them if they ever got out. Most of these pictures made Roseanne Barr look like a *Sports Illustrated* swimsuit model but that didn't keep most officers from going right to the photo album whenever conducting a cell search. Later in my career they were no longer allowed to receive pictures of any girl displaying her cervix and I guess they just had to rely on their photographic memory . . . or check out the way our jumpsuits accentuated our curves.

Inmates are not allowed to have money other than on their books for making purchases in canteen or from vendors. Of course there *is* cash in the joint but they have to be as careful hiding it as they would be with dope or a weapon. Some inmates prefer to do their own laundry instead of the weekly laundry service we provide them, and they can buy detergent for it at canteen if they prefer to do it in a bucket themselves. We had received information that one felon had a fairly large amount of cash hidden in his cell, so we did a thorough search and finally found the roll of bills stashed inside a container of the detergent. And I thought all the crooks into "money laundering" were in the federal prisons.

Frequently, part of an inmate's sentence would involve paying restitution to their victims. If they had a job that paid, a percentage of their salary would go towards restitution. The few that did get paid only made about 18 cents an hour, so it could take a while for those pennies to roll in. Usually, when a friend or relative would send in a money order to be put on their books, about half of it would be deducted and go to the victims. The inmates, who weren't concerned about the welfare of their victims when they did whatever they did to get incarcerated, were still not moved by the plight of these folks.

So they would have the money orders sent into a friend who would then go to canteen and give the goodies to them for a portion of the plunder. I always took this matter seriously and tried to prevent them from getting one over on the system. If I overheard a convict giving someone on the phone another inmate's name, number and housing address to send a money order to, I would relay that information to the squad. When felons came in from the yard with sacks of groceries from canteen I'd make them show me the receipt, which I scrutinized to make sure he hadn't already settled the deal by giving away most of the groceries before entering the building. If they didn't have one, I would confiscate the sundries and send them to the sergeant. When they did have a receipt and were legit, I couldn't help clowning them by examining the tab and exclaiming loudly, "They're charging $10 now for a jar of cellie jelly (Vaseline)?" I never allowed any of them to go to yard with groceries intending to circumvent restitution from collected or to settle debts with canteen.

I mentioned that ramen soups are one of the main currencies inside. This goes along with freeze-dried coffee crystals. Soups satisfy, especially during lockdowns or at bedtime. There is one faucet that dispenses hot water, and plenty of dudes fill up Ziploc bags at 0900 when dayroom closes and it's time for ni-night. If they're on lockdown or for some other reason can't get to that faucet, they can use a stinger to heat up the water.

Inmates on occasions want to end their lives, and it's not that easy with counts, security checks, rationing of meds, psych staff intervention. My buddy, C/O K. Henderson, described an incident at Folsom that was creative and effective. He was sitting in the program office early in the morning when an alarm went off in a nearby housing unit. He, along with other staff, responded to the unit and immediately upon entering the building were struck with a strong, pungent, electrical smell.

He yelled for the control booth cop to throw the circuit breaker switch to the cell where all the other staff was gathered. This despondent inmate had decided to take his own life and had cut off all the wires from his TV, radio, and fan, and stripped the wires of their insulation so they were bare copper. He'd wrapped the wires around his arms and ran them into his mouth, in which he had put a wet rag to further facilitate conductivity like they did in the electric chair. He then sat there on his bunk, holding the remaining male part of the wires he had encapsulated himself with, bit down on the rag in his mouth, and shoved the plug into his extension cord. *ZOT!* Quick and painless, apparently.

Inmates need to be able to communicate with each other about some matters that could get them in a wreck if we intercepted the communiqué. So they had various codes that were constantly changing. Usually, it would be a list of numbers or letters corresponding with another letter of the alphabet. For instance *A* might be represented by *K* or 17, depending on the current code being used. If inmates suspected the code had become compromised, they would change it but had to make sure all knew which being used at all times. If we found a list depicting the latest code, we would try to sneak it out of the cell to a copier and return it to its hiding place without them suspecting that we had found it. We would then give a copy to the squad and the first watch control booth cop so he could look for any coded messages in their outgoing mail. It was like obtaining an German Enigma machine in WW2…

Sometimes they could communicate to someone nearby or on

another tier by using tapping sounds. The most common tapping code was to tap the same number of times that the intended letter fell in the alphabet. For instance, *C* would be three taps or *O* would be fifteen taps. Inmates could use a more sophisticated code if they both were on the same page. They had ways of indicating the start of a new word or sentence. They could also talk through the vents to other inmates, but they had to be either next door or directly beneath them on the next tier. That way was easy, but the conversation would not have any privacy, and at the Creek, with all its double agents, it was risky to try to convey anything not intended for universal consumption.

I also mentioned that just before an inmate paroles, his family or friends will frequently send in some "dress outs" so he can walk out in street clothes. If they don't get dress outs, they can leave in prison blues, but the cost of those clothes will be deducted from their gate money. Sometimes the box of dress outs will have some dope stashed inside by the sender. There are usually one or two inmate workers in R&R, and they're the ones who take the boxes and put them on the storage racks. The inmate's name and number will be on the box, and they know which one the dope is in so they just open it up, take the dope and tape it shut again.

Inmates would occasionally go on hunger strikes as an effort to protest something, but usually that move was intended to get a bed move or more meds. Whenever they did this, they would be confined to their cell and provided the latest meal, which they would refuse. They would also be weighed daily and have their vital signs taken. Almost without exception, the inmates would actually *gain* weight! This was due to the fact that although an inmate was refusing the State food offered in his cell, he was not refusing all the chips, cookies and food brought from the chow hall and passed under their cell door by his homies, or goodies or that his cellie would bring to him.

Another tactic of protest or disruption was flooding, especially in Ad Seg. If they wanted attention, they would stuff towels or other items in the toilet and flush it repeatedly until it overflowed the bowl, ran onto the floor, and out onto the tier. Sometimes a whole section would do it and it would create quite a mess, disrupt programs, and force staff to deal with it. If it was on the second tier, it could be a bigger problem. The tier tenders and porters would have to mop it up, and it could become a security issue if it continued. A veteran floor cop knew which inmates had priors for flooding and would anticipate the act if the inmate was pissed about something. The cops would open the plumbing chase next to his cell and shut off his water supply. This game was later circumvented when the state installed devices in every cell that only allowed three flushes every 30 minutes or so. If an inmate was having some intestinal distress it could be tough, as they would have to wait to send it down and those toilet trout would be swimming around that bowl for a while. Many had to adopt the doctrine that had become common during the various droughts we've endured in California: "If it's yellow, let it mellow. If it's brown, send it down."

Tattoo artists are plentiful inside and this profession can be a good way to supplement one's fortune. It's against the rules, mainly to reduce the spread of HIV and Hep C, but also to prevent conflict brought on by debts not getting paid. That doesn't stop them though, I've seen guys come into the system mostly devoid of skin doodles and a few years later they're covered with graffiti.

They can make a "tat gun" by taking the motor out of a tape player, attaching it to an ink pen barrel with a short section of the thinnest guitar string inside it for the needle. If they could get ahold of a needle through a careless or dirty staff member, that was a bonus. They got the ink by draining pens, so we kept a lookout for containers of it in their cells, and the convicts were discreet about disposing the empty pen barrels.

Giving a tattoo requires time and privacy. That means an inmate getting into a cell with the artist without being noticed or missed from his cell at count time. It was easier in the older times when we ran our unlocks differently. Back then, we would open their doors for five minutes, allowing them to go inside, get or drop off items or change clothes while we stayed on the dayroom floor. After five minutes, inmates would have to close the doors and either stay inside, go onto the dayroom or onto the yard. This allowed the opportunity for assaults, sexual encounters or tattooing. Now we walk the tier and open each door, let them go in or come out, and close the door. After making the entire trip on a tier, we would repeat the process again, making it nearly impossible to enter a cell that is not your own or is occupied by more than two residents. If there were officers working on overtime or a swap who didn't know whose house it was, this gave the inmates opportunities to pretend to live there. The artist's actual cellie would have a slumber party at the recipient's house while the work was being done. Frequently, because it's a time consuming, laborious process, they would do a cellie swap for the overnight hours. During the counts, they would just cover their identity with their blankets. As long as the counting officer saw skin, he would not suspect anything was afoot. The cell where the work was being done would have the neighboring inmates keeping an eye out in case the floor cops were walking the tier and they could alert the businessman by saying, "Man walkin'." They knew the likelihood was that the only visits they might have from staff would be at 0030, 0230, and 0430 for the counts. This overnight cellie swap tactic was also used for romantic liaisons.

We kept our eyes out for fresh tats and ones that might reveal gang affiliation. Most officers would not write up the fellas for having paraphernalia but would just get rid of it in the "hot trash" bin, kept up in the control booth. Hot trash was anything that could be used to make a weapon or was dangerous in any way. About once every month or two, a yard cop would come by when the yard was not open and take all the hot trash out to a dumpster in the vehicle sally port. They wouldn't bother to write them up because the lieutenant hearing the beef would usually dismiss it. A notation about it might be made in the logbook or on the bed card kept on each inmate in the control booth. That card would show the dates of all the bed moves he'd had and things such as verbal counseling about delaying lock up or chow release disciplinary issues he might have had. Some would also jot down any personal observations about this chap such as being a prick, asshole, or general problem child.

People frequently ask me what the teardrop tattoos mean. The truth is they can mean a multitude of things. Most often, it means that convict has killed somebody but can also mean they've done time. It can also mean they've lost a family or gang member. Sometimes it means they got "turned out," which means being forced to be used as a sex object. If the tear is not filled in and is just an outline, it can mean this person had a buddy killed and is seeking revenge. In reality, only the wearer knows what it represents.

In addition to tattoos, there are numerous inmates with skills who provide services at a price for the fellas. One guy supplemented his existence by fixing radios and was quite good at it. He was so skilled he could alter them to work on a shortwave frequency, which allowed inmates to communicate with people outside the walls without being monitored. This was very helpful before the influx of cell phones and will always be a handy capability to have.

Even in prison, appearance was a big deal. Our house "royalty" was always trying to get away with wearing make-up. Some C/Os didn't sweat it, but I always made them clean it off. If a sergeant saw them on the yard or in the chow hall wearing it, and knew she lived in my housing unit, I would get jacked up about it. Some inmates with artistic talent could be approved to receive art supplies from vendors and the queens would either purchase or obtain the pastel colors from the artists for "favors." They would also use the Kool-Aid from the sack lunches. No doubt there were some dirty staff members that brought make-up in for their favorite queens too. Sometimes they would melt down the black plastic chess and checker pieces to use for eyebrow pencil. They would also use hydrogen peroxide from acne medicine to bleach their hair.

Many of the blacks would want their hair slick and processed, and they could get things like Jheri curl or those Afro-sheen substances at canteen. If they got sent to Ad Seg, they wouldn't have their property or personal hygiene items because they were bagged up and stored until they came out of the hole. In order to keep their hair from getting dried out, they would use the mayonnaise packets from their sack lunches on their hair. It was gross and after a day or two really started to smell quite bad. As a white boy, I never understood what they thought was attractive about that coif, but then again, I'm sure they thought the same thing about our Vitalis or Dixie Peach pomade.

    All in all, our inmates were quite seasoned at trying to pull one over on us. I'd like to think we got pretty good at stopping their shenanigans, but I'm sure there were plenty we knew nothing about . . . and didn't want to know.

Weapon Stock

IN PRISON, HAVING or making a weapon of some sort could be a bonus or necessity for some incarcerated people. We have to do our best to keep inmates from acquiring weapon stock that they could fashion into something with which to inflict damage on each other or staff. There are two basic types of shanks: a stabbing device and a slashing device. One of the easiest and best tactics was getting ahold of a spoon from the chow hall back when we still used metal utensils. It was, however, time consuming and took a little elbow grease to sharpen it into a point, and then make a handle out of cloth, torn from a shirt or sheet or wound string for a righteous shank.

The discontinuation of using metal eating utensils eliminated a good weapon source but there were plenty of other options available to a resourceful convict. In the main kitchen as well as the ones in each facility, there are big butcher knives that would make Michael Myers envious, but they are locked up and hung on shadow boards, which are inventoried before and after each shift.

The kitchens have many rolling racks that trays slide in and out of, and the flat pieces of metal that hold each tray can be worked loose and removed. If an inmate can manage to get the metal out of the kitchen, it can then be sharpened into a shank. The rolled edges of the sheet pans were also worked loose and turned into puncturing devices. The way that the kitchen workers were searched before getting off work varied with different staff members. There's no set policy on that, and some kitchen cops don't strip them all the way out but just make them strip to their boxers and check their clothing by basically patting them down. I always stripped them out completely whenever I worked that position, because I didn't want any of them putting blade into me or other staff. The workers would always throw in some gay references about us enjoying checking out their equipment or portals, and moan about being stripped out in an attempt to get us to cut them slack. We tried to inspect those food racks regularly to see if any parts were missing.

I mentioned earlier that dental floss has many uses in prison other than dental hygiene. I knew of an inmate residing in Ad Seg and just before getting released back to A yard, he used floss along with some tooth powder to saw off a nice slab from the steel shelves inside the cell. Convicts will use scouring powder to increase the abrasive quality to saw through solid steel. The officers didn't thoroughly search the cell after he left, and the guy performed a very gory sticking the next day on A yard that got him sent back to the hole. Inmates usually do the rubbing on the cell walls for sharpening and the OGs know to do it under the shelves, sink, or bunk to avoid us noticing the tell-tale scrape marks.

There is also a nice steel rod on a three-hole punch used for cutting holes in paper to insert into a binder. We had to keep a lookout on the hole punches to make sure the rod hadn't been removed. Typewriters used in offices (some by inmate clerks) also have a long, steel rod in them. Some inmates could be approved to have a small electronic typewriter in their cell for legal or literary works, and they had to be checked regularly to make sure that the rod was still in there.

Newspapers can be wetted, bound up really tight and allowed to dry then wrapped tightly with elastic from socks and can be transformed into a really strong spear or arrow. I've seen videos during our annual training where inmates can utilize the elastic taken from socks, underwear waistbands, or even rubber bands to make an effective bow and arrow. I've seen them shot 30 to 40 feet and puncture the target. A friend of mine and helpful adviser to this writing, Officer Starnes at the time but now Lieutenant Starnes, was issuing meal trays in Ad Seg at CMF in Vacaville when he was stabbed in the back of his neck with a spear that measured 58 inches long and had a three-inch tip on it made from a metal strap from the back of a wheelchair. The metal piece was passed to the perpetrator by an inmate worker in Ad Seg and is one of the reasons why most pens no longer allow inmate workers in Ad Seg. Starnes was hit because a group of cops had rushed this inmate's cell a week earlier for refusing to return his tray from the meal, and he had decided to hit any "nonwhite" cop. Even though Starnes is Portuguese, his complexion was dark enough to qualify. Starnes tried to blow his whistle upon realizing he'd been hit but there was so much blood coming out of his mouth, it got inside the whistle and wouldn't work.

There were also mop buckets that porters used in numerous areas that had a metal rod on the part used to squeeze out excess water on the mop, and they provided a tempting target for anyone intent on making a stabbing device. It wasn't that hard for inmates to work them loose and only required sharpening a tip and fashioning some sort of tape or cloth handle. Any time I saw one of those buckets in the area I was working, I would check to make sure that rod was still there. If it disappeared, I would know when it happened and that limited the list of suspects.

Screwdrivers are great because they already have handles on them and only require being sharpened to a nice point. Yard crew, plumbers and maintenance inmate workers use them. They also are hung on shadow boards and inventoried each shift, but somehow, sometimes, we found weapons made from them. There's an inmate plumber on each yard who pushes a car full of parts and tools around to each building. Whenever they entered my housing unit, I would have them come to me immediately and would check each drawer with the inventory sheet that hung from the side of his cart. The majority of times they were in my unit was because we'd called their boss and had them sent over to unclog toilets.

Inmates are allowed to have razors, which provide them with sharp, metal objects even though the razors the state gave them have very narrow blades. They can still be taken apart and used to hurt themselves or others. They have box cutters in R&R like the ones used by the 9-11 terrorists that are used to open dress-out and quarterly package boxes. There are two inmates who work in R&R, and they are rarely stripped out prior to returning to their housing unit. I guess the cops that worked in there either felt the workers were trustworthy or thinking they didn't have ample time or opportunity to acquire such items. They have been known to acquire blades from box cutters, which also have found their way onto the yards. A favorite slashing weapon was to heat up a plastic toothbrush handle and insert the blade into the melted plastic. After it cooled and hardened, it was a really good device with which to hit someone across their neck and open the jugular vein. Sometimes, in order to increase the chance of infection or worse, these blades would even be covered with feces.

I mentioned earlier that putting a few *D* batteries in a sock made a good weapon too. If the inmates lived in the gym or a dorm that had lockers, a padlock could be used instead of batteries. Both could do some serious damage when swung around and applied upside someone's head. Since none of the components are considered contraband, they're commonly used as weapons.

There were plenty of scissors around in offices and education but we broke off the sharp tips and smoothed them into blunt ends. Even with that, we still had to keep close watch on them, because a blade is still a blade and could be sharpened into a point again if an inmate could get a pair back to their cell unnoticed. Sometimes staff in education or other administrative areas could get careless and leave them lying on a desk.

In my early days at the Creek, ribs and pork chops would be served for dinner every once in a while, but it was a chore trying to account for all the leftover bones, which made pretty good stickin' instruments. Those items were removed from the menu permanently after an inmate got stuck in the neck the day after ribs were the dining selection.

Another easily acquired and effective item is the top of a tin can, such as a tuna can with a pull top. This product is readily available from canteen, and if an inmate opens the can and rolls up the metal lid really tight, it can be a good stickin' device.

Around the time I joined the department, there was a glut of new joints being built, and a lot of the newer cops were transferring to them in order to have better seniority. Whenever a new institution opens, before they even start receiving inmates, the staff spends weeks searching the yards and units for tools, nails, straps, screws and numerous other items dropped or left behind by construction workers that can be fashioned into a weapon. No matter hard long and hard they searched, we were still finding them years later.

In the joint, practically anything can become a weapon.

Interesting and Dirty Staff

CORRECTIONS IS BUT a microcosm of society. There's both good and bad, but really, I think the scale is tilted towards the good. We all had our backgrounds investigated, and if there were any glaring transgressions, you would be rejected. If you're an idiot, it's pretty hard for there not to be some sort of record of it by the time you're going through this check. Anybody harboring racist, sexist or abusive traits probably have shown evidence of them at some point prior to then. Those need to be weeded out before they can inflict harm on any staff or residents. Nowadays, the applicants even have to go through a psychological evaluation. Thank goodness that wasn't the case when I went through the selection process.

I'm going to tell stories here that are shocking, but the ones who were dirty are the exception and the vast majority of staff goes about their job with vigilance, courage and are resolute in their execution of maintaining security, preventing escapes and protecting the public. We also try our best to encourage and facilitate those prisoners who want to leave the lifestyle behind and get out to be good fathers and citizens. There's a whole world outside the Beast's belly that doesn't revolve around the worst aspects of human selfishness, greed and aggression.

First off, whenever a staff member is discovered or suspected of being dirty in any way, the term is that they got "walked off." This would almost always be accomplished by the squad lieutenant and sergeant stopping them at the entrance building by the employee sally port as they arrived for their shift. I can recall many times arriving for work and seeing those squad supervisors hanging around the area. We all knew what that meant. No matter who you were, there was a little knot that formed in your gut, wondering if it was you that was going to get pulled over. Even if you knew you were clean, it didn't mean someone hadn't made allegations against you in order to accomplish some devious agenda. The target would then be escorted into the Administration Building, informed of the charges and relieved of their ID and badge.

Usually, the staff member would be offered the choice of resigning at that time or, if they chose to fight the charge, they could be terminated at the end of the process. If they resigned, they would still be eligible to keep their retirement and benefits. Most chose that option when confronted with the totality of evidence against them.

In addition to probably losing their job, a great many of the staff member's peers were going to see it happen, and the word would spread throughout the joint like wildfire. You'd hear, "Did you hear so and so got walked off today?" There was a binder at the entrance station showing the ID picture of all who were being denied entry. Any of us could check it whenever we wanted. Getting walked off didn't always mean someone was through, as sometimes the ongoing investigation didn't prove guilt. Those individuals were allowed to continue their careers, usually getting all back pay they'd missed while out, with interest.

I always wondered if these dirty officers really believed they were going to get away with it, because as far as we knew, they were going to get popped eventually. It's possible there were some that did it for years without detection but I doubt it. As I said, there are no secrets inside the Beast and inmates aren't going to allow any dirty staff member to try and go straight and cut off the flow of whatever they're providing, whether it is dope, information dispersion or sexual favors. Usually, the cop would have gotten his or herself into a financial bind or just thought maybe this was a good way to get that new Evinrude outboard motor they'd been lusting after but seemed just out of reach. If you're willing to take the risk, lots of money can be obtained. Beats working those ten OT shifts month after month, I guess.

One of the ways staff gets busted is the squad will put a "wire" on an inmate who will try to get the targeted staff member to say something incriminating. I've heard of Keystone Cops situations where the wire fell out on the dayroom floor but was undetected by the dirty staff member. Another tactic is to use an inmate's boom box. When they get one of them from a vendor, the "record" function was always disabled in R&R so it couldn't record anything that could be smuggled out. But sometimes, the gooners would reconnect the record capabilities of the box and the inmate would be holding it as he conversed with the dirty staff member. If they didn't notice the red light on the box or the tape rolling, they deserved to get busted.

There was one officer who got busted for providing drugs to the fellas and was delivering the goodies right to their cells. Apparently, this cop was a full-service outlet and was smuggling in heroin, coke, weed, tobacco, steroids and cell phones. When this individual got popped, they went to his/her home and apparently there were bindles all prepared with individual cell numbers written on them, and phones were getting delivered right to the front door.

Sometimes the package officer would allow a floor cop from the housing unit to bring inmates over and administer the contents of the package as long as all the items were chronicled on his property card. The dirty cop might tell the package officer that this particular inmate worked during the hours the package room was handing out packages and maybe the package cop was really swamped about getting packages delivered and was grateful, as well as trusting, to have some assistance. When I was the Plaza officer I helped issue packages when I had a lull in escorts.

Another guy, who was nearing retirement, got in a wreck and lost his job. Seems he was bringing in all the drugs that our guests enjoy along with some other sundry items. There were even allegations that he was getting blow jobs from one of his inmate workers. This is a very risky practice not only from a disease perspective; I've also heard of times when this act was being performed on a male officer. Upon achieving climax, inmates have been known to produce a Ziploc bag, spit the ejaculate into it, seal it up and then get that cop through DNA. It's gotta be pretty hard to explain why a convicted felon residing in the same California State prison you happen to be employed by would have your DNA. Once they have achieved that leverage, they can escalate the shopping list of items they'd make that lame bring in.

Another officer was stopped at the entrance building for being a "mule" and bringing drugs in for the fellas. As the process of the bust was underway, word spread inside, and as members of the squad were headed to his house to search it, a phone call was made from inside the walls (I won't say from what area) to this chap's abode to alert his wife that the posse was en route. He lived in a remote area and it took a while for them to arrive, so she had plenty of time to get rid of the evidence. The identity of the individual who placed that warning phone call is fairly well known by many staff members, but the individual is still working there. This person sent me a friend request on FB a while back, but I have zero respect or need for any staff member who puts all of us in danger like that.

We had a free staff worker who got himself into such a mess that it's almost funny. He had a serious drinking problem and would frequently call in sick if he was too hung over or too drunk to show up. He started allowing his inmate workers to tattoo each other in the office, and before long, they were giving him tats too. He started bringing in tattoo patterns and items needed to accomplish the artwork. Soon he was bringing in dope and booze. Then one of his workers paroled and moved in with him and his wife. Next thing you know, they threw *him* out so the parolee and the lush's wife could cohabitate in bliss. Finally, the gentleman got so deep into the mess, he went to his supervisor and spilled the frijoles on the whole situation. He was fired and I hope he has gotten himself right because in my interactions with him he was a pleasant enough guy.

As I stated earlier there were many female staff members who lost their jobs for getting involved with inmates. The term used was "Over familiarity". Some of them treated inmates in a pretty harsh manner, so we were all shocked when they got walked off. There were maybe two males I remember who also got in wrecks for having romantic feelings for the felons. Frequently, if a female staff member suddenly lost a bunch of weight and started coming in all dolled up, it was an indicator.

When I had been at the Creek for only about a month, I was working out at the Level 1 dorms on Third Watch. After the last count cleared, I went up to the program office to await my relief. I thought I was supposed to take the mailbag containing the reroute mail in it to the office, so I toted it up there with me. My relief showed up about 10 minutes late, and as we were exchanging equipment he noticed the mailbag. He asked, "Who brought that mailbag up here?" I responded, "I did, I thought I was supposed to." He sees his chance to play on this fish cop and states, "Well, I'm not taking it back to the unit, you are!" He probably only had about a year in himself but had to take advantage of one of the few officers with less time in than he had. I'm thinking if he hadn't been 10 minutes late, I might have complied, but because he had been tardy, I told him that he could handle that task himself. As I was walking out the door, I hear him say, "Prick!" Oops, that changed everything. Growing up in my neighborhood, if you called someone a name like that, you better be ready to do something about it. I stopped and leaned back into the office and informed this lame, "I'll be outside in the parking lot if you have anything else you want to say to me." After standing out there for a few minutes, I walked down the road towards the minimum parking lot. My blood was boiling by the time I got to my car. I drove back up to the office and was going to go into Dorm 2 with the intention of puke-slapping this dork, but the sergeant stopped me before I could get to the dorm and talked some sense into me. It's a good thing he did, because my career would have probably ended with just a few months of seniority.

Interesting and Dirty Staff

I heard of watch sergeants at other prisons calling up an officer towards the end of his shift and telling him that they were short of staff for the next shift and they were being held over. The watch sergeant would then proceed to that officer's abode, where the poor officer's wife was waiting for her sergeant lover to show up to administer a cavity search. I also heard of staff members calling their wives or husbands and claiming they were being held over, then picking up their mistress and heading to a late-night bar for a few pops before culminating the indiscretion. Apparently, on more than one occasion, the cheater would be swigging a few cocktails with his lover when they would see their spouse walk in with her own secret lover. The divorce rate was pretty high in these locales, as was the alcoholism.

We had a pretty high-ranking custody staff member who transferred to the Creek from one of these isolated prisons. He was the most even-tempered person I ever met... he was always mad. He had started as an officer at a different pen, and I heard from some of my buddies who had worked there that at the end of his shift they would frequently have to "freeze the gate." This means stop letting staff out until this dude could leave before getting socked up with some parking-lot therapy. One night, after he became a supervisor at a isolate joint, a few officers decided to go over to his house and set his fence on fire. They were drunk, and one of them had his ID fall out at the scene of the crime. The target took "a fence" to the vandalism and also took 10 percent of the cop's salary for a year. You got that coming for being felony stupid.

MCSP tried to hide one C/O who was quite obese. I think while in school, he ran out of lunch money by breakfast. I guess he had an eating disorder, he was a bulimic amnesiac. He'd binge, but then forget to purge... If he got in a race with a pregnant woman, he'd come in third. Having good hearing is important in order to be an effective officer but this guy was as deaf as a bat. They put him in a post where there would rarely be any opportunity to have to move or get physical in any way. He was an older white guy, a pleasant chap. He always had a briefcase with him. When I worked at the entrance building one day, he opened it for me to check for contraband. It was full to the brim with a complete assortment of candy bars. I never had a trick-or-treat bag look this full. I'm not sure if it was the institution, the union or CDC that initiated the issue, but somehow, someone became concerned about his ability to run (he had the top-end speed of a glacier) to a disturbance or fight with inmates, so they told him they wanted to give him a physical ability test. He basically admitted there was no way he could do anything they would challenge him to do, so he just resigned.

I stated earlier that CDC employs representatives for each of the major religions. The Catholic one tried on several occasions to bring wine inside with him to hold communion ceremonies. When his briefcase was inspected at the entrance building, he would raise heck when informed that this would not be allowed. Eventually he agreed to use grape juice instead. A few of the vintners we had residing at the Creek could have provided him with a challis of quality fermentation, with a 2:30 yesterday vintage, for just a few soups.

The work change area of the vocational program provided plenty of opportunity for characters to convey their observations in an amusing way. This is the place where the inmates involved in the various vocational programs get stripped out every time they leave the area, mainly due to all the weapon stock they have access to, and we wanted to avoid it making its way onto the yard. There was one colorful officer who worked in there and every morning he'd walk towards the area, he'd shout, "Meat inspector! Meat inspector coming through!" He claimed he could identify any convict on the yard by his dumbstick and was able to determine which of our guests were lefties or righties.

We all did "Pat downs" or as CDC likes to call them, "Clothed body searches" on a daily basis. When we were checking the inside of the pant legs, how far up towards the crotch we went varied from cop to cop. Apparently, one of our brethren took it to the limit and beyond when checking the upper extremities of the inner thigh. One convict told me after being searched by him, he thought this officer was like a carnival worker and was "Trying to guess the weight of my balls". Maybe he was just thorough...

There was one loveable, big ol' country boy who graduated from the academy and showed up at the Creek toward the end of my career. Big Country stood about 6'4" and tipped the Toledo at about 370 pounds, depending which hunting and fishing season it was and how many boxes of "Silage Helper" he'd cooked up lately. I wanted to include a photo of him but didn't want him to be reduced to being "click bait" for some GQ magazine ad. He was known around the joint as "Big sexy" and looked like he was in his fifth trimester. A cannibal's dream, he had just the right amount of marbling to be a delicious meal. He always claimed he was a light eater. I'm guessing that meant when it got light, he started eating. He did not receive the embarrassment gene and talked about and did things that nobody else would admit to. His life centered around evacuating his lower GI. He was either pooping, about to poop or just finished pooping. I'm not sure if it was his personal magnetism or if, due to his physical mass, he had his own gravitational pull. His family had lived in the area for many generations and he related a story about a local character from long ago who had a real weakness for the ladies of the night. Back then, money wasn't always the compensation used in exchange for services rendered. According to folklore, this fellow, on at least one occasion was feeling the need for some lovin' but was devoid of cash at the moment. The object of his desire noticed a deer he'd recently shot in the back of his pick up and offered a trade of venison for vagina...He accepted, always looking to get more bang for his buck...

I had not arrived at the Creek yet when this incident occurred and I'm glad I wasn't. There was an officer who had a bit of a unique understanding about his role of being a Correctional officer. One day he was the control booth cop in a housing unit when he got on the dayroom PA system and announced, "Attention in the unit, I want everybody in here to know that I consider all of you political prisoners and will not shoot any of you under any circumstances!". The disclosure was met with disbelief from both residents and staff. I would have closed the dayroom, locked up the felons in the building, called my yard sergeant and told him to either get somebody over here to relieve him...or me, because I wasn't going to remain on that dayroom floor after such an invitation was extended for any inmate to hit any or all of the staff OR convicts in that building. That gentleman resigned shortly after his proclamation.

The following situation could not exist in CDC anymore because of the random drug tests administered to all staff members now. But myself and all officers that came into the department before or shortly after I did were not subject to such testing because of a "grandfather" clause. I had an officer friend who felt comfortable enough around me to admit and describe in detail how he used to get stoned at work occasionally. He stressed to me that he never did it when he was in a post where he had to deal with inmates, which provided me with great relief.

He was working in a perimeter tower on first watch and would bring in a film container with some green bud in it, along with a push-pin type of thumbtack. He would also have a canned soft drink, and at some point during the night would chug down the drink, remove the tab from the top and push in part of the can, forming a small bowl. Utilizing the tack, he'd punch a few holes in that part of the can. After opening all the windows and making sure a central service S&E wasn't walking under his tower conducting a perimeter fence check and that the Outside patrol sergeant was inside the perimeter, he would take a lung-buster hit. He'd crush the can with his foot, put it in a zip lock bag to avoid any odor, and hide it in the bottom of his lunch pail. I assume he would then lay waste to the multitude of treats in that lunch pail. He also had Visine and chewing gum to further mask his indiscretion. He told me that on occasion he would blaze up on his way to work, pull over on some side road near the joint, flush his eyes with Visine and pop some gum in his mouth before having to sign in. He had to be wary of other staff seeing him pulling off to the road or returning to the main road that might cause suspicion.

I really didn't have a problem with him doing any of this as long as he didn't do it when having to do with inmates or providing security for me or any other staff member . . . or convict either, for that matter.

The majority of trash talk within the Beast revolved around boasting about how big their pork sword was or how much short shrift their verbal adversary had. Apparently in the day of the round table, it was considered a sign of ignorance to be encumbered with an oversized serpent. A rumor no doubt initiated by a few needle-dick kings and nobleman. That story was passed down to me from my direct bloodline great, great Grandfather...the village idiot.

I was known to participate in some hijinks as well, believe it or not. One of my favorite stunts involved a novelty, an incredibly stinky liquid called "Morning Breeze." It's an extremely potent, concentrated, sulfur-based substance that smells like someone stuffed a rotten egg up some diseased corpse's ass then passed gas around it. I'm not sure if you can still buy it but I used to find it at some magic stores. I sometimes brought a bottle of Morning Breeze in with me. One miserably hot day, a bus came into R&R and unloaded about 25 criminals. They were herded into a large holding tank awaiting processing and placement into their new home. Since there is no air-conditioning in R&R, they put a really large floor fan in front of the door of the tank, which were just bars like an old cell door. Can you see where this is going? I would stand behind the fan and open the bottle up. I didn't take long for them to start yelling all sorts of accusatory exclamations towards the other felons and staff, wondering who had such toxic waste gurgling within their digestive tracts.

Frequently I would bring in Jalapenos or other peppers to augment my lunch. The convicts (Especially the Hispanics) would beg me for one, they loved to put them in their Ramon soup. One time I brought in a Habanero and one of my residents really wanted that one. I told him I'd let him have it but he had to eat the whole thing in front of us. He agreed, I gave it to him and he chomped it down on the spot. After about ten minutes, he wasn't looking so good and asked if he could go in his house. As he was walking towards his casa, I yelled up to the control cop "Give 133 a one way". I then yelled over to him as he approached his cell door, "If your cellie comes down here on the next unlock complaining about his dick being on fire, we're all gonna know what time it is with that!".

DVI runs a dairy that provides milk for all the joints in California and is run by inmate workers. I loved to tell the convicts, "I wouldn't drink that if I were you. That dairy is run by a bunch of horny inmates working around all those milking machines...That's not milk, it's half & half and you don't wanna know what the other half is.".

All in all, some staff could be as interesting—and as dirty—as the inmates.

Sports

SPORTS ARE A big part in the Correctional environment for both residents and staff. From the felons playing on the yard, there were leagues involving Football, Basketball, Soccer, Horseshoes, Volleyball and handball, as well as pick-up games going on constantly. To staff and the Annual Summer Games, it was always part of all of our reality. Betting is also a huge pastime of the fellas and staff.

Everybody knew which football, basketball and baseball team that everybody rooted for. The inmates frequently had their team's logo tattooed on their tumbler, and their cells were often decorated with that team's paraphernalia. Staff usually had something on their lunchbox, and one way or another, everybody knew everybody's teams. It was a good source for much trash talk throughout the year.

Betting was a large revenue producer for the bookies in each housing unit. The inmates were always trying to get ahold of the sports section of my paper in order to see what the betting lines were on upcoming games and how those lines were moving throughout the week. There were always a few staff members who ran a little game among themselves, but it had to be kept on the down-low because it was not appreciated by the administration, probably due to concerns about staff getting into debt with other staff and potential conflict which could follow. I knew of staff having bets with inmates but it was never for anything more than pushups or maybe an extra sack lunch or two.

The convicts had leagues with teams being based on which housing unit they lived in, so there were frequent beds moves made as each unit tried to load up a roster with ringers for whatever league was going on at that time. The floor cops in those units sometimes would get involved in these moves just from having pride for their housing unit. Geocentricism prevails again..

The Annual Summer Games were a really big deal to staff members. Every year, usually in August, a different joint would host the games. It was a great time to catch up and party with old classmates from the Academy. It was really quite like the Olympics as there were so many events. You did have to work at the specific prison you played for though, you could be an electrician or plumber as long as you worked at that pen. Along with all the usual sports there was shooting, bowling, fencing, golf, boxing, Judo, track and field even a Tug-O-War. The competition was fierce. I was approached on more than one occasion by high-up administrators and supervisors wanting me to transfer to their joint in exchange for a cushy position (even promotions) along with great days off. I only played softball, but one year I also played basketball. That wasn't too smart, not only because it took so much energy but I showed up with my old super-short trunks from the old days. My teammates, along with the competition, clowned me mercilessly about them. They thought I was the guy who stood on the ladder next to the peach basket and pulled the ball out after each score. Someday they'll be back in style and I'll claim credit for bringing it back.

Mule Creek absolutely sucked butt at softball for the longest time, but after a while enough new players showed up and we became very good. After being the welcome mat for so long, it was cool to be one of the medal contenders every year. We took the silver medal in the Bay Area and, two years later, won the gold when Chino hosted down near San Bernardino. Right after that, CDC stopped having the games. So I guess we're still the reigning champs.

Sports

Mule Creek gets it's first medal in softball! This year we won the silver medal and two years later we took the gold. Author is back row right.

After that we all started focusing on the Police Games, which were even more competitive. You had to have a peace-officer certification but could be a fireman, EMT or cop and could play for any team you wanted. It involved teams from all over the western region of the United States, not just California. That made for a bunch of loaded teams.

The associate warden at DVI put together an all-star team from all the Northern California joints. He got us some nice uniforms with "NorCal" across the chest. Did that make us Nortenos? There was a SoCal all-star team too, and we spanked them a couple times. Sometimes the Busters DO win. We had all been playing against each other for so long, the DVI Assoc. Warden knew the players he wanted. He picked about three from Folsom, four from DVI, three from Sierra in Jamestown and three of us from Mule Creek. We never won the gold medal at the Police Games but did take the silver a couple of years.

The Day We're All Waiting For

THERE I WAS, sitting in my driveway, wearing my jumpsuit with the upper half unzipped and the sleeves tied around my waist, boots on for the last time, trying to analyze what I was feeling. I had beaten the odds and was at this moment a retired correctional officer, a man of leisure. The odds had made it unlikely that I would even get through the selection process due to my wild and rebellious earlier days, not to mention driving back and forth to Ione on the narrow, winding country roads of Amador County in fog, rain, sleep deprivation and dodging idiot drivers for a quarter of a century. All you needed to see was the numerous roadside memorials along the way to realize how dangerous it was. I had witnessed many wrecks, including fatalities. Then, factoring in that I had gotten through the physical, academic and emotional challenges of the academy, followed by 25 years with the prospect of being stabbed, beaten, experiencing stress-related issues, taken hostage, gassed, sued—by inmates *or* staff—and being fired for myriads of perceived transgressions once at the institution. I had made it! I was fortunate.

And so I sat, reflecting on all that had transpired and how I felt about it. I'd expected to become emotional and misty, but I didn't, and I wasn't going to force it.

The day began as so many had before with the alarm clock terminating my sleep at 4:15 a.m. and me rolling out of the rack, packing my lunch into my cooler, stepping into my jumpsuit, lacing up my boots and heading out the door. My sweet golden retriever/yellow Lab mix, Bailey, knew what seeing me putting this outfit meant. I patted her head and gave her the reassurance that I would be back soon. She would never see me put that uniform on again. I frequently carpooled with several other staff members who lived in my area, 32 miles from Ione, but on this day, I went alone. The drive took about 40 minutes going in and about 50 minutes coming back depending on what watch I was on. It was good to have that time to get into character on the way in and to decompress on the way home. The drive was a pleasant one through rolling pastures with grazing cattle along the Jackson Highway, Ione Road and into Mule Creek State Prison. Having driven this route for 25 years, most of it on this early shift, I knew exactly what time I should reach various checkpoints along the way to know if I was on schedule. I saw tail lights well ahead of me and headlights in the distance behind me, I could with reasonable certainty surmise who was driving. However, the danger was always present on that country road, even once arriving at the prison's driveway. A few years earlier, two officers who were husband and wife turned left into MCSP and were T-boned by a truck, killing the wife instantly. Her husband never did return to service.

I popped into the local Stop & Rob convenience store in Rancho Murieta for food, drink and newspaper. There was a very nice, gregarious gent working there who would offer me a, "Be safe today" wish as I left his store on such mornings. I resisted the urge to make him aware that his job might be more dangerous than mine.

On this day, I was working as a floor officer in one of the mental-health housing units on Bravo yard, just as I had for the past few years. My partner and I would relieve the first-watch officer, ask them if anything of importance had occurred overnight, and then walk the tier on a security check, mostly looking for bleeders or hangers. The last count had taken place ninety minutes earlier and there wouldn't be another

The Day We're All Waiting For

one for another ten hours. It would be embarrassing if an inmate were hanging or had bled to death, with the coroner determining that he had been dead for many hours. Within 15 minutes or so, our building was called for chow release. The control-booth officer opened the doors and the prisoners would file out to walk the track to the chow hall. Whenever there was a lot of movement and bustling, it was a good opportunity to move on someone who had drawn another's' ire, so we were especially vigilant. It's more common for prisoners to hit someone while returning from chow than on the way in due to everyone being still drowsy; plus, if a hit occurred prior to chow, there could be a long delay until the uninvolved inmates got their breakfast, which doesn't sit well with hungry prisoners. That individual who felt his actions were wise could be the recipient of a good sticking later on. Two things inmates don't like are anyone messing with their food or their visits.

I certainly was not in the mood for any foolishness on my last day, so I posted up on the dayroom floor, looking as menacing as I could, making sure the prisoners all knew I was on point. I should point out that I'm 6-feet-5 and around 255 pounds.

After the prisoners had vacated the building, I went outside the sally port door and watched the inmates from other housing units in their procession on the track towards the chow hall. It was a chilly morning on the final days before New Year's, and I was reflecting on all of my morning, afternoon, evening and overnights shifts. The sounds of screeching seagulls pierced the morning air, as they knew that the inmates would soon be exiting the chow hall. Many of the fellas would toss them some of the bread from the sack lunch they received upon exiting the chow hall. So many of the convicts trudging along the track—bundled up in their coats with "CDC Prisoner" stenciled on the back—had been there before me and would likely be leaving on a "Toe tag" parole. I could identify most of them by their shape and gait. What went through their minds as they continually got up for yet another day, just like yesterday, knowing the next day would be the same? The aromas wafting into my nostrils reminded me of the rains lone had experienced overnight and amplified the sensory overload people frequently feel at impactful moments of their life. I looked at the surrounding hills, which were now becoming faintly visible with the sunrise as well as illumination from the yard lights. I had enjoyed gazing upon those rolling hills from so many perspectives around the joint over the years.

Once the prisoners returned from chow, they locked up for a while until a work/school release was done. At 0800 the yard opened and most headed out to play basketball, soccer, volleyball, run or walk the track. There would also be drug deals, sex acts, threats issued and carried out.

It was my last day, so many staff members were coming by to hang out since I had come in with many of them and would never see most of them again. When you are in potential life-or-death situations with these folks, you get pretty close to them. An announcement was made over the speakers, institution-wide, that it was my last day, so I had tons of phone calls and people dropping by with their best wishes. There were two other officers retiring that day too, one was C/O J. Baker and he was having a party that night so it didn't seem so final.

The shift that day passed quickly, but I can certainly remember some that seemed to last for days. Usually that was because it was a crummy position, was sick, stifling heat, or I didn't care for my partner. As the shift was nearing its conclusion, my inmate clerk had arranged for a collection of drag queens to come into the building as his boom box blared "Let's Get It On." They danced and tried to flirt with me. I fanned myself with a paper, feigning arousal, and everyone in the unit howled. Nice to have some "royalty" paying their respects.

My partners were urging me a take off early so I wouldn't get caught up in anything should an incident occur, which often happened during the bustle of a shift change. I checked in my handcuffs, pepper spray, keys and baton, waved at all the convicts, and they gave me an ovation as I headed out the sally port onto the yard. Not sure if it was out of appreciation or relief that they wouldn't have to deal with me anymore.

The Day We're All Waiting For

My inmate clerk wanted to escort me off the yard, saying he didn't want anything to happen to me on the way out. I think he just wanted the prestige of being in on the moment and I wasn't the least bit concerned about any such possibility. I told him I wanted to be alone with my private thoughts and he understood. It was the only time I ever shook an inmate's hand. I took the long way around the track, passing the housing units on that yard, all of which had some sort of memory attached to them. First watch, second watch, third watch, shift swaps, overtime. There had been hilarious moments, sad ones, tragic ones, tense ones. As I strolled along, many inmates passed along their good wishes and appreciative thoughts. Some of the staff members came outside to witness a moment that seemed like it would be forever before they would experience it themselves. I guess the yard gunner had alerted everyone on the radio and they were actually clapping and cheering as I passed. It touched me deeply.

The Bravo yard gunner saluted me from his gun perch as he popped the gate and I passed through it. I didn't recognize him but he looked young and new, and I couldn't help but think about how much longer it would be before he would reach this day. He was probably having similar thoughts as he watched this grizzled veteran of so many incidents and decades of correctional awareness pass beneath his gun tower. As I exited the yard gate and began the walk through the plaza towards the Main Control sally port, a female counselor I had known for many years happened along and we strolled arm in arm. She had been the officer I rescued several times from that creepy, leering sergeant in Tower 7 years earlier. I checked my mailbox for the last time and saw the daily movement sheet in it showed me marked as "retired!" Good to know they weren't going to call me in the morning and report me as AWOL.

As I went through Main Control sally port, and then onto the final perimeter sally port, had my ID scanned for the last time and strolled out into the parking lot, I stopped and looked back at all the concrete, gun towers, chain link and razor wire, feeling extremely grateful for all that Mule Creek had provided me. I also felt proud that I had done my job. Even on those shifts when I was exhausted coming off working 16 or more hours, was sick, working in sweltering heat, freezing cold and rain, partnered with someone weak or unlikeable, wading into a tempest of violence, or dealing with any inmate or supervisor intent upon ruining my day, career, or life—I had done my job. I had completed my 25-to-life sentence! Where was MY gate money?

In the beginning, I'd been new and clueless and couldn't imagine having so much time to do. However, for the last several years I had been the final remaining member of the seven officers from my academy class. The rest had either retired, resigned, taken a medical retirement, transferred, one had been murdered by her C/O husband or promoted out. Now there were none.

I got in my car and drove that so very familiar route back to Fair Oaks. It was December 28, 2012, and I'd done my time.

END OF WATCH

Epilogue

IT'S BEEN EIGHT years since I walked out of that last sally port. I've only been to the joint twice since and didn't go past the entrance building. Once was to pick up my concealed weapon permit and the other was to have Sgt. L. Gambill take the photos of me for the back cover of this book a few months ago. I still fit into my Class A uniform after 8 years of the good life.

So many stories ended up on the cutting room floor, if anybody enjoys this book, there are hundreds of stories yet to share, many from my eventful, foolish youth.

I've planted a bunch of banana trees and other flowers and bushes, built a deck and incorporated the whole Tiki bar cliché tropical setting at my hovel. A buddy and I built a lovely redwood bar, got a nice big BBQ (Freud would have something to say about a man and the emphasis on the size of his BBQ) put in some nice, adjustable lighting, a music system, Tiki torches, a hammock and water fountains. I have small gatherings of four to five couples several times during the summer, and it's always a great night at the Tacky Tiki. One great thing about sweltering days in Fair Oaks is they turn into warm, sultry nights . . .

On that note... I have been divorced from Pam for about 10 years or so now and she lives five minutes away in the house she grew up in with my daughter, Gina. Her dad died a few months ago on his 103rd birthday. Both girls sacrificed a great deal of their social life taking care of him the last couple years of his life. He was an amazing man who always treated me great even during and after the divorce.

Both my parents have moved on, but I want to extend my profound appreciation about how fortunate I was to have been raised by them. You gotta choose your parents carefully. Daddy always used to say that there weren't any parenting classes or books when they became parents. While they both would say they made mistakes on choices they made in raising us three hellions, I believe they always did what they thought was the best thing and that's all you can ask of anyone. We Davidson boys were no bargain. I was provided every opportunity to flourish and along with my brothers had everything we needed to achieve happiness and success. Any bumps in the road along the way were strictly of our own doing. We always felt loved and appreciated. My dad told me that if your word ain't worth nothing, you ain't worth nothing. My mom taught me to persevere through challenging times and keep a sunny disposition in everyday occurrences, both good and bad.

My children are absolutely the best thing that have ever happened to me. They're both so sweet that it makes me wonder how they could have come from my loins. Sam has been working at North Ridge Country Club, got his degree from CSUS and has found a job in his career field. He got his a bit faster than my 14-year paper chase. His passion is bird photography and he has the eye for capturing them in unique angles, poses and lighting. He's published calendars for the last three years and now has a coffee table book out too. Sam took the photos of Folsom's East gate sally port that Karen Phillips, the graphic designer, was able to manipulate into the cover of this book. He's my hockey buddy and we watch all the Shark games together.

Gina just graduated from UC Davis on the dean's honor roll and has been accepted into USC grad school. Now I know she didn't come from my loins. She also worked at the campus police station. She is my theater buddy and during the summer, we're at the Fair Oaks Theater Festival most weekends in their cute little intimate outdoor amphitheater. She and Sam are here frequently for the WWE shows and we enjoy the characters and plots. Gina was born too late—she loves the music from the sixties and I took her to the 50th anniversary display of the Summer of Love at the de Young Museum in Golden Gate Park last summer. She wanted all the fashions displayed there and also loves going to Haight-Ashbury.

I don't want to get too political here but I'll put out a bit of a Big D manifesto. I don't fit into anybody's convenient category politically. I'm conservative on some issues and liberal on others. When it comes to crime, I'm pretty far to the right, and of course, taxes are too high and nobody wants the government interfering in our lives by telling us what we can or cannot do. Unfortunately, there are people and corporations that need to be told that certain behaviors mess everything up for everybody else. If everybody treated each other with courtesy and consideration, we wouldn't have to place regulations on everybody in order to keep a few greedy, inconsiderate, self-absorbed pricks from screwing things up for the rest of us.

Okay, enough about that . . . I'm getting ready to head for the course and a wonderful 18-hole walk. I could suck or kick ass or anything in between, but I'll treasure it regardless of my score. They say golf and sex are the only two things in life you don't have to be good at to enjoy... You'd think my game would have improved dramatically after retiring and it has to a degree but I've finally given up on attaining my two dream careers...Golf pro and Jockey. I just bought a nice new kayak and it's a peaceful way to relax and a new way to get in a workout. I'm getting the Tiki Bar and hammock dialed in for a summer of soirees and got my bags packed for the adventures the horizon beckons me for.

Like most folks, some people are impressed with me and some... not so much. It's like that renowned philosopher, sage and soothsayer Ricky Nelson said, "You can't please everyone so you got to please yourself.

A few nuggets of wisdom before I walk out the sally port.

I try to adhere to these beliefs (sometimes successfully).

If it's not yours, don't take it.

If it's not true, don't say it.

If it's not right, don't do it.

I'm older than I once was but younger than I will be.

I'm accountable for me...and to me.

When you lose, don't waste the failure. Learn from it.

I'm living proof that one can grow old without growing up.

The best things in life aren't things.

People will do anything for a T-shirt.

Life gets more precious when there's less of it to waste.

It's better to look out the windshield than the rear view mirror.

I subscribe to the philosophy... everything in moderation . . . including moderation.

With apologies to Forrest Gump, Life is like a roll of toilet paper. The closer you get to the end, the faster it goes.

Lower your shields and take a chance. Chances lost are hopes' torn out pages.

Acknowledgements

I WANT TO thank everybody that I had any sort of encounter with during my career. From every staff member I ever worked with to every convicted felon with which I interacted. If it weren't for a few lucky breaks, we might have been cellies. Every one of them contributed something to the experience and my awareness into the world of incarceration.

Special thanks to Jeff Baker, Cornell Beatty, Desiree Dupree, Kevin Henderson, Dave Starnes, Neal Clark, Lori Gambill, Debby Swanson, and K.T. Smith for all taking the time to sit down with me, sharing stories, and clarifying situations along with imparting their own observations. Lori was my carpool partner for much of my career and at the time of this writing, she is the Outside Patrol sergeant at the Creek. This couldn't have happened without their contributions.

To Cindy Sample and Janet Fullwood, two great writers and humans. Janet was the travel editor for the Sacramento Bee for years. They were very helpful in grinding out this memoir.

To Rena Lowry, who provided several good ideas about the sequence and flow of this story, along with numerous other wonderful ideas. I NOW know to put the knives blade down in the dishwasher. And, well...the Firepit knows...

Special thanks to Bill Walden, along with his wife, my cousin Linda Davidson Walden. Bill is the sharpest guy who knows something about everything and was extremely helpful (and patient) in this project, even though he went to Georgia Tech... Thanks for bringing him back from Georgia Linda.

Extra special shout out to Judge Thomas Wallner. He lived in the hood and his daughter, Martha, who was the first person to get me stoned. He plucked me out of the clutches of John Q. Law several times and I probably wouldn't have been able to pass the background check if he hadn't intervened. There were a few times when I got myself in a wreck and he would just step in and make it go away. Geocentrics at work, I was from his Hood. Thanks Tom, for allowing me to mature at my own plodding gait and to experience prison from a staff perspective rather than as a resident.

Much gratitude to Lt. Angelo Gonzales, the Public information officer at MCSP for providing the photos of Mule Creek State Prison. I remember when he showed up as a runny nosed rookie.

My parents, Ross and Micky. They provided every opportunity to get educated, travel the world, and be loved, accepted, and appreciated. I chose them well.

My protégés, Sam and Gina. No father could ever be prouder of two people that, in spite of all my shortcomings, have become the sweetest, rightest, respected, admired, and most grounded humans I know.

Acknowledgements

My sweet pups, Sam and Gina Rose at one of our favorite settings..Capitola Beach!

To my only (as of this writing) female cohabitant, Pamela Castori. A truly unique and exceptional human. She epitomizes all the traits that make this world the best orb in the universe.

To Sundi Mohr for all her support and connections within the department. Thanks Sundi, for introducing me to Bloody Marys at Zeldas' in Capitola...

To Karen Phillips, the graphic designer who endured a lot of my changes of mind for the eye catching cover of this memoir. She was patient and receptive as we narrowed down the options before we captured the image I wanted to convey about the book's content. Check her out at Phillips Covers.

All my friends, current, past, and future. Every one of you contributed to the formation of this twisted example of human frailty. Special shout out to my buddy Ben Wade and his sweet and lovely partner, Brenda L. Clark. He's my golf, craps, and general hangout buddy that lived across the street from me in high school and was one of my cellies at the Teichert "Farm" house. We each have too much dirt on each other to ever feel completely safe. Bob Beheler, my camping, golf, and hilarity buddy. See ya soon for the annual "Wild Boys" camping trip. We had to cancel it for the first time in about thirty years due to Covid 19. It's probably for the better, that's at least ten pounds of excess I didn't acquire this year.

To every woman that was ever a part of my life, regardless of the degree or duration of involvement. Every one of you gave me something precious. I've had a couple of close calls as far as becoming fully domesticated and sharing an address but something, so far anyway, has made it seem (usually to both of us) that it was not in the cards, at least not at that time and circumstance. We all mature at different rates and I certainly took the scenic route. Of those, more than once the reason was alcohol abuse. Volatile tempers, negativity, and verbal abuse are never going to be a part of my living environment. I'm no saint by any stretch and enjoy drinking, but it should be fun and relaxing. If I'm walking on eggshells and trying to stay out of her crosshairs, well I have more lofty expectations for the rest of my life than that. Alcohol, when abused, has destroyed more families, lives and relationships than all other drugs combined. Still thinking that wonderful woman is out there as we continue to seek each other out... It would be nice to find my cellie to serve out the rest of this term together...inside the heart of THIS Beast.

Acknowledgements

Cheers! Every day is a celebration after 25 years inside, The Belly of the Beast...and no, that's not Pruno...

To all Earth's residents, past and future. Every person I interacted with from fleeting eye contact to lifelong friends and family. Each one of you added an ingredient to this bowl of gruel.

Farewell to 2020. Some great things occurred during it but as I always (sometimes) say, "There are better days ahead".

www.ingramcontent.com/pod-product-compliance
Lightning Source LLC
Chambersburg PA
CBHW050855240426
43672CB00019B/2982